The Ethics Of Immediacy

PSYCHOANALYTIC HORIZONS

Psychoanalysis is unique in being at once a theory and a therapy, a method of critical thinking and a form of clinical practice. Now in its second century, this fusion of science and humanism derived from Freud has outlived all predictions of its demise. **Psychoanalytic Horizons** evokes the idea of a convergence between realms as well as the outer limits of a vision. Books in the series test disciplinary boundaries and will appeal to scholars and therapists who are passionate not only about the theory of literature, culture, media, and philosophy but also, above all, about the real life of ideas in the world.

Series Editors

Esther Rashkin, Mari Ruti, and Peter L. Rudnytsky

Advisory Board

Salman Akhtar, Doris Brothers, Aleksandar Dimitrijevic, Lewis Kirshner, Humphrey Morris, Hilary Neroni, Dany Nobus, Lois Oppenheim, Donna Orange, Peter Redman, Laura Salisbury, Alenka Zupančič

Volumes in the Series:

Mourning Freud
by Madelon Sprengnether

Does the Internet Have an Unconscious?: Slavoj Žižek and Digital Culture
by Clint Burnham

In the Event of Laughter: Psychoanalysis, Literature and Comedy
by Alfie Bown

On Dangerous Ground: Freud's Visual Cultures of the Unconscious
by Diane O'Donoghue

For Want of Ambiguity: Order and Chaos in Art, Psychoanalysis, and Neuroscience
by Ludovica Lumer and Lois Oppenheim

Life Itself Is an Art: The Life and Work of Erich Fromm
by Rainer Funk

Born After: Reckoning with the German Past
by Angelika Bammer

Critical Theory Between Klein and Lacan: A Dialogue
by Amy Allen and Mari Ruti

Transferences: The Aesthetics and Poetics of the Therapeutic Relationship
by Maren Scheurer

At the Risk of Thinking: An Intellectual Biography of Julia Kristeva
by Alice Jardine, edited by Mari Ruti

The Writing Cure
by Emma Lieber

The Analyst's Desire: The Ethical Foundation of Clinical Practice
by Mitchell Wilson

Our Two-Track Minds: Rehabilitating Freud on Culture
by Robert A. Paul

Norman N. Holland: The Dean of American Psychoanalytic Literary Critics
by Jeffrey Berman

Psychological Roots of the Climate Crisis: Neoliberal Exceptionalism and the Culture of Uncare by Sally Weintrobe

Circumcision on the Couch: The Cultural, Psychological and Gendered Dimensions of the World's Oldest Surgery
by Jordan Osserman

The Racist Fantasy: Unconscious Roots of Hatred
by Todd McGowan

Antisemitism and Racism: Ethical Challenges for Psychoanalysis
by Stephen Frosh

The Ethics of Immediacy: Dangerous Experience in Freud, Woolf, and Merleau-Ponty
by Jeffrey McCurry

The Ethics Of Immediacy

Dangerous Experience in Freud, Woolf, and Merleau-Ponty

Jeffrey McCurry

BLOOMSBURY ACADEMIC
NEW YORK • LONDON • OXFORD • NEW DELHI • SYDNEY

BLOOMSBURY ACADEMIC
Bloomsbury Publishing Inc, 1385 Broadway, New York, NY 10018, USA
Bloomsbury Publishing Plc, 50 Bedford Square, London, WC1B 3DP, UK
Bloomsbury Publishing Ireland, 29 Earlsfort Terrace, Dublin 2, D02 AY28, Ireland

BLOOMSBURY, BLOOMSBURY ACADEMIC and the Diana logo are
trademarks of Bloomsbury Publishing Plc

First published in the United States of America 2024
Paperback edition published in 2025

Copyright © Jeffrey McCurry, 2024

For legal purposes the Acknowledgments on pp. x–xii constitute
an extension of this copyright page.

Cover design by Daniel Benneworth-Gray
Cover image © Markus Spiske / unsplash.com

All rights reserved. No part of this publication may be: i) reproduced or transmitted in any form, electronic or mechanical, including photocopying, recording or by means of any information storage or retrieval system without prior permission in writing from the publishers; or ii) used or reproduced in any way for the training, development or operation of artificial intelligence (AI) technologies, including generative AI technologies. The rights holders expressly reserve this publication from the text and data mining exception as per Article 4(3) of the Digital Single Market Directive (EU) 2019/790.

Bloomsbury Publishing Inc does not have any control over, or responsibility for, any third-party websites referred to or in this book. All internet addresses given in this book were correct at the time of going to press. The author and publisher regret any inconvenience caused if addresses have changed or sites have ceased to exist, but can accept no responsibility for any such changes.

Library of Congress Cataloging-in-Publication Data
Names: McCurry, Jeffrey, author.
Title: The ethics of immediacy : dangerous experience in Freud,
Woolf, and Merleau-Ponty / Jeffrey McCurry.
Description: New York : Bloomsbury Academic, 2024. |
Series: Psychoanalytic horizons | Includes bibliographical references and index. |
Summary: "Argues that modernism can be seen as a therapeutic
project for transforming human experience, and draws from
Freudian psychoanalysis, Virginia Woolf's criticism and fiction, and Maurice
Merleau-Ponty's phenomenology"– Provided by publisher.
Identifiers: LCCN 2023010057 (print) | LCCN 2023010058 (ebook) |
ISBN 9798765107249 (hardback) | ISBN 9798765107256 (paperback) |
ISBN 9798765107225 (ebook) | ISBN 9798765107218 (pdf) |
ISBN 9798765107232 (ebook other)
Subjects: LCSH: Human beings–Philosophy. | Philosophical
anthropology. | Phenomenology. | Modernism (Literature) | Freud, Sigmund,
1856–1939. | Woolf, Virginia, 1882–1941–Criticism and interpretation. |
Merleau-Ponty, Maurice, 1908–1961–Criticism and interpretation.
Classification: LCC BD450 .M3473 2024 (print) |
LCC BD450 (ebook) | DDC 128–dc22
LC record available at https://lccn.loc.gov/2023010057
LC ebook record available at https://lccn.loc.gov/2023010058

ISBN: HB: 979-8-7651-0724-9
PB: 979-8-7651-0725-6
ePDF: 979-8-7651-0721-8
eBook: 979-8-7651-0722-5

Series: Psychoanalytic Horizons

Typeset by Integra Software Services Pvt. Ltd.

For product safety related questions contact productsafety@bloomsbury.com.

To find out more about our authors and books visit www.bloomsbury.com and sign
up for our newsletters.

This book is dedicated to my family, Mom and Dad, Aunt Jo, my late Grandfathers, and especially Jennifer, Peter, and Zoe

Contents

Acknowledgments	x
Introduction An existential revolution: An ethics of experience	1

Part I
Freud Before Freudians

Chapter 1 Toward unsettled life: Anomaly and quandary in Freud	15
Chapter 2 Toward insane life: Immorality and incoherence in Freud	23

Part II
Freudians Beyond Freud

Chapter 3 Toward creative life: Recalcitrance and futurity in Woolf	73
Chapter 4 Toward wondering life: Mystery, miracle, and menace in Merleau-Ponty	117
Conclusion The Freudian age: A contemporary horizon	173
Notes	187
Index	206

Acknowledgments

In one way or another, I have been writing this book for almost a decade, and I want to thank many people living and lost.

Thank you to my many fine teachers: Jason Lueth at Washington High School in Sioux Falls, South Dakota; Gwen Myers and the late Paul McHale at Mound-Westonka High School in Minnetrista, Minnesota; Edward Griffin at the University of Minnesota; J. B. Schneewind, Nancy Struever, Susan Wolf, Frances Ferguson, William Connolly, the late Allen Grossman, and the late Richard Macksey at Johns Hopkins University; Stephen Fowl and Frederick Christian Bauerschmidt at Loyola University of Maryland; Stanley Hauerwas, L. Gregory Jones, J. Kameron Carter, Reinhard Hütter, Romand Coles, Ellen Davis, and Kenneth Surin at Duke University; Ronald Jalbert, Thomas Janoski, Eleanor Irwin, Janet Mooney, David Orbison, Mario Fischetti, and Bruce Fink at the Pittsburgh Psychoanalytic Center.

Thank you to my many great intellectual friends: from days in Minnesota, Megan Anderson, and Behzad Afshar; from days in Maryland, Teal Anderson, Zachary Calo, Josh Obstfeld, and Sarah Hedges; from days in North Carolina, Abraham Nussbaum, Jason Byassee, Sara Olack, Traci Smith, Charles Del Dotto, Joel Schickel, Jana Bennet, David Liu, Robert Koerpel, Phil Morice Brubaker, Sarah Morice Brubaker, Daniel Barber, and David Cloutier; from days in Pennsylvania, Patrick Miller, Erik Garrett, Terra Merkey, James Swindal, Justin Pearl, Rita Mockus, Daniel Burston, Derek Hook, Kevin Smith, Patrick Driscoll, Sharon Leak, Athena Colman, Angelle Pryor, and Meirav Almog.

Thank you to Duquesne University Presidents Charles Dougherty and Kenneth Gormley, Provosts Ralph Pearson, Timothy Austin, and David Dausey, Deans Christopher Duncan, James Swindal, and Kristine Blair, and University Librarians Laverna Saunders and Sara Baron for their support over the years that has enabled me to be a teacher-scholar-administrator.

Thank you to my colleagues at Duquesne who have made my work possible by providing the essential conditions for my work: light, cool, warmth, water, clean and safe space, food, and technology. Of the many facilities engineers, housekeepers, baristas, and computer technicians, I especially thank Jeff, Dave, Walt, Aaron, the Union coffee crew, Terry, and Charita.

Thank you to my colleagues at Duquesne and beyond from and alongside whom I have learned phenomenology: H. A. Nethery IV, Kevin Smith, the late George Kline, Fred Evans, Daniel Martino, Erica Schiller Freeman, Alessio Rotundo, Lanei Rodemeyer, Frederick Wertz, Jessica Wiskus, Richard Wilson, Tone Roald, Michael Barber, Amanda Lowe, John Raczkiewicz, Travis Hall, Fr. Brian Cronin, C.S.Sp., Fr. William Ogrodowski, James Wolford-Ulrich, Chelsea Binnie, Frank Lehner, John Peacock and Fr. Elochukwu Uzukwu, C.S.Sp.

Thank you to Jonathan Lear, Louis Sass, Iain McGilchrist, John Caputo, Rowan Williams, and Adam Phillips for their insights and inspiration that have contributed to this book, even if their influence is not always evident and may even have forms of which I am unaware.

Thank you to the organizers and participants of the many groups and conferences at which I first presented versions of my research for this book—sometimes in woefully inadequate versions: the Society for Phenomenology and the Human Sciences, the Organization of Phenomenological Organizations, the Interdisciplinary Coalition of North American Phenomenologists, the British Society for Phenomenology, the Duquesne University Student Counseling Center, the Pittsburgh Psychoanalytic Center, the Center for Interpretive and Qualitative Research at Duquesne University, the North American Society for Early Phenomenology, the Society for European Philosophy and Forum for European Philosophy, and the Polish Phenomenological Society.

I am very grateful to Prof. Victor Molchanov, Editor of the *Russian Yearbook for Phenomenological Philosophy*, Volume Six (2021), for publishing some of my preliminary research for this book in "Perceptual Life. Merleau-Ponty's Aim in Writing Phenomenology" in a Russian translation by Olga Ivashchuk. I am also very grateful to Mr. Pavan S. Brar, Editor of *Middle Voices*, Volume 1, Issue 1 (2020), for publishing some of my preliminary research for this book in "Experience beyond the imaginary: Reading Freud's 'Elisabeth von R.' with Lacan's 'The Mirror Stage.'"

Thank you to the co-editors of the Psychoanalytic Horizons book series, Mari Ruti, Peter Rudnytsky, and Esther Rashskin, along with Haaris Naqvi and Hali Han at Bloomsbury, for bringing the project into the series. I especially want to thank Mari Ruti for her strong support of my project, and for her grace toward me through the process of writing and rewriting this work.

For generously providing feedback on versions of parts or all of this book project, sometimes in very different forms from the final product, a deep thank you to Robert Koerpel, Tom Sparrow, Johan Bodaski, Pippa Letsky, Mari Ruti, Kevin Smith, John Hitchcock, Erica Schiller Freeman, Susan Wadsworth-Booth, Alessio Rotundo, Mario Fischetti, Janet Mooney, Justin Pearl, Jennifer Peters McCurry, and the anonymous readers of the manuscript for Bloomsbury whose critical feedback helped me to significantly improve the book.

For support of a different but vital kind, a heartfelt thank you to L.L., A.T., and especially David Moore and Stacey Wettstein.

In addition, because my ability to cross the finish line with this book has been difficult, I am especially grateful to Mari Ruti and Stacey Wettstein, again, and to Jennifer McCurry, for their support and reassurance in the home stretch.

Lastly, my deepest thanks go to my family: to my parents, Diane and John, to my aunt, Jody, to my late grandfathers, Jack and Melton, and, especially, to my immediate family, my wife, Jennifer, and my children, Peter and Zoe. Thank you all for all your love and support during the years I have been writing this book.

Lastly, I must also thank anyone whom I have forgotten to thank by name, and I must insist that no one whom I have thanked is responsible in any way for this book's inadequacies.

Introduction
An Existential Revolution: An Ethics of Experience

Another Kind of Revolution: Existential

History is a site of revolutions. Some occur at the planetary level, like from Holocene to Anthropocene. Others appear at the level of institutions and systems, as with from feudalism to capitalism. Others still involve transformations in artistic culture, such as from classicism to romanticism. Yet others still happen at intellectual levels, for instance from Aristotelian to Newtonian physics. And not to be forgotten are worldview revolutions, for example, from nature as a divine sign to nature as a material machine.

Often intertwined with these kinds of revolutions, however, affecting them and affected by them, are existential revolutions. In these times, human beings embrace a new definition of what it means to be human. Nor is this primarily an intellectual process. When human individuals and communities arrive at a new vision of self-definition, they acquire this new self-definition less as a datum of cognitive awareness and more as "an almost tactile sense" of being alive in a new way.[1] These revolutions transform the character and quality of human subjectivity itself. In a process that can take decades or even centuries, human beings leave behind one way of experiencing self, other, and the world and take up another. They leave one form of what it feels like to exist and have possibilities and embrace another.

One mark of existential revolutions is the transformation of which specific kinds of lived experiences human beings value and privilege. For human existence at any given time and place takes on its particular shape in large part because individuals decide to hold up a certain kind of experience as being more central to human identity than others—to be a compass for life. The momentums and deliverances of one register of lived experience become more central and trustworthy sources of orientation than those of other registers.

Lived experience, after all, is plural, not monolithic. Experience can be affective, ratiocinative, perceptual, recollective, anticipatory, imaginative, intuitive, practical, theoretical, contemplative, technological, and bodily, to name a few of the experiences that permeate human life. And the pressures of these different moments of lived experience can and do come into conflict. One of the most apparent instances of such conflict concerns what experience should be privileged. Hence Western moral philosophy's perennial debate regarding the relationship between emotion and reason when the energies and contents of emotional and rational experience stand in tension.

For this reason, choices concerning which kinds of experience to privilege are imperative and unavoidable. Human beings in any time and place, when they find themselves in situations of intractable conflict—psychological or moral, for example—must decide to esteem and trust the data and power of some lived experiences more than others. A specific concrete form of human life will possess its unique shape—politically or architecturally, for instance—in large part because of determinations, made implicitly or explicitly, regarding which kinds of lived experience are most central and authoritative, on the one hand, and which kinds are not.

While such patterns of subjectivity—the privileging of some kinds of experience over others—can stably persist over extended periods in a culture, they rarely, if ever, persist forever. Over time, frustration and discontent arise within even the most stable patterns of judging the value of different kinds of experience. Then, more or less consciously, humans in one time and place begin to feel that the specific way in which they value and privilege different kinds of experience now entails an intolerable amount of suffering.

At these moments, the time is ripe for an existential revolution. Frustration and pain motivate human beings to seek new ways of valuing different kinds of experiences and ordering these experiences. Their discontent and suffering move them to revise, more or less consciously, their sense of which types of experience are most significant, most trustworthy as sources for shaping their identities and guiding their lives, and most likely to give them the chance to enjoy an existence with less suffering. People come to see registers of their experience that were once central for defining their human identity as less central; they find themselves deemphasizing, subordinating, or even suppressing the call of these registers in areas of their actual life—religious life, social life, and so on. In turn, people come to see other registers of their experience that were once less definitive for their human identity and action as more definitive; they find themselves following the data and energies of these registers in their actual life—domestic, educational, and so on.

Yet even if existential revolutions have therapeutic aims and effects, these new possibilities always appear dangerous. An old form of existence and identity, which has been a home, has to be relinquished, and leaving home is always challenging. Familiarity feels safe, and the foreign feels hazardous—even when, as psychoanalysis teaches, a familiar home has been a painful place. Another reason existential revolutions are dangerous is that, by embracing a new kind of subjectivity, people not only leave behind the pain of the old kind. People also have to leave behind some of the benefits of the old one, benefits that the new way of life will not replicate, perhaps cannot replicate. Any enduring form of evaluating and privileging experience, and the form of human life bound up with it, enables us to address and negotiate at least some fundamental needs and dilemmas in at least somewhat constructive ways. Hence, abandoning an established pattern of experience and the form of life that embodies and expresses it means abandoning the goods and securities of that pattern. Yet although the risks involved with leaving a home will impede people from embracing an existential revolution, the perhaps even more important reason that existential revolutions are dangerous is that they frequently require their participants to embrace precisely those kinds of lived experiences that they had previously considered the most perilous and problematic. Existential revolutions summon individuals and societies to embrace dangerous experience.

Here a historical example might help. Consider the radical existential revolution in ancient Greece, as Homer's and Plato's texts express and embody its contours. Homer's *Iliad* encapsulates and articulates a human existence that privileges individualistic, aggressive, practical, affective, subjective, assertoric, instinctual kinds of experience—and the heroic, agonistic, violent form of life that went with them. Generated out of a frustration with the chaos and discord that characterized Homeric existence, Plato's *Republic* stood on the other side of an existential revolution, in which Greeks came to be committed to more social, cooperative, dialogical, theoretical, rational, objective, justified, and reflective modes of experience. Subsequently, a more placid civic life emerged along with them. To Homer's Attic form of life, Plato's Classical form of life's valuing of social, cooperative, theoretical, rational, and reflective experience was indeed dangerous. The embrace of such experience entailed a vastly new and strange form of existence. In fact, as someone like Nietzsche believed, the turn promised to ruin everything that had made Homeric life glorious and vital; it welcomed just those weak, abstract, and disembodied experiences that Homeric life believed undermined authentic human existence.

Exploring Existential Revolutions: Cultural Sources

What is the evidence that existential revolutions have happened? The brief mention of Homer and Plato shows that works of literature, philosophy, fine art, and music provide rich material for identifying and understanding existential revolutions. These sources not only objectively report on the transformations in the way we evaluate different registers of experience; more powerfully, they evoke the transformations among their writers and readers.

Such sources work on at least four different levels: renunciation, definition, contrast, and evocation. First, a source can show a culture rejecting an existential grammar it has come to find problematic: the culture tells itself what it once was but is no longer, what kinds of experience it once wanted to privilege and value but no longer does. Second, a source will articulate the new existence it is embracing. Third, this articulation will often contrast the present and the past. Humans often do not understand their new form of life until they have contrasted it with the past they have left behind, just as they will often not understand the old form of life until they have left it behind for something new. Only in the light of each other do old and new existential forms become visible. Finally, a source can inspire and evoke a new state of existence and its experiential life in those who encounter it. In all these ways, a cultural source is one way that a form of life, at any given historical moment, articulates, embraces, deepens, and develops what it takes to be its ideal form of existence in contrast to other possibilities that it is foreswearing.

Again, the central point is that cultural sources are more than journalistic: they do not just report on forms of existence and these forms' evaluations of experience that preexist their artistic or philosophical embodiment. Instead, these sources bring the new existence more fully into being by inspiring a new vision of human identity and experience. In the terms of Charles Taylor and Hubert Dreyfus, cultural sources are not only denotative but also constitutive of a form of life. A concrete pattern of human existence becomes what it is and what it is not by articulating itself through its cultural artifacts.[2] This constitutive articulation operates in both the creation and the reception of the cultural work: both in the experiences of writing, composing, and making and in those of reading, hearing, and viewing.

We can return to our Greek example by looking at the first book of Plato's *Republic*. There, in Socrates's debate with Thrasymachus about the nature of justice and its relationship to self-advantage, Plato's text gives voice to and summons a new sense of identity and existence, one which, Plato believes, offers more inspiring possibilities for human life than the Homeric paradigm it is trying to displace. In this way of reading Plato, whether Socrates dialectically refutes Thrasymachus is irrelevant. What is crucial, instead, is seeing the way the dialogue elucidates and recommends a shift from one ideal of human existence to another, a shift from prizing certain kinds of experiential registers to prizing others—in this case, from the individualistic and aristocratic state of existence with its high esteem for appetitive and agonistic experience to the political and civic state of existence with its high regard for rational and cooperative experience. The point, furthermore, is not only that the ancient Greeks may have understood the contrast between the former and latter forms of life only when Plato articulated it. The point, more radically, is that political and civic life—with the new overriding value of cooperative and rational experience as the compass for identity and action—came into its own in ancient Greece through the cultural efforts of Plato and others. The existential revolution became real as Plato imagined it and wrote it in texts that his audience read, appreciated, recognized themselves in, and appropriated.

The Freudian Age: A Recent Revolution

A history of the many existential revolutions the world has undergone would make for a fascinating project. However, the focus here will be on a relatively recent and profound existential transformation that took place in Europe during, roughly speaking, the first half of the twentieth century. It had been gathering force for centuries.

In this age, Europeans between *c.* 1895 and *c.* 1945 began to give a specific kind of experience an increased centrality, as they fashioned their identities and enacted their lives. The emphasis was on *immediate* experience.[3] Understanding what comprises this kind of experience is the task of this entire book, but we can make a first gesture at defining the experience here. I take immediacy to have two closely related meanings, both of which have to do with the lack of mediation. First, an experience is immediate if it is "undistanced" or "unabstracted" from the object it is experiencing. So, the perception of an object is immediate while reflective thought about the object, which takes place on the basis of the perception, is distanced and abstracted from the object as perceived. If one is thinking about the object conceptually, then one's contact with the object is mediated through the concept, whereas in perception there is no mediation, as the object is experienced directly. This scheme of understanding the relation between perception and conceptual thought is controversial, but it is how phenomenological philosophy sees the situation. Second, an experience is immediate if it is one that we simply find ourselves in even before we know it, one that comes upon us suddenly and unexpectedly, often anomalously, one that we undergo, at least initially, unselfconsciously. If one is experiencing a thought, desire, or feeling immediately, then one's experience of that thought, desire, or feeling is not yet mediated by processes of reflection, evaluation, or understanding that can only come temporally after the fact of the immediate experience itself. So, in the first sense of immediacy, which we might call ontological, a conceptual idea is arrived at through a deliberate process of abstraction and is thus not an immediate experience of whatever object it is an idea of. But, in the second sense of immediacy, which we might call genealogical, the same idea might be suddenly undergone in the flow of consciousness; here the idea, which has not yet been mediated by any form of further reflection or evaluation, could be an immediate experience. Since my investigation combines—in a way that I hope is somewhat harmonious—what we might call the ontological and genealogical senses of immediacy, an initial definition of the phenomenon might go this way: *immediate experience is the realm of somehow unmediated, pre-reflective, pre-evaluative, unselfconscious phenomena—thoughts, feelings, perceptions, wishes, dispositions—that arise in the flow of human consciousness.* At some level, the register of immediate experience—what it is and how it works—had always existed. Still, there was a radical shift in how human beings came to a newfound and robust appreciation of its deliverances and aspirations and began to stake their existence and identity on the priority of this specific register. Its contents and energies became the primary compass for making personal and social meaning, for inspiring private and public action, even for understanding the ultimate nature of human being itself. Human being was not just intellectually reconceived; it was existentially reconfigured. In a way that was not only thought but felt, the field of immediate experience now stood at the heart of what it means to be an authentic human person and live a thriving human life.

This revolution manifested itself in many different ways, but in this project we will investigate, with focus and depth, three of its cultural expressions by attending to a set of concise but profound texts. These texts are Sigmund Freud's case studies of 1895 on the phenomenon of hysteria, Virginia Woolf's essays from 1923 to 1925 on the nature of modernist fiction, and Maurice Merleau-Ponty's statement in 1945 of his conception of phenomenology. In their different regions of psychological, social, and philosophical reality, these works when taken together give profound articulations of a radically changed human existence that was now grounded in immediate experience.

These works were intense and significant moments in Europeans' attempt to overthrow a form of existence they had inherited—one that rejected the power and guidance of immediate experience. They took up another, one that respected such power and guidance. In this way, these authors' work was therapeutic. Through their words, they sought to dismantle problematic conceptions and embodiments of psychological, social, and philosophical existence, respectively, in which the content and forms of non-immediate experience had the authority to dominate or destroy the content and forms of immediate experience. In turn, their works summon a different, and to their minds more constructive, imagination and realization of psychological, social, and philosophical life in which the data, energies, logics, and purposes of immediate experience would take a salutary lead.

In this book I call the period of existential revolution exemplified in the work of Freud, Woolf, and Merleau-Ponty "the Freudian age." This name seems fitting because it was Freud's work that, perhaps for the first time, named and encouraged a radical embrace of immediate experience in content and form. His work was the lever, at least in intellectual and cultural discourse, that interrupted the complacency of an established existential trajectory. His work crystallized and inaugurated—as both its sign and cause—the new existential paradigm.

Even so, Freud's work by itself did not define the existential revolution. It was only one moment, essential and foundational but not exclusive, within a broad groundswell of intellectual and cultural life. The Freudian age as a kind of zeitgeist was an age only because his work inspired others to follow him in staking human existence on the truth and force of immediate experience. The meaning of Freud's work itself becomes fully evident only when we see how it echoed beyond itself.

Although many remarkable figures took up the essence of Freud's work, my project is focused intensively on Woolf and Merleau-Ponty—who both explicitly engaged Freud's work at some level. Their explicit interest in Freud is worthy of exploration, but the interest here is how their literature and philosophy, respectively, interpreted, appropriated, expressed, and advanced Freud's deep and broad focus on immediate experience within the depth-logic of their work, not just those moments when they engaged Freud by name. My argument is not an attempt at psychological criticism. Instead, I argue that Woolf and Merleau-Ponty worked within a Freudian grammar. Whether unconsciously or consciously, they saw their work as Freudian in this way is an interesting question, but not important here. These authors took up the spirit of Freud's focus on immediate experience in profound and provocative ways that did not merely repeat or reiterate Freud's ideas. More interestingly, they took up his ideas, developed them, deepened them, extended them, and applied them to dilemmas in human identity and action that went far beyond clinical psychology. The hope is that concentrating on the work of Woolf and Merleau-Ponty will offer a fruitful path—as broader but less detailed attention to a wider range of figures and works would not be—to gaining a keen and subtle understanding of the overall spirit and logic of the Freudian age and its continuing impact.

Because cultural texts—at least in one way of reading them—constitute new forms of actual human existence, the texts of Freud, Woolf, and Merleau-Ponty are signs that both signaled and engendered a seismic shift in human mentality that was happening among Europeans generally. That is to say, these works pointed to and summoned a pivot in actual "on the ground" human existence that involved a new and widespread consciousness of the increased value of immediate experience in every dimension of life: not only in psychological theory and practice, literature and fine arts, or philosophy but also in everyday political, social, romantic, familial, and religious life too. The limits of this project do not allow me to prove that Freud, Woolf, and Merleau-Ponty represent a broad shift in ordinary everyday life, but my intuition is that their texts do show a growing cultural consensus, perhaps more often implicit than explicit, on the rights and authority of immediate experience, which went far beyond the specialized and rarefied realms of either Freud's Vienna, Woolf's Bloomsbury, or Merleau-Ponty's Sorbonne.

This was indeed revolutionary because immediate experience, which had always been one kind of lived human experience, had been historically suspect. The data and impulses of this realm, the standard thinking went, were too often irrational, skeptical, immoral, chaotic, and even insane. Left unchecked and unregulated, this kind of experience was thought to lead to an ignorant, individually and socially destructive, chaotic, mad form of life. Common wisdom advised against making unreconstructed immediate experience the polestar for fashioning identity and making meaning if human flourishing was the goal.

Across the standard Classical, Christian, and Enlightenment paradigms, immediate experience held a subordinate place. Immediate experiences of mind, self, knowledge, and world were allowed purchase in human existence only if they submitted to other ostensibly more valuable kinds of experience; these often comprised reflective and evaluative kinds of experience—for example, rational or moral. Their force and logic were preeminent: they set the possibilities for other ostensibly less valuable kinds of experience. Thus, human existence gave the rational and moral the right to regulate and determine the value of immediate experience. Whether it was judged beneficial or destructive for human life—and whether it was therefore validated, sublimated, reshaped, ignored, suppressed, or even, if possible, annihilated—the fate of every moment of immediate experience lay outside itself in the authority of some other kind of experience that has higher prestige and authority.

In the existential revolution of the Freudian age, this inherited paradigm was called into question. As the works of Freud, Woolf, and Merleau-Ponty show, intellectuals in this era had begun to realize, more or less clearly, that valuing immediate experience only in the light of other forms of experience that were often hostile to it did not ultimately advance the best possibilities of human life. Instead, forcing immediate experience into a subordinate position led to various problems: dishonesty, inauthenticity, immorality, and perhaps worst of all, needless suffering.

The texts of Freud and others show individuals coming to embrace another paradigm to replace the rejected paradigm, one in which immediate experience, just as it presents itself—psychologically, intersubjectively, rationally, perceptually—is given primacy of place in the value-hierarchy of different kinds of experience. The works of Freud and his fellow partisans express and evoke the advent of a new form of human life in which the first-order energies and the effects of immediate experience were now central resources for determining the ideal shape of emotional, social, and philosophical life. For human life in Europe, this specific register of experience would now become the primary compass for orienting human feeling, social intercourse, and thinking. The contents of immediate experience would now make up the criteria by which to judge the value of the contents of other kinds of experience.

Preview: Questions and Chapters

I will not summarize the chapters in detail here.[4] The project's claims need to be fleshed out and justified within the chapters to become intelligible. Even so, I do want to offer readers a horizon to help guide them as they read the book and a preview of the topics of the chapters.

This horizon is a set of thematic questions to guide exploration of the emergence of the Freudian age. What comprises immediate experience? What is it like? What are its truth, essence, and logic? How does it exist differently in different areas of human existence—in affective life, knowledge, and social interaction, for example? How have we attempted to negate the truth and force of immediate experience? Why does humankind find this register of experience so dangerous? How do people develop and deploy strategies to ward off what they perceive as the threatening pressures of immediate experience? How are these strategies bound up with illusions concerning the nature of psychological, social, and philosophical truth and life? What are the negative consequences of such strategies? How and why should people—as they fashion identity and make meaning—privilege and value immediate experience instead of denigrating or shunning it? What happens when people relax their defensive strategies against immediate experience? What new kind of human life becomes possible when individuals and societies tarry more deliberately with the truth of immediate experience and live with the grain of immediate thoughts, desires, and feelings? In each chapter of the book, I try to answer these questions in different ways.

The book is divided into two parts. In the first section on Freud, a concise first chapter shows how Freud opened up the possibility for a new engagement with the realm of immediate experience by both acknowledging and articulating the existence and logic of this kind of experience.[5] In a longer second chapter, I explore Freud's path-breaking work on hysteria to see how he perceived the truth of immediate *psychological* experience, its reality and logics. We will see why Freud thought people find this type of experience so dangerous and why they build defensive illusions and ideals that need to be therapeutically dismantled—illusions and ideals to which human life is prone and which comprise strategies to protect against the dangers of immediate psychological experience and to keep distant from it. We will see how he imagined that people's lives could become new and different once they allow themselves to tarry with the grain of this kind of experience rather than self-contradictorily battling against it. The focus of this chapter is on the content and form of human life's emotional and desiring existence, and how this existence is transformed when we embrace more deeply the advents and vicissitudes of psychological immediacy and its logics.

Since immediate psychological experience is only one kind of immediate experience, in the book's second section we explore two other varieties of immediate experience. In the third chapter, the focus is Woolf's literary criticism and her inquiry into immediate *intersubjective* experience. In this chapter we look at the ways in which our *social* existence can be transformed when we welcome more intentionally the leads and pressures of intersubjective immediacy and its logics. In the fourth chapter, the topic is Merleau-Ponty's phenomenology and his investigation of immediate *perceptual* experience. Here we pay attention to the ways in which our *philosophical* existence can be changed when we welcome the presence of perceptual immediacy and its logics.

In the conclusion I suggest that Freud, Woolf, and Merleau-Ponty did not just intellectually explore and articulate the truth of immediate experience in different areas of human life. Nor did they merely describe the kind of existence we take when we invest more intentionally in such experience. Instead, in an explicit way that was novel in European life, they endorsed immediate experience and its logics as having ultimate significance in human life; thus, they initiated a new ethics, a new way of life.[6]

Freud and the others were offering an ethics of experience, one concerned with the optimal way to engage life's register of immediate experience. They pushed individuals to welcome and embrace immediate experience, to privilege this register of experience as a primary source and compass to guide their attempts to fashion personal identity and find meaning in life. To suggest that Freud, Woolf, and Merleau-Ponty are ethical thinkers is not to claim that they address the kinds of questions usually perceived as belonging to the traditional discourse of moral philosophy that figures like Aristotle, Hume, Mill, and Nietzsche engaged—questions of virtue and vice, good and evil actions, moral obligations and prohibitions, noble and base ends, and so on. Their work was intensely ethical in a different, perhaps even more primordial, threefold sense: first, they articulated a specific vision of a way of life, a form of existence that humans could embody and express; second, they defended the superiority of this way of life; and, third, they imagined and offered different kinds of therapeutic practices that, when taken up, would make the way of life they were articulating and defending not only possible but actual.[7] In these ways, Freud and his followers worked, both explicitly and implicitly, to contribute to the formulation of an ethic for modern European life, a summons to a new existential paradigm that they believed individuals could and should embrace.

Nor is the development of this ethic of only historical interest. From the second half of the twentieth century until the present, there is much evidence that North Atlantic humanity—and beyond—has more and more deeply embraced this ethic of intentionally living from the sources of immediate experience. The radically innovative existential paradigm that Freud and the others' work expressed and advanced is very much alive, as individuals in Europe and all over the world have increasingly allowed this paradigm to set the terms for the ways in which they negotiate more dimensions of their existence. The existential revolution that was named, created, explored, and espoused in the Freudian age may define human life in the present even more than it did in the era when it was first created, so we need to understand this age's ethic—the vision of life it bequeathed, the benefits this vision claimed to deliver, and the therapeutic practices required to make this vision real—if we hope to understand ourselves.

Part I

Freud Before Freudians

Chapter 1

Toward Unsettled Life: Anomaly and Quandary in Freud

Introduction: Something Like a Phenomenology

To discuss the place of immediate experience in human existence, we need to know, in an initial way, what it is about a lived experience that makes it make sense to categorize it as immediate. We need to have a tentative understanding of what this kind of lived experience is like. We need to perceive provisionally what distinguishes immediate experience from non-immediate or mediated experience.

This kind of investigation might be called phenomenological. A phenomenological investigation involves at least four dimensions. First, the inquiry attends exclusively to the plane of lived experience on its own terms; it does not attend to supposed or speculated realities that may exist outside that plane. Second, the inquiry focuses on a specific region of lived experience. Third, the inquiry describes as richly as possible the character of this region of lived experience—as opposed to theorizing about its operations or explaining its causal origins. Fourth and last, the aim is to precisely define the particular kind of lived experience being investigated in order to distinguish it from other types of experience.[1] To start pursuing this phenomenology, or something like a phenomenology, we can briefly engage a foundational text by Freud, the "Preliminary Communication," which he wrote with Josef Breuer.

The Logic of Immediate Experience: Interruption and Anomaly

How does Freud distinguish immediate experience from other kinds of experience? In one sense, all subjective experience is immediate, at least from a first-person perspective. If it were not immediate, it would not be subjective, at least not for the particular subject who is experiencing it. However, only some kinds of experiences are genuinely immediate in another sense.

We can see how Freud conceives the realm of immediate experience by considering a very brief vignette that he offered in the "Preliminary Communication": "We may take as a very commonplace instance a painful emotion arising during a meal but suppressed at the time, and then producing nausea and vomiting which persists for months in the form of hysterical vomiting."[2] This sentence is rich in meaning, and several terms in this passage merit fleshing out. Filling in Freud's example, we will imagine the painful emotion as rage. The first key term is "emotion." To speak of emotion is to dwell within the realm of first-person experience. When speaking of rage, one is in the qualitative realm of human subjectivity: first-person feelings, ideas, wishes, reveries, fantasies, emotions, dispositions, and so on.

A second keyword is "arising." Here there are two issues. First, the experience itself is the main subject of the action, not the person having it. The person feeling the emotion is passive: they receive the emotion; it comes into their mind involuntarily, unanticipated, and unsolicited.[3] In a real sense, the individual is not the subject of the experience; they are subjected to it. The experience comes on the scene in a way that the person who has it feels imposed upon; they are more passive than active, more victim than agent. We commonly speak of people as subjects who have experiences, but that way of speaking in this scenario does not seem accurate. It is not so much that the person at dinner has the experience of the emotion of anger; it is better said that the experience of the emotion of anger has them.

In addition, the term "arising" denotes that the experience carries a sense of otherness and exteriority. The emotion, as it comes into mind, feels anomalous. Somehow the experience is not just uninvited and unexpected; it comes on the scene as an interference, an interruption that feels foreign and unwanted. Freud does not mean that the angry person believes psychotically that their anger was magically injected into their head by some malign other, only that the experience (for example, the rage) is mystifying.

A third key term is "painful." The unrequested and unforeseen emotion is not just anomalous; it is anomalous in a way that hurts. Thus, the person suffers the emotion not only because they feel subjected to something strange that seems to come from outside themselves; they also find the emotion itself distressing.

The fourth keyword is "suppressed." Because the anomalous experience to which Freud's hysteric is subjected stings so much, the person who suffers it refuses to allow it to remain within the realm of conscious awareness. They try, instead, to eject it out of consciousness—an attempt that is successful as far as it goes. The person's emotion as an emotion vanishes from conscious awareness. In this way, the person erects a defense against the strange, unsummoned, and unpredicted emotion so as to avoid the suffering it threatens to bring. Since the rage is painful and out of character, the self attempts to eliminate it.

The fifth key term is "producing." We avoid unrequested, anticipated, painful experiences by inventing a different experience within consciousness. In this way, we remove ourselves from our original, primordial experience. In a kind of cover-up, an original experience is replaced by a secondary, derivative one, with the very purpose of the latter being to self-deceptively conceal and cancel the problematic presence of the former. Thus, a situation of inauthenticity and untruthfulness results; an individual trades a naïve and innocent experience for an artifice to displace and hide it.[4] By trying to deny and circumvent a fundamental and significant dimension of their existence like their anger, in the shape in which it first arrived, the person ends up, in a real way, losing themselves.

The sixth keyword is "hysterical." The productive consequence of suppression is not a happy one. The act of suppression does not shield the individual from pain; it forces them into a different form of pain. The victory attained through suppression was pyrrhic. The attempt at eliminating the primordial experience is unsuccessful. Fleeing suffering, the individual just finds a different kind of suffering. The person at dinner consciously but only momentarily felt a surge of murderous rage come over them. However, this rage felt so foreign and painful they defensively tried to eliminate it from conscious awareness almost as quickly as it arose. After this defensive suppression, the rage no longer existed in their life as rage. But the consequence was that they were now, unfortunately, trapped in a different kind of derivative experience just as painful as their anger had promised to be. By ridding themselves of a painful emotion, they have brought on a bodily agony that is itself painful: they have made themselves nauseous, and the affliction has no end in sight. It seems that, no matter what they do, they cannot avoid pain.

The last key term is the first main word in the sentence: "commonplace"—indeed "very" much so. Here Freud may be saying that the process he is describing is not atypical or rare. It may not even be a process that is interesting or relevant only to psychiatry and psychology. The possibility of going through this kind of process—

suffering and then defending against an unasked-for, unanticipated, distressing, anomalous experience in a way that delivers only a pyrrhic victory—may be, instead, an intrinsic dimension of what it means to be a human being. This is not to say that Freud thinks the process will always culminate in a full-blown hysterical symptom. It is to say that Freud may be describing an existential pattern that all human beings have to negotiate in some manner in their lives—whether it is rage or some other experience.

Freud's illuminating words, then, are rich with meaning. They help us to formulate an initial definition of what we can call the region of immediate experience that Freud was discovering and exploring. Immediate experience is the intrinsic dimension of human being that consists of all the uninvited and interfering content in first-person consciousness that interrupts our life, content to which we unavoidably find ourselves subjected and against which we inevitably but inauthentically, untruthfully, and ultimately pyrrhically try to defend ourselves.

This brief foray into Freud helps us formulate an initial definition of experiential immediacy. This definition is neither exhaustive nor final, but it helps identify the experiential terrain we are investigating. It also reveals something important: immediacy is not defined only by its contents—emotions, desires, thoughts, for example—but also by the logics across its contents. Immediate experience always involves theme and form.

Dangerous Experience: An Evil?

Now we can address a question that has been hovering around this discussion. Why is immediate experience often dangerous experience? Adam Phillips is correct to say that Freud's work shows how "We fear the immediacy of experience." The fear is so great that it can compel individuals to try to eliminate from conscious awareness the immediate experience that interrupts their lives. But why exactly is this immediacy frightening? Phillips's answer is that it is because so much of this immediacy expresses "the uncontainable."[5]

What Phillips means is that any given form of human life permits an acceptable range of possible lived experiences. All the individual's lived experiences must match up to a standard for what all their lived experience can and should be. This standard provides a kind of outer boundary and limits the experiences allowed in this form of life.

Specific experiences will be desirable and others will be undesirable, some will be expected and others unexpected. Most radically, specific experiences will seem possible, and others will seem not only undesired or unexpected but impossible.

Immediate experience as anomalous experience is dangerous experience. Indeed, anomalous experience is frightening experience almost by definition. The threatening nature of the anomalous is even embedded in the word "evil." Whereas the Proto-Indo-European root of the word "good" is g^hed^h, which could mean "to unite, be associated, suit," the root of the word "evil" is *upélos*, which could mean "going over or beyond (acceptable limits)."[6] An experience would be good and welcome when it is somehow fitting and appropriate—if it sticks to whatever is the norm, the nomos, for what experience should be. An experience would be evil and frightening, on the other hand, if it is somehow excessive and exceptional—if it exists outside or over against whatever is the norm, the nomos, that claims the right to determine what content lived experience is permitted to have.

The key is that an anomalous experience can seem evil precisely because of its form—although content can matter too. A moment of immediate experience can seem frightening because it exceeds the stable and established boundaries and limits, patterns and pathways, for lived experience, whatever they may be. Such a moment can, in turn, seem good because it fits into the inertia of established boundaries and limits, patterns and pathways, whatever they may be. Whether an immediate experience is good or evil depends upon whether it can be contained or not.

Feeling Stymied: Three Quandaries

Human life, then, can land in some awkward quandaries when it comes to the phenomena of immediate experience. One quandary concerns how this experience is both inevitable and dangerous—a painful interruption in human life that can nevertheless not be eliminated. Another quandary relates to how we cannot avoid engaging this kind of experience when, once it arrives, our preference would be not to engage it at all. We have to engage something we are resistant to engaging. A final quandary concerns how our preferred strategy for engaging the immediacy we resist engaging is itself problematic, a strategy that is ultimately futile and inflicts its own havoc and damage.

The first quandary concerns the situation in which human life finds itself. As we said, any form of human life includes a nomos (a law or custom, the word comes from classical Greek) that determines the boundaries and limits for possible lived experience in that form of life. Despite this nomos, uninvited, unexpected, seemingly impossible experiences do happen in human life. Human subjectivity inevitably contains the uncontainable. As analyst Donnel Stern says, in a different context, "unbidden experience is more the rule than the exception."[7] This point is one with which the analyst and philosopher Jonathan Lear concurs when he speaks of how mental life often operates "ateleologically."[8] For Stern and Lear, subjectivity by definition frequently includes experiential content that deviates from established and customary, ostensibly reasonable and plausible, more or less habitual and automatic, experiential trajectories. Various moments of experience fail to abide by the nomos, the established law and custom, which is claiming the right to set parameters for what is allowable experience. Immediate experience, as we have tried to define it, is *a-nomos*—anomalous, errant and lawless, unbidden and ateleological, strange and extraordinary, and thus frightening and evil. In sum, lived experience frequently and inevitably colors outside of its own settled lines—even when doing so is painful because life prefers, at least prima facie, to color within the lines. Although individuals find extraordinary moments of lived experience painful, the breaking in of just these extraordinary moments is itself an ordinary occurrence.

Now the second quandary. If any form of life is always finding itself painfully interrupted by the data of immediate experience, then that form of life will have to negotiate in some way the stubborn presence of this experience. It cannot be eliminated. Yet because this experience cannot but be frightening, humans find themselves in a distressing position in which they must deal with a set of phenomena they would like to avoid dealing with at all.

Finally, the third quandary. Freud's example suggests that we favor, somewhat understandably, one particular strategy for dealing with what we would rather not deal with: suppression. Here the endeavor involves attempting to escape a painful moment of immediate experience by trying to eject it out of conscious awareness altogether. Freud's vignette of the diner whose suppressed anger turns to stomach upset shows that suppression is an ineffective strategy for humans to deploy when they find themselves in the situation we are exploring. Suppression gives pyrrhic victories at best: an individual forces one specific painful moment of immediate experience to leave consciousness only to find another moment has replaced it. Suffering remains; it simply changes form. Individuals who deploy suppression to avoid suffering the anomalous and uncontainable cannot avoid the consequences of doing so. A moment of immediate experience, once it arrives on the scene (as it always does), will not be denied some kind of existence, some sort of purchase. Just when tempted to deny the reality of such a moment through suppression, we are tempted to do the impossible.

Conclusion: Unsettling Experience, or Beyond the Quandaries?

At this point, another word might help to capture the essence of immediate experience: "unsettling." A moment of this kind of experience unsettles human life, by interrupting and destabilizing—upending and overturning the individual's sense of existential gravity. And immediacy does these things in a way that can create extreme fear and anxiety in the subject. This immediacy can be so unsettling that individuals who cannot escape it nevertheless try to do so; through suppressing this experience, they try to revert to being subjects who have never had the experiences they have indeed experienced—even though this strategy to avoid pain then brings different pain.

Here we can define something crucial about immediate experience. *The unavoidable, ineliminable, and undeniable phenomena of immediate experience are so unsettling to human life's stabilities and inertias that life often surrenders to the temptation to attempt the impossible task of avoiding, eliminating, and denying these phenomena a place in human existence altogether.* This definition is also not exhaustive or definitive. Nevertheless, it shows why human beings find themselves trapped in the quandaries of immediate experience just described.

At this point, questions arise. Are our only options either to be damned by the immediacies of experience or to be damned by the refusal of them? Is there a way to avoid being damned? Is there any possibility we might escape the quandaries outlined in Freud's vignette?

Chapter 2

Toward Insane Life: Immorality and Incoherence in Freud

Introduction: Freud and Consciousness

Sigmund Freud's name is often used as a synonym for the unconscious. For him, the real story of the mind and its travails is never on the surface of conscious experience. Instead, the true nature of the mind—including its possibilities for sickness and health—reveals itself in hidden and unacknowledged "depth" structures and operations, agencies, energies, and intentions behind or underneath first-person awareness.

Although this familiar narrative is true, it is also incomplete, as recent work by Jonathan Lear has taught us.[1] For Freud investigated consciousness as much as he did the unconscious. As Jean Laplanche has noted, the early Freud saw the unconscious as the creation of consciousness; it was ushered into existence through our dysfunctional engagement with what were, first of all, conscious contents.[2]

The story of Freud's angry diner in the previous chapter already revealed the nature of human conscious life in several ways. We learned that immediate experience is a fundamental dimension of human consciousness. We discovered features that make certain moments of conscious experience immediate, and this experience's sudden, unanticipated, uninvited, anomalous, unsettling, painful nature.[3] We saw how the individual has little agency vis-à-vis the advents of immediacy in consciousness; they are passively subjected to the phenomena in first-person awareness. We noticed the temptation for us to resist and deny immediate moments a place in consciousness because of how the momentums and deliverances of these moments deviate from and endanger the inertia and stability of established, habitual, and tightly held experiential trajectories for conscious life. We ascertained the ultimate futility of giving in to this temptation. We recognized the real and challenging existential quandaries that consciousness presents, quandaries in which life can be stymied in the unavoidable confrontation with disturbing immediacies. And finally, we wondered if there was any escape from these quandaries.

The aim of this chapter is to move from considering immediate conscious experience in general to considering one particular kind of conscious immediacy: immediate *psychological* experience. Looking closely at Freud's account of this kind of experience will reveal that, although he thought human beings might never be able to completely escape the difficulties and quandaries presented by this kind of consciousness, he did believe human beings could engage the region of this difficult and perplexing experience in a more constructive way. Thus, in his early case studies on hysteria, Freud diagnoses a destructive path for conscious life to engage immediate psychological experience, a path that mires life in hysterical suffering. But he also reveals a more salutary way for individuals to engage immediate psychological experience, a way that leads their consciousness beyond the grip of hysterical neurosis. In this strategy, the aim is to confront the difficulties of immediacy and resist the temptation to try to somehow eliminate it from consciousness because of these dangers. In this existential modus operandi, the individual honestly faces the pain of immediate experience in a way that does not so much eliminate the pain as open up room for joy to exist alongside it within consciousness.

Although Freud believed that an actual psychoanalytic treatment would best facilitate this process, he also offered his writings as a therapeutic resource for individuals who wanted the chance to experience themselves and their consciousness in this new and different way. The study of these writings is an invitation to readers to find a new form of life: *conscious life*. In conscious life, neurotics would experience more of their immediate psychological experience in a fully aware manner—to experience moments that a powerful part of the self would prefer to have never become conscious in the first place.

One caveat. While I do believe Freud's work offers us profound truths about the human mind, I do not think Freud's theory or technique stands beyond criticism. Thus, I will not offer a wholesale defense of Freud's thought. I will instead attempt to show how Freud explicitly turned to the register of immediate experience to imagine what psychological life could look like when this life is lived in alignment with, rather than against, the grain of immediate emotional and desiderative experience.[4]

Suffering Virtue: The Origin of Hysteria

We can explore Freud's thinking on this topic by considering two papers he published in 1895, from the years in which Freud was first discovering and formulating his psychoanalytic theories of mental functioning and therapeutic action. One is a mainly theoretical paper, the famous "Preliminary Communication," which Freud wrote with his sometime friend Josef Breuer. The other is a case study he wrote by himself, the equally famous "Fräulein Elisabeth von R.," in which he meticulously detailed how a patient in his neurology practice fell into hysterical neurosis and then found her way out of it.[5]

How, then, did Freud and Breuer formulate hysteria's genesis and cure? In these texts, Freud's focus was on the shape of human existence as much as it was on the vicissitudes of psychological symptoms—or, rather, his focus was concerned with the way the former and the latter are always connected. In his existential and psychological investigation, Freud thematizes what we can call the neurotic form of life, which is the context in which the advent of hysterical symptoms must be understood.

From his time in Paris with Charcot, Freud had learned that hysteria is neither an organic disease nor a form of malingering by the patient. Instead, it is a psychological disease: it has a psychological cause and, for this reason, is amenable to a psychological cure. (Originally, for Charcot and Freud, this cure was hypnotic suggestion.) Freud aimed "to investigate a great variety of different forms and symptoms of hysteria, with a view to discovering their precipitating cause," their *psychological* cause (3). Refusing to believe that hysteria was either random or inexplicable, Freud believed that if he could discover the real explanation for why hysteria came about and how it functioned, he could also discover how to cure it. What we will find, however, is that Freud never considered hysterical neurosis as simply an issue concerning the neurotic's realm of thoughts, wishes, and feelings. Instead, hysteria was an issue concerning the neurotic's entire existential orientation. How so?

Here we can return to Freud's example of the cause of a hysterical symptom to help us see the most critical aspects of this phenomenon: "We may take as a very commonplace instance a painful emotion arising during a meal but suppressed at the time, and then producing nausea and vomiting which persists for months in the form of hysterical vomiting" (4). The keyword to engage here is "emotion." We are in the realm of psychology: affects, thoughts, wishes, reveries, fantasies, impulses, temptations, and the like.

We can imagine a context for the situation Freud described in this way. A young man is insulted by his father at dinner and, in response, feels a surge of murderous rage come over him. However, this feeling of anger is so painful to the young man that he eliminates it from his conscious awareness almost as quickly as it arises. This feeling now no longer exists as a conscious psychological phenomenon. After suppressing his rage, he becomes sick to his stomach, and this affliction has no end in sight.

If the young man's story is psychological, not physiological, how did Freud understand it? Why was the feeling of rage so painful? Why and how did he suppress it? Why and how did this suppression lead to a hysterical symptom? How might psychoanalytic treatment dissolve this distressing symptom?

To answer these questions, we need to see how Freud conceived hysterical neuroses as "traumatic neuroses" (4). Here the causes "for many if not for most hysterical symptoms ... can only be described as *psychical* traumas" (6, my italics). What are these traumas? For Freud, "Any *experience* which calls up distressing affects—such as those of fright, anxiety, shame, or physical pain—may operate as a trauma" (6; my italics). Again, note how "experience" has the nominative position. The traumas at the origin of hysteria consist of the self's unbidden and distressing emotions, desires, feeling, fantasies, reveries, and wishes themselves. These traumas can have external or internal sources, but they are always grounded in experiences. The interesting point is that, while extra-mental violence often precipitates trauma, Freud believes that, precisely speaking, it is the intrapsychic experiences themselves—usually but not always caused by and correlated with external violence—that comprise the core traumas from which hysterics suffer.[6]

Concerning the nauseous young man, Freud would say that it was not only or even primarily his father's harsh words at dinner that traumatized him. Those words were an external stimulus that was a necessary but not sufficient condition for the young man's suffering. The ultimate trauma was the young man's own involuntary and sudden rage.[7]

Here, however, we need to question why some moments of immediate psychological experience—such as the young man's rage—prove traumatic while other moments do not. After all, people feel strong emotions such as rage all the time without necessarily feeling traumatized by them. Why and how does one individual find the same emotion, like rage, traumatic in one situation but not so in another?

Here we have to remember what we previously learned. Forms of life, individually and collectively, settle upon modi vivendi that value and defend specific patterns of experience. Yet, in every form of life, what we are calling *immediate experience* is stubbornly present. This experience is anomalous and disruptive; its contents ateleologically deviate from and upend the inertia of habitual experiential trajectories. Conflict arises when the insistent yet discordant contents of immediate experience clash with forms of life that believe they can sustain themselves only when they defend against such dangerous contents. Within this context, this feeling toward this person in this situation is unthinkable; it is out of the realm of possible experience the individual believes they ever could or would expect or summon.

What form of life, then, does the hysteric aim to defend against the interruptions of immediate experience? Freud wrote, "among hysterics may be found people of the clearest intellect, strongest will, greatest character and highest critical power" (13). The neurotic form of life is committed to a virtuous pattern of conscious experience, one in which all conscious experience is virtuous. The neurotic's ultimate pride is pride in their virtue, a virtue that extends throughout all areas of their existence without qualification. When this form of life goes well, all subjective experiences will follow the norms and principles of the right and good. The established pattern of experience—inertia—will be praiseworthy in the eyes of both self and others.

Here Freud is neither denying nor condemning the fact that, experientially speaking, human beings, at least sometimes, can, do, and should consciously inhabit moral space.[8] When it is relevant to do so, Freud would say human beings must consciously inhabit moral space—must be consciously conscienced, we might say. In this space, individuals have experiences—actions, intentions, ends, dispositions, desires, feelings, and so on—that, in different ways, they will perceive and classify as holy or sinful, good or evil, virtuous or vicious, noble or base, right or wrong, praiseworthy or blameworthy. When individuals have such experiences, whether embodied and expressed in action or not, they believe they are dwelling within a special realm of perception, a domain where evaluations cannot be reduced to judgments of personal preference and taste. To have a moral experience or an experience that is moral is to dwell within a region of ideals, and their corresponding requirements. Within moral space, the individual can fail to be moral. Whether an individual is holy or sinful, good or evil, virtuous or vicious, noble or base, right or wrong, praiseworthy or blameworthy is not the question. The issue is only whether they, when it is relevant to do so, in fact evaluate their life and its possibilities in moral ways, whether good or evil behavior is in question. Someone can be a so-called bad person, whether they are riddled with guilt or happy in sin and remain firmly ensconced in moral space.

The issue Freud diagnoses in the neurotic life is different.[9] The neurotic does not live in moral space only when it is relevant to do so. Instead, they believe that they do and should live in nothing but moral space. They must understand and evaluate every one of their experiences as either moral or immoral, good or evil. The terms of morality and immorality, which are appropriate in the proper experiential contexts, are given the right to colonize and govern all experiential contexts. The possibility of conscious human experience that need not and should not be understood in or abiding by moral terms is unthinkable for the neurotic.

One kind of experience that Freud thinks can and does get colonized by moral space in the neurotic's life is psychological experience, their feeling and desiring life—that is to say, it is not only their behavior that the neurotic perceives in moral terms but the full content of their psychological life. Every thought, feeling, desire, or daydream is always either moral or immoral, either good or evil. The relevance of moral evaluation is comprehensive in human life; there are no limits to this evaluation's reach. Thus, it seems unthinkable that psychological experience would not merit moral evaluation.

Yet the neurotic's condition goes beyond even this picture. In Freud's estimation, the neurotic holds not only that moral space is the only kind of space that human life can inhabit; they also believe that their ideals of virtue have the right to set the terms for the logic of their psychological or "inner" life. Experience must be not holy or sinful, good or evil, virtuous or vicious, noble or base, right or wrong, praiseworthy or blameworthy, but without qualification, *only* holy, good, virtuous, noble, right, and praiseworthy. The neurotic feels that not only their action and behavior must be virtuous; their entire range of psychological experience, including everything unintended and involuntary, must be virtuous also. It is not sufficient for the neurotic to act peaceably and avoid violent deeds; they must also avoid having fantasies about engaging in violence, even when these fantasies have no real or possible connection to behavior. And, in their inertial experiential patterns, the neurotic does have what they take to be a moral psychological life, a psychological life with exclusively moral desires, thoughts, and feelings.

Just here is where Freud thought the neurotic is ripe for trouble. For just this existential situation makes trauma possible; in fact, Freud believed, it makes it inevitable. Trauma happens when the neurotic suffers within their consciousness an immediate psychological experience that flagrantly interrupts and contradicts the neurotic's belief that they can have a perfectly virtuous conscious psychological life. Freud calls these immediate experiences "distressing things" (10). Because the neurotic form of life stakes its entire existence on having virtue *in its conscious psychological life*, any feeling that erupts suddenly into consciousness that seems inconsistent with moral ideals will be seen as a profound threat. Thus, in the face of the advent of certain consciously experienced emotions that cannot be perceived as in some way virtuous, the neurotic becomes terrified and even unintelligible to themselves. To have a genuinely immoral feeling sends a stinging signal to the neurotic that they are not who they think they are; their entire identity is brutally upended. It is for all these reasons that even the mere presence of some affective content within the neurotic's conscious awareness will constitute a trauma.

However, concerning this whole scenario, we need to clarify something: the content of the morality at play in the evaluation does not matter much or at all. Freud's interest in the moral and the attendant dilemmas involved was purely formal. The religious person and the secular person may disagree markedly on what is good or evil, right or wrong, and so on. But they can both become neurotic if their existence—particularly their psychological existence—takes the shape Freud thinks it does in the neurotic form of life. The issue is that a moment of immediate psychological experience, according to the criteria of the horizon of the neurotic's settled moral aspirations, seems immoral.

Our young man, then, finds himself experiencing what he considers a deeply immoral feeling, one that feels immoral just because it contests the habitual terms of his moral experience, as that experience just happens to be. This feeling is simply impossible for him to have. In light of his principles regarding filial love and respect, his fierce rage, even when it is only psychological, is so unacceptable as to be unthinkable. His moral principles and ideals forbid him to insult his father in actual word or deed; they also forbid him to have any emotions, even in the privacy of his mind, that might fantasize about doing so.[10] The young man must never feel anger toward his father, no matter how unfairly he feels his father has treated him. Taken to its radical conclusion, the young man's sense of the demands of filial piety may be so strong that he is never even capable of fathoming the possibility that his father *could* ever mistreat him. For such a feeling would make the emotion of anger toward his father justified in some contexts, just as it cannot be if he wants to sustain his identity as a loving and grateful son, all the way down.

Just here, the problem is that the young man does find himself feeling an emotion that flagrantly contradicts his sense of permissible psychological experience. For he must honor his father without qualification not only in deed but also in the privacy of his mind. When the son suffers the sudden surge of murderous rage during dinner, he experiences a trauma. His rage is traumatic for himself, even as a purely psychological experience, because he feels that all his experience in emotion or fantasy must obey the principles of his moral experience. Otherwise, he would lose his ability to be a good son, which means he would lose his potential to be a moral person living a moral life, which means that he would lose his chance to live a meaningful life within the existential framework that defines his life. In this framework, his rage at his father constitutes an attack on the young man's entire sense of identity, of who he is and wants to be. It is so out of character that it threatens nothing less than existential death.

What is such a person to do? Here we arrive at one of Freud's most famous ideas. Sensing that the existence of their identity, their whole possibility of living a meaningful life, is vulnerable, the neurotic takes desperate action against the troubling emotion that, uninvited, is invading consciousness. This threatened self, Freud says, "intentionally repressed from his conscious thought" the feeling that was initially conscious but traumatically undermined the neurotic's identity and form of life (10). Nor is this repression unreasonable in itself. For the one experiencing it, the anomalous emotion seems to come from elsewhere, from outside the self. It feels as if an invader is on the scene. The emotion threatens something almost like demonic possession. It constitutes an existential threat, and the neurotic self will try to avoid existential annihilation by rejecting it however they can. Repression is the neurotic's tool for sustaining and saving the ability not only to live a completely moral life—that is, in deed but also in conscious thought, feeling, and desire—but to live the only life the neurotic can recognize as their own, the only life worth living for them, the only life that seems real.

Refusing Emotion: The Symptom

For Freud, hysterical symptoms include "disorders in the nature of *tic*, chronic vomiting and anorexia[,] … various forms of disturbance of vision, constantly recurrent visual hallucinations" (4, original italics).

We could add paralyses, aphasias, and aches and pains to this list, but here our focus will still be nausea. The key is that the phenomena appear without physiological explanations. We have physical symptoms without physical causes.

When a moment of immediate psychological experience vanishes through repression, it is because the neurotic has taken a particular stance toward it—or, rather, not taken a specific stance toward it. Freud writes, "patients have not reacted to a psychical trauma because the nature of the trauma excluded a reaction" (10). What does it mean to exclude a reaction to a traumatic emotion? Is not repression itself a reaction to traumatic content?

By "reaction" Freud means something particular. When the neurotic allows their mind to have a proper "reaction" to a moment of its immediate contents—that is, a first-order, spontaneously emergent emotion—this mind affirms this moment as its own.[11] In other words, in reaction a concrete emotion finds itself directly experienced as an emotion. The individual is willing to feel and does feel their emotions just in the form in which they first arise in conscious experience.

When a moment in consciousness arises that the neurotic individual perceives as a radical threat to their identity, they can choose to withhold the "reaction." Freud writes that the individual's psyche refuses reaction "because social circumstances made a reaction impossible or because it was a question of things which the patient wished to forget" (10). Here, the neurotic self refuses to accept and affirm a moment of their own conscious content, a moment of their own immediate emotional life. Instead, they try to repudiate and disown such a moment. Even though their mind somehow generated the moment within its conscious flow of experience, the neurotic will refuse to own it. Repression consists, first, of this disowning and repudiation.

When the psyche embraces and affirms the immediate emotions, they become free to remain in the mind's ongoing conscious life as memories. When the psyche disowns them, however, when it leaves them "unreacted," they leave what Freud calls a kind of "amnesia" in their wake (12). No conscious memory remains of the uncomfortable moment. Stephen Mitchell and Margaret Black bring out the point clearly: "In Freud's early theorizing, the center of the repressed was an actual experience, the memory of which, because of its traumatizing impact, could not be allowed into consciousness."[12] "Memory," then, is a consequence of "reaction." A psychological experience becomes a conscious memory when the psyche has reacted to it—that is, accepted and owned it—rather than rejecting it. When there is no reaction, however, there is no memory. Even though the emotion initially and manifestly appeared within consciousness, the work of repression has ensured it was there for only the briefest of moments. It is now, for consciousness, as if it had never been there. Or so it seems.

So, the nauseous young man refuses to feel his own rage. Since his identity and form of life center on what he understands to be his moral commitment to filial respect, he finds his anger toward his father so dangerous that he cannot allow it to exist in his conscious life. In a desperate attempt at identity protection, he tries to eject this distressing emotional moment out of his consciousness. Experiencing it consciously for but a moment, he represses it out of the same conscious awareness in which it first emerged. His rage does not become a memory. He is no longer personally aware that he felt rage at all. As far as he is consciously concerned—he thinks—it is as if his rage never happened.

Now, Freud asks, does this kind of repression make for a truly effective defense against threatening mental content? Does the act of repression succeed in ejecting disturbing content out of the mind? In one sense, the answer is yes. The mind can rid itself of an unbidden, renegade, threatening emotion—as an emotion. Repression, that is, can make an emotion disappear in the form of a conscious psychological phenomenon.

Making an emotion disappear from consciousness as an emotion, however, does not make it disappear altogether. Hence Freud's comment: "We must presume ... that the psychical trauma—or more precisely the memory of the trauma—acts like a foreign body which long after its entry must continue to be regarded as an agent that is still at work" (6). For Freud, total amnesia is impossible. Repression is an ejection that is not a real ejection. The neurotic cannot make a painful moment of consciousness vanish without trace or effect.

The issue is then how does the disquieting moment remain in the mind? A common interpretation of Freud would say that the moment remains in the mind by going underground. The disturbing emotion leaves the realm of conscious awareness and takes up residence in a different realm of the mind, viz., the unconscious.

This account is not wrong, but it fails to fully capture Freud's early understanding of how the unconscious works. When emotions, through repression, become unconscious, they continue to exist in a powerful way by becoming what Freud labels "*abnormal states of consciousness*" (12; original italics). Thus, although it is true that Freud thought repression created the unconscious, here Freud says something subtly different. He claims that repression creates not an unconscious but a *different consciousness*. Making an emotion unconscious means making it *differently conscious*. It is more a lateral move across the horizon of consciousness than a vertical move from the surface of consciousness down into the depths of the unconscious.

Freud's point is that repression is successful only in pushing traumatic psychological phenomena out of the mind's psychological consciousness. It is not effective in making traumatic feelings vanish from consciousness altogether. As Freud writes: "If the reaction is suppressed, the affect remains attached to the memory" (8). When a traumatic emotion is initially consciously experienced and then repressed, that emotion continues to exist in a powerfully and even traumatically conscious way. The repressed emotion remains conscious, but not as an emotion. The emotion remains somewhere within the conscious experience. The way the emotion remains in the conscious mind, however, is no longer psychological. Repression is the mind's mechanism for protecting its identity by transmogrifying a painful moment of psychological consciousness into a painful moment of a different, nonpsychological kind of consciousness.

This nonpsychological but still conscious experience is, Freud famously proposed, the experience of the hysterical symptom.[13] In other words, the experience of the hysterical symptom is still a conscious experience, but now it is a physical, bodily experience. The body concerned is not the organism studied by biology, which German calls *körper*—related to what English calls "corpse." The body that hysteria afflicts is the lived body: the first-person and subjective body, the felt and sensed body, the pleasured and pained body, which German calls *Leib*. When the mind does not allow itself to feel a psychological experience as a psychological experience, or an emotion as an emotion, the mind's only recourse is to experience the emotion as a physical pain in the lived body.[14] Symptoms are the individual's way of experiencing elements of emotional life that it does not want to experience but must, even if by other means.[15]

This distinction between the abnormally or differently conscious and the unconscious is subtle. What are *unconscious* are the repressed psychological phenomena *as* psychological, feelings *as* feelings that seem so dangerous the psyche cannot allow them to remain conscious. In contrast, what are *differently conscious* are these same psychological phenomena, these same threatening feelings, only now transmogrified into the form of nonpsychological sensations—that is, painful somatic symptoms in the lived body.

Freud believed that every immediate psychological experience insists that life accept, affirm, and own it in some way. Humans must give at least some reaction to everything that arises in their consciousness. Yet because every immediate psychological experience is protean enough that it can morph into a bodily experience, the mind always has the choice to embrace its troubling emotions in physical rather than psychological ways. Psychological immediacy will get its rights and expression. Conscious emotional experience demands to be consciously experienced, in either emotional or physical terms. Thus, the self will suffer, in every sense, its immediacy. The question is only what form this suffering will take.

The young man's anger, then, did not disappear. It just moved to a different plane. Instead of the anger wreaking havoc in his psychological life, it began to wreak havoc in his bodily life. Since he refused to experience anger as an emotion, he now must experience it in the form of nausea and vomiting. Hence Freud's belief that repression always fails. What is repressed always returns, even if it does so in a different form.

In this context, we can understand one of Freud's most famous ideas, the idea of repressed memories. He writes, "*Hysterics suffer mainly from reminiscences*" (7; original italics)—painful mental experiences that the psyche refuses to remember mentally through memories and instead remembers physically through hysterical symptoms. These reminiscences become "pathogenic ideas" (12) located not in the mind but in the body.

Here we can articulate one of Freud's fundamental points about hysteria: the hysterical symptom is the way the neurotic experiences their emotion indirectly. A difficult immediate psychological experience must be consciously embraced; the only choice is to embrace it directly or indirectly. Embraced indirectly, it is still embraced in a real way, albeit one that is problematic.

Whereas in a direct embrace, the subject consciously feels an emotion as an emotion, in an indirect embrace they consciously experience the emotion as a physical phenomenon. When transmogrified into another form that is not an emotion, the emotion is disguised and distorted into something other than itself; it appears as something other than what it truly is. It is an emotion that has been forced into an unemotional form.

To sustain what he takes to be his identity and very existence, our young man shuns his rage in the way it originally and suddenly appeared in his consciousness as an emotion. He trades his direct psychological experience for an indirect psychosomatic experience;

he endures a psychological phenomenon in a nonpsychological form. He chooses to experience his anger in a state other than anger— that is, nausea. Instead of experiencing the anger authentically and truthfully, he decides to experience it in a disguised and distorted way as psychosomatic vomiting. In this way, he has to pay the piper for his commitment to allow the terms of virtue to have a complete, unrestricted, and unconditional privilege to determine his conscious existence and identity.

Neurotic Life: Inauthentic, Insensible, Interminable

Freud never thought of the symptom as a self-enclosed phenomenon, in which one isolable psychological moment whose pain is too unbearable to experience directly becomes one isolable physical moment whose pain is borne more easily. The symptom is a sign of a pervasive existential structure within conscious life. The symptom exists only within an enduring form of identity that it expresses and encapsulates.

We have already seen two intrinsic dimensions of Freud's vision of the neurotic form of life. First, the neurotic is committed to the value of virtue: virtuous experience is the condition of possibility for the content of all kinds of experience, including conscious immediate psychological experience. Second, because of the way that it values morality, this form of life necessarily generates the painful hysterical symptom as a defense to ward off painful emotional experience that threatens the synchronicity of moral and psychological experience.

Now we need to unpack some other intrinsic dimensions of neurotic life that are essential to Freud's understanding of it. The first concerns this form of life's lack of truthfulness and authenticity. It does not engage psychological reality on that reality's own terms.

Specifically, in Freud's account, the neurotic does not engage emotions as emotions. They fail to allow the emotional phenomena to be the phenomena they are. Human beings in neurotic life will entertain emotions only once they have forced them into disguised and distorted forms. The bizarre situation is a form of life in which an emotional creature refuses to feel emotions. Yet because the human being as an emotional creature must feel emotions in some way, it feels the emotions in a nonemotional way. There is no authentic engagement with authentic emotions; there is no truthful feeling of emotional truth. In short, there is no authentic or truthful psychological *life*.

Another issue is the quality of the neurotic's emotional life. In short, it is stunted and impoverished. The neurotic refuses to feel emotions as emotions and blocks the ability to have a whole emotional life because certain emotions that arose in consciousness have gone missing from conscious awareness. Moments of what Freud would consider unnatural insensibility ensue. The symptom may keep the neurotic away from many kinds of emotional experience, as their consuming focus is their physical pain. Repression can not only diminish the presence of one specific disconcerting emotion in a person's life. It can diminish the full register of a person's emotional life and can threaten the possibility of a full psychological life in general.

The problem goes even deeper. This untruthful and inauthentic way of dealing with immediate psychological experience can also usher in a more all-encompassing insensibility. Why? Freud believed that every symptomatic neurotic, like the nauseous young man, is someone who, through their symptom, is "re-living the scene to which the actual onset of the illness was related" (14).

In the neurotic person, consciousness does not allow a reaction or a discharge to occur concerning painful content and thus lodges that content in a psychosomatic symptom. The problem then is that, once the symptom is on the scene, Freud thinks the neurotic's emotional life becomes forever stuck in it. Here it is not only that the neurotic cannot devote attention to emotional existence because they remain imprisoned in psychosomatic physical suffering. It is even more that the neurotic is intractably caught in the single painful emotion they have repressed—that is, the neurotic unconsciously remains imprisoned in the experience of a given emotion (such as rage) even while consciously this imprisonment has a quality other than emotional (such as nausea). The neurotic has ensured that they cannot escape the feeling by not feeling the emotion directly but instead hystericizing it. We are not in a situation where it is a case of trading in one moment of disturbing emotion in return for one moment of psychosomatic suffering; this is not how subjectivity works. Rather, it is a case of remaining trapped, consciously, in the hysterical symptom, because one remains trapped, unconsciously, in the one specific emotion indirectly experienced in the symptom.

This state of affairs has an ugly consequence. The neurotic suffers a kind of physical and emotional arrest and repetition. When the neurotic trades in an emotional experience for a psychosomatic symptom, they do not just deny themselves the one particular emotional experience. Instead, since repression and symptom formation entail that the neurotic will experience only one emotion, they will suffer from a complete emotional immobility that limits their ability to have much of a variegated emotional life at all. Indeed, at some level, they cannot have a conscious emotional life at all because they have trapped themselves in the consciousness of ongoing physical pain—pain that is, even while it is psychosomatic, nonetheless a phenomenon of the consciously lived body. The angry nauseous young man is nothing more or less than just an angry nauseous young man as long as he remains in the grip of hysterical conversion.

Symptom Relief: Memory, Psychology, Language

If neurotic consciousness is physically painful, emotionally arrested, and altogether inauthentic, how does Freud think humans can escape it? The question here, to be clear, is not just how the individual escapes one discrete symptom. The question is more far-reaching. How can humans relinquish, or even renounce, one problematic form of conscious existence (neurotic life) to adopt another more satisfying form of conscious existence?

We need to see how Freud conceives non-neurotic psychological subjectivity in general. This subjectivity engages its immediate psychological experience differently than subjectivity does in neurosis: it engages it directly. Freud writes, "By 'reaction' we here understand the whole class of voluntary and involuntary reflexes ... in which, as experience shows us, the affects are discharged" (8). Once we trade the mechanistic language of "reflexes" and "discharge" for a more qualitative and human language of "choice" and "feeling," we can see that this sentence encapsulates the existential logic of psychological subjectivity without neurosis. In this paradigm, when a disturbing emotion arises in the mind, the psychological process is not over—it is only just beginning. As Freud's language of "voluntary" implies, the mind must freely choose to affirm and welcome unanticipated and disquieting emotions as real moments in the individual's psychological life, even when these moments call into question the mind's established self-understandings and meanings. This affirmation is the completion of the emotional experience. Indeed, there is no full emotional experience (or experience of an emotion, properly speaking) without this affirmation and completion. The human mind needs to voluntarily feel all its involuntarily arising emotions, especially the painful ones, as emotions; painful emotions require the mind to regard and feel them as emotions.

When moments of immediate psychological experience arise, these moments demand that the psyche acknowledge and embrace them.

Freud the scientist, then, descriptively outlined two possible structures for human psychological existence when it comes to consciously engaging immediate experience. In the first possibility, the psyche chooses to directly feel its emotions that arise in consciousness and, because of this reaction, does not have reason to generate symptoms and neurosis. In the other, the psyche chooses to engage its emotions indirectly and, because of this withholding of reaction, brings about neurotic life with its symptoms. The critical point is that the human mind is not intrinsically neurotic. Neurotic life and its symptoms result from a contingent, not necessary, process involving a misguided (even if understandable) existential choice on the part of the sufferer.

Yet Freud was never just a scientist. He was a compassionate therapist too. He wanted to help people escape neurotic pain. And the theory he used to explain the origin of hysteria also included a way of thinking about how to cure it by helping an individual move from a destructive structure of psychological existence into a different, less painful one. The name Freud gave to this process was *abreaction*.

What defines this therapeutic action? To begin, it goes straight to the intractable experience imprisoning the neurotic. The neurotic symptom creates something like an inescapable time loop: the neurotic is caught in "re-living the scene" where they inchoately felt the emotion they could or would not allow themselves to feel fully. In their current life, they have put themselves in a situation where they can experience only the one single painful emotion that they refused earlier and the distressing symptom that encapsulates it. Indeed, they now both experience and do not experience this emotion as they suffer the nonemotional pain of the psychosomatic symptom.

Surprisingly, however, Freud thinks that the problem here is not simply that the neurotic is reliving the scene. The problem is that they are reliving the scene in a specific way: indirectly. This indirect way is a superficial strategy that seems to offer an easier method of handling a dangerous immediate psychological experience, but it ultimately vitiates life.

To escape the trap of the symptom, the hysteric needs to relive the scene of their original pain more intensely and fully than ever before. They need to experience their original emotion in a direct way that gives it the "reaction" that was withheld the first time around. "The psychical process which originally took place must be repeated as vividly as possible; it must be brought back to its *status nascendi*" (6; original italics). Since psychoanalytic treatment had facilitated this return, Freud thought, "*we had succeeded in bringing clearly to light the memory of the event by which it was provoked and in arousing its accompanying affect*" (6; original italics). The neurotic relives the experiential scene at the source of the neurosis and gives it the acknowledgment they refused to give it the first time around. So the neurotic lives this scene or experience authentically for the first time in all its nasty glory. The neurotic remembers their experience. Abreaction allows the experience to become, for the first time, a memory rather than a presently self-reiterating experience. Ironically, the problem is not that the neurotic is trapped in the memory of a trauma; they have no actual memory of the trauma; they cannot remember it as something past because it remains so intrusively present. Counterintuitively, perhaps, the neurotic needs to remember more, not less. When the mind is hospitable to the whole gamut of the individual's own life in this way, when the present intrusion becomes a memory of past trauma, Freud wrote, "*each individual hysterical symptom immediately and permanently disappeared*" (6; original italics).

In this way, Freud's therapeutic abreaction fostered for the neurotic analysand a fuller experience of their immediate psychological experience, which they had hitherto refused to experience. This kind of complete and direct experience of a hitherto incompletely and indirectly experienced painful emotion is the neurotic's only path forward beyond the symptom. By exchanging the repression of an unexpected and disturbing emotion for a reaction to it, the neurotic breaks the time loop of symptomatic affliction that has entrapped them.

In addition, Freud does not think it therapeutically efficacious for the patient simply to remember their anger cognitively. Analysis is not an invitation to the analysand to report a moment in their psychological history dispassionately or journalistically. He writes: "Recollection without affect almost invariably produced no result" (6). Healing occurs when an emotional moment of consciousness is emotionally remembered. Again, the goal is for a fuller memory, an actual memory, rather than a reiterative present. In abreaction, the past can become truly past for the first time.

Returning to the nauseous young man, we see that relief will come in only one way. He needs to allow himself to feel his original anger at his father as anger, in contrast to experiencing it as nausea through a process of hysterical conversion. Only when he feels his rage in a direct, truthful, and authentic way will he find some physical and psychological peace. Furthermore, now that he is not trapped in place in a repetitive emotional and somatic stasis, he may discover that he is now able to recover and develop a deeper and broader emotional life in general.

An important point to emphasize here is how Freud thought this process of abreaction must take place in a particular way: linguistically. Healing arrived when *"the patient ... put the affect into words"* (6; original italics). The original arrested experience has to be re-experienced with all its passionate feeling through speaking it, through reliving it in and through language. The patient puts the affect into words not by speaking descriptively about it dispassionately and objectively but by speaking it affectively. The affective experience has to be experienced in speech as it was not before. Hence Freud's insistence that the incompletely experienced immediate psychological experience finds completion and reaction only through an act of speech, what Freud calls "verbal utterance" (6; original italics).[16] The issue is not only the content that is spoken in speech, it is also the manner in which the speech is uttered.

In this way, the original full-blooded emotional experience that the psyche allowed itself to experience only indirectly—by forcing it to go underground, or to go to a different ground—in a toxically psychosomatic way is finally directly experienced. Freud summarizes his position: "It will now be understood how it is that the psychotherapeutic procedure which we have described in these pages has a curative effect. *It brings to an end the operative force of the idea which was not abreacted in the first instance, by allowing its strangulated affect to find a way out through speech*" (17; original italics).[17] Relief from the symptom comes only when the individual directly brings themselves to experience their immediate psychological experience; their psyche welcomes this experience in affective speech and thereby feels emotions as emotions. The psychological subject now explicitly owns their psychological immediacy and experiences it directly by speaking it emotionally—angrily, sadly, passionately, or however the situation merits.

For Freud, the idea that conscious psychological life must abide by the ideals of virtue is an illusion to be diagnostically unmasked and therapeutically dismantled. The analysand realizes through their analysis that the rules of virtue have no rights over psychological life. These ideals of virtue, the neurotic must see, are generated by a misguided fear of the chaotic anomalies of immediate psychological experience even as, once generated, these ideals reinforce this misguided fear. The sometime neurotic renounces the self-contradictory, destructive fantasy that the ideals of virtue have an all-extensive authority over their conscious psychological life. This fantasy, this illusion, is the condition of possibility for the trauma that lies at the origin of the painful neurotic symptom. The therapeutic elimination of this illusion lies at the heart of the dissolution of this symptom.

Psychological Life: To the Deep and Dynamic

I suggest that Freud's analysis tried to facilitate the recovery—by living it directly and completely in consciousness for the first time—of conscious emotional experience through abreaction. Yet I emphasize that Freud's goal was not limited to eliminating isolated hysterical symptoms or recovering isolated repressed emotions. His interest was more radical: to invite the neurotic to welcome and embrace painful moments of psychological experience in the most direct way possible in a new form of mental life. In this process, the sometime neurotic gains an authentic psychological life for the first time.

The first dimension of psychological life that Freud charts in the "Preliminary Communication" should already be clear. The sometime neurotic will dwell more fully and deeply within immediate psychological experience. They will give this experience more of the reaction it demands and merits. In doing so, the individual's emotional life will be both deeper and broader. They will more intentionally welcome into consciousness and embrace all their feelings, even when these feelings have arisen anomalously or suddenly. Whatever the varying contents may be, they are welcomed and embraced. The individual's subjectivity thereby opens to a richer experience of individual emotions, which now belong to the individual as a part of their existence and identity. The individual no longer feels these emotions are foreign invasions. They also open to a broader experience of a more polychromatic emotional life in general.

Freud's point is profound. In a real sense, abreaction allows the self to feel emotions in a fully conscious way for the first time. When taken as foreign, when lodged in the symptom and unconscious, an emotion is only partly and incompletely conscious and only partly and incompletely the emotion it is; it exists in a stunted, truncated, diminished form. To exist fully, the emotion has to find reaction or abreaction within conscious life. Reaction does not simply receive an emotion passively; it consciously unfolds the emotion into its fullness. Abreaction does not make an unconscious emotion become conscious in the same form it was when it was unconscious; it does not remember an emotion that fully existed in consciousness before the mind repressed it. Instead, the state of the emotion when it sprang into consciousness was incomplete;

it needed reaction to become complete. When this reaction was not forthcoming, when the mind refused the emotion this reaction, the emotion went into the unconscious in a truncated, half-existent way.

Here we can see why the idea that abreaction simply "makes the unconscious conscious" or "remembers a traumatic experience" does not capture Freud's precise understanding of abreaction. When this phenomenon makes conscious something unconscious through remembering, it makes something that has only partial existence in the unconscious or something that is abnormally conscious in the symptom into something that fully exists within authentic emotional consciousness. When abreaction makes an emotion conscious through remembering—when the mind accepts and owns the memory both intentionally and directly—it allows this emotion to exist more profoundly than it ever has before. The emotion is now what it always had the potential to be but had only incipiently been before in the unconscious and the symptom. This completion of the emotion, through reaction or abreaction, develops psychological experiences (including immediate psychological experiences) into their fullness as phenomena that psychological life can consciously experience profoundly and richly.[18]

In fact, it is unclear whether the language of memory and remembering is even appropriate here. In some sense, abreaction not only allows an emotion to exist in a fuller manner; it may allow the emotion to exist in a real way for the first time. The reason is that, in some sense, when the mind experiences an unexpected and intolerable upsurge of feeling that it then represses, there has been no anger as anger that ever existed that the mind could later remember. Abreaction is not making forgotten anger present again, because there was never any genuine emotional experience of anger, to begin with. When we remember that an authentic experience of an emotion requires moments of upsurge and reaction, we see that abreaction is not so much remembering a moment of anger in the past as it is making anger itself, as a real emotion, present for the first time. Abreaction is doing in the present what reaction could have done in the past. We might say that the goal of Freud's analytic treatment is to remember what did not happen. Put differently, the goal is not so much to retrieve a memory of an emotional experience that occurred as to create a memory, to turn the initially arrested experience into a memory for the first time, to make the past moment into what it always should have been.

Here we can mention a further paradox that characterizes the phenomenon of forgetting and remembering memories. Although

Freud did want analysands to remember their traumatic experiences, he also wanted them to forget these experiences—at least in a certain way. Freud writes, "The fading of a memory or the losing of its affect depends on various factors. The most important of these is *whether there has been an energetic reaction to the event that provokes an affect*" (8; original italics). It might seem as if the way to leave a painful immediate psychological experience behind is to try to forget it—that is, to repress it. But Freud counterintuitively holds that the way to move beyond a painful psychological experience, lodged in a symptom or not, is to experience it more, not less, directly and intensely through welcoming it into the realm of conscious psychological experience.

We might say that Freud wants to replace amnesia with forgetting. Amnesia, on the one hand, is a disappearance of a painful emotion from consciousness that is not actually a disappearance. Abreaction, on the other hand, allows a painful moment of consciousness, having now been experienced directly, to disappear from consciousness, to cease being the focus and colonizer of conscious awareness. Freud's counterintuitive claim suggests that, on the one hand, the way to forget a painful memory is to remember it, and on the other, that if the mind cannot remember a painful memory, the mind will never be able to forget it. Hence while we think of a memory as something one can remember, for Freud it is also something one can forget (but not until it is first remembered!).

This kind of forgetting is not absolute. The original painful experience, now fully experienced in abreaction, will still be available to the conscious mind as a memory. Yet it will not consume conscious life in an ongoing, interminable way. The emotion can fade in focus and intensity when felt directly when it arises—or when abreacted in analysis later.

Abreaction benefits the neurotic by alleviating their symptom and diminishing its distressing emotion. When the mind directly embraces an immediate psychological experience, not only does the symptom start to disappear but the affect itself, by receiving the reaction it demands in abreaction, loses much of its insistence and force when finally discharged. When the mind embraces its painful emotion directly, it escapes both the hysterical symptom in the body and the painful emotion's dominance in the mind.

This kind of remembering and forgetting does not leave the mind blank. When a painful emotion is abreacted, the mind creates room for other emotions to gain a place in conscious life. Conscious life can become a variegated process of different emotions that come and go.

One painful emotion has become a memory, and then another, perhaps less painful, emotion can come into focus. When the mind directly feels an emotion as an emotion and gives it the response it demands, the emotion, even if painful, becomes only one moment in an ongoing and differentiated chain of emotional moments. It no longer insists on colonizing consciousness.

One way to crystallize the point starkly is to say that the analysand in abreaction gains a new mind. In particular, the neurotic, by more directly experiencing their immediate psychological experience, gains a mind that has a future, not only a past and a present. Consciousness becomes—either again or for the first time—dynamic rather than static; it develops a conscious life that is an ongoing flow of different moments, which in its vicissitudes can bring more satisfying emotions along with painful ones. Abreaction restores (or ushers in for the first time) what we might call emotional motion. The psychological self gains the capacity to experience a rich, broad, and ever-changing range of emotions—with positive and negative valences.

Thus, Freud's therapeutic goal went beyond symptom relief. His ultimate goal was for his analysands to consciously embrace their immediate psychological experience and thereby find a new psychological life: a richly polychromatic and dynamic emotional life, saturated with rewarding and also distressing emotions. Psychological existence has a new center: the goal of experiencing all emotions, whether gratifying and upsetting, as consciously and directly as possible as they continually arise and fade in intensity and focus.

Our young man, in this light, finds himself trapped in a constricted emotional life. He is intractably stuck in his nausea, which prevents him from feeling his anger. Beneath and within this physical pain, the young man remains, unconsciously speaking, intractably imprisoned in the experience of just the one painful emotion of anger—anger that, to a large degree, he has never actually allowed himself to feel. In Freud's terms, by not remembering his rage, the young man cannot forget it, and by refusing to forget it, he can remember nothing else. We might even put it provocatively and say that the very meaning of the young man's life, the only meaning of his life, in his neurotic state, is to vomit and rage.

Abreaction offers him a way out of his symptomatic suffering and his unceasingly painful way of life. When he feels his anger fully as anger, he can leave behind his nausea as the all-consuming experience of life. When trapped in an anger that continually reiterates itself symptomatically, interminably, and mercilessly as nausea, his mind had no future in any meaningful sense, no possibility to feel anything other than the anger it, indirectly, felt. Now, however, having felt his anger at his father directly as anger—for the first time!—his mind can experience a future with a broad range of emotions toward his father and others.

Reaction and Abreaction: Saving Virtue

Abreaction has another benefit for Freud. It is related to the issue that generated the neurotic symptom in the first place. Abreaction can be the paradoxical means of restoring the neurotic to a fully moral life.

We need to remember that an existential stance lies at the origin of neurosis in Freud's mind: the neurotic's unstinting commitment to virtue. This commitment is so fervent, thoroughgoing, and even fanatical that every moment of the neurotic's psychological life has to be perfectly virtuous, as they understand virtue to be. This commitment then motivates the repression of whatever insurgent emotional moments went outside the lines, so to speak, and caused these emotional moments to return indirectly and problematically in the form of painful hysterical symptoms.

After abreaction, where is the neurotic vis-à-vis the issue of morality and virtue? First, the neurotic, through abreaction, will realize that, in all likelihood, they are already a virtuous person. They come to see that emotions do not threaten anyone's ability to be a virtuous person. They learn that moral criteria are relevant at some times but not others. They discover that emotion in itself does not merit or welcome moral evaluation. Even if they fantasize murder, an angry feeling simply cannot be, in itself, vicious. Indeed, an emotion can appear vicious only when seen in the light of ideals and principles of virtue that are inappropriate to it. For Freud, these ideals and principles give criteria appropriate only for the realm of human action and behavior. Moral issues and questions are not yet in play when an emotion simply as an emotion burgeons in consciousness. A feeling experienced as a feeling—nothing more, nothing less—is neither morally good nor morally evil. When experienced psychologically, psychological data neither enhances moral identity nor diminishes it. Emotions and other psychological realities are often amoral phenomena. Thus the neurotic may find that their immediate psychological experience does not and cannot inherently threaten their moral identity.

Another point is that Freud's work shows how, by engaging their immediate psychological experience directly, the neurotic may find, in addition to an experience of being at peace with their conscience, the capacity to become an even more virtuous person. The renunciation of moral fanaticism can enable virtue in the realm where virtue is an intelligible concept: behavior and action. For Freud, the form of psychological existence he was promoting—which does not pressure psychological life and experience to match up to the demands of virtue, which lets psychological life entertain all its contents—may serve to safeguard and promote the project of leading a virtuous life.

How does Freud think abreaction safeguards and protects moral life? The answer has to do with the precise form of abreaction. Abreaction instantiates and expresses emotions in passionate speech. It places speech where symptoms were, but it also places speech where unchecked actions may be. Here, Freud writes, "language serves as a substitute for action; by its help, an affect can be 'abreacted' almost as effectively" (8).

What is the implication of seeing abreaction as a practice of speech and language? Abreaction can relieve not only a neurotic symptom but also a need to enact violence. The life of psychological reaction and abreaction, in which human beings feel their emotions directly as emotions, saves humans from violence directed against the self in crippling neurosis and violence against the other in destructive behavior. Reaction and abreaction protect life from unnecessary mental suffering and from vicious behavior. When our young man experiences his murderous anger toward his father as reaction or abreaction, he lessens the possibility that he will murder his father.[19]

In addition to warding off vicious behavior, abreaction can promote virtuous behavior. The reason is that the neurotic, by misguidedly insisting upon perfect virtue in psychological life, may be undermining the goal of pursuing virtuous life more broadly. Trapped in intractable and repetitive conscious symptomatic suffering and unconscious negative emotion, the hysteric cannot have much of a moral *life* in terms of *action*. The hysterical symptom will consume all the energy, time, and focus that might otherwise be available for moral action. Abreaction frees up this formerly unavailable resource of time and energy, which the neurotic may now choose to pour into action that reflects their moral ideals. Thus, the possibility of a virtuous life requires the capacity to accept so-called vicious immediate psychological experiences.

The angry young man, confused about the relationship between morality and psychology in the first place, may unconsciously think that by trading his conscious rage for conscious nausea he is protecting and advancing his moral identity. Yet the fact is that it will be difficult for him actually to be a devoted and respectful son—or anything else, for that matter—if he is consciously immobilized by nausea and unconsciously imprisoned by anger. The moral identity he was insistent on sustaining is more of a fantasy than a reality. However, when the young man feels his rage, something else can happen. The rage can dissipate, and he will find more inner resources to be a moral person in his actions and relationships, including the relationship with his father that he originally meant to protect through repression of his rage. By feeling the full fire of his anger toward his father, he becomes more capable of loving his father—and, beyond that, more capable of living some kind of meaningfully virtuous life in general.

Refusing Desire: Sex and Aggression

Having explored the vicissitudes of conscious immediate psychological experience when it is emotion, now we turn to when it is desire. Here we can look at Freud's case study "Fräulein Elisabeth von R." His study of this young woman, one of his first patients, reiterates themes in the "Preliminary Communication" while also going beyond them.

Who is Elisabeth? Why does she need treatment? She is a young, single woman who enjoyed mental and physical health until a few months ago. At that time, her beloved older sister died. Soon after, Elisabeth suffered horrible leg pains that made it almost impossible for her to walk.[20] She sought out Freud because these pains seemed to lack any physiological basis, to be psychosomatic. In Freud's terms, she appeared to be suffering from hysterical neurosis.

The origin of Elisabeth's hysteria has all the features we saw Freud outline above. First, her "illness and her actual symptom ... have been caused and determined by ... experiences" (138). Elisabeth has had an immediate psychological experience, sudden, unanticipated, and undesired. As Freud says: "It seems to me that the concept of a 'defence hysteria' in itself implies that at least *one* moment of this kind must have occurred" (167).

Second, this originally (if only momentarily) conscious experience was so anomalous that it was traumatic. Elisabeth felt that the experience threatened to destroy her established psychological identity, governed as that identity was by the strict demands of virtue that forced her to try to think, feel, and desire only what seem to her to be praiseworthy things. Freud writes, "her behavior, the fact that she had fallen ill in these circumstances, was sufficient evidence of her moral character" (157).

Third, to avoid the trauma that has begun and which threatens to overwhelm her, Elisabeth represses any psychological content arising in her consciousness that seems to defy her norms and ideals of virtue out of consciousness. She attempts to save her virtuous identity by ejecting whatever comes into her conscious awareness that seems to contradict and undermine her integrity. Thus Freud writes of "The incompatible idea, which, together with its concomitants, is later excluded and forms a separate psychical group" (167).

Concretely, however, what was the specific and concrete conscious content that Elisabeth had perceived to be so threatening that she believed that, if she were to allow it to remain within her conscious awareness, it would destroy her? What was this trauma that she was desperately fighting off by repressing it? What was her difficult, disturbing, and dangerous immediate psychological experience?

Freud discovered that Elisabeth had several desires pass through her consciousness. The foundational one was Elisabeth's ardent desire for the happiness of love. "Here, then, was the unhappy story of this proud girl with her longing for love" (143). Elisabeth wanted a passionate marriage to a good man. This desire defined her existence.

Furthermore, and here is where her trouble began, Elisabeth believed that her sister had exactly what she wanted. She felt "the contrast between her own loneliness and her sick sister's married happiness." This contrast was "painful to her" and gave her "a burning wish that she might be as happy as her sister" (151).[21] Furthermore, in her conversation with Freud, she remembered that she once took a walk with her brother-in-law, in which "She found herself in complete agreement with everything he said, and a desire to have a husband like him became very strong in her" (155). She has wanted deeply and desperately to be a wife just like her sister, who is married to a husband just like her brother-in-law.

Yet her wishes' true nature and extent appear only when Elisabeth walks into the bedroom where her sister's dead body lies. Freud writes that she

> stood before the bed and looked at her sister as she lay there dead. At that very moment of dreadful certainty that her beloved sister was dead ... at that very moment another thought had shot through Elisabeth's mind, and now forced itself irresistibly upon her once more, like a flash of lightning in the dark: 'Now he is free again and I can be his wife.'
>
> (156)

This moment crystallizes and manifests the true nature of her desiring vis-à-vis her sister and brother-in-law. In a moment of manifest sexuality and, in addition, aggression, Elisabeth finds that she not only has wanted to be like her sister with a man like her brother-in-law but also has wanted to take her actual sister's place to be with her real brother-in-law.

When this wishing becomes conscious, Elisabeth has to confront a moment of not only manifest but flagrantly forbidden sex and aggression.[22] Freud wrote, "her love for her brother-in-law was present in her consciousness like a foreign body ... a tenderness whose acceptance into consciousness was resisted by her whole moral being" (157). Her death wish toward her sister, too, could only be felt as a wicked intrusion, one incompatible with all her moral commitments. Elisabeth lusts after someone she believes is off-limits; she harbors a death wish toward someone she loves. To her way of thinking, she wants to do something evil: to murder the sister she loves in order to steal her spouse.

Elisabeth's conscious experience of her sexuality and aggression is so morally abominable to her in light of her aspirations for the content of her desiring life that its presence in consciousness for even a few seconds is traumatic. This brief instant is so devastatingly self-alienating that she is convinced that, if allowed to remain in consciousness, it will shatter her whole personality. It is a threat that she feels she must deflect at all costs.

Upsurges of Madness: Insanities of Desire

Here we can clarify at a deeper level the reason that Elisabeth finds her sexuality and aggression so traumatic and interfering with her emotional and bodily life. The logic goes beyond her desires' sexual and aggressive nature to the broader overall quality of her desiring life. This quality is insanity. Freud believed that the content and the logic of conscious immediate *psychological* experience, in its anomalous goings and comings of desire, has a manifestly *psychotic* character. So, even in the neurotic, Freud believed a certain kind of insanity exists—*neurotic insanity* as opposed to psychotic insanity.[23]

For Freud, psychotic elements belong to conscious psychological life both inescapably and intrinsically. Neurotics, he writes, "in their hypnoid states ... are insane, as we all are in dreams" (13). The hypnoid states, we remember, are the symptomatic states in which a repressed desire is achieving its rights through the symptom. Freud can speak of times "where we meet with an acute hysteria, a case which is passing through the period of the most active production of hysterical symptoms and in which the ego is being constantly overwhelmed by the products of the illness (i.e., during a hysterical psychosis)" (263). Acute hysteria is indeed hysterical psychosis. Freud sees many of the dangerous ideas, emotions, and desires of immediate psychological experience, phenomena once conscious but now repressed, as fundamentally psychotic: "Whereas ... our dream-psychoses have no effect upon our waking state, the products of hypnoid states intrude into waking life in the form of hysterical symptoms" (13). An insane moment of consciousness is what failed to receive reaction—and thus is getting its rights by other means, by expressing itself indirectly and untruthfully in the psychosomatic symptom.[24]

If the hypnoid state is insane, then the indirectly expressed desire in this state is insane. Thus, it is no surprise that Freud speaks of "the fear felt ... by all neurotics of going mad" (88). Significant facets of the neurotic's mental life are indeed mad. From Elisabeth's perspective, her wish to kill her sister and steal her sister's husband is insane.

The reason can become evident when we consider "sanity" etymologically. The word "sane" comes from the Proto-Indo-European *swā-n-, indicating wholeness.[25] From this root was derived the Old Dutch *sōna, which could signify peace and agreement, and the Proto-Germanic *sōnō, which could refer to reconciliation and atonement.[26] The "insane" would then indicate the partial, the fragmented, the agonistic, the conflicting, the disagreeing. Psychological insanity would represent an unreconciled battle between different, unrelated, and unreconcilable moments of desire.

These etymological insights help us pinpoint why the language of insanity is appropriate here. It is not because Freud thinks an insane desire is insane because it is offensive, scandalous, or (as the cliché goes) "crazy." It is also not because he thinks an insane desire, in its fundamental nature, is always delusional or hallucinatory. On the contrary, in Freud's mind, an insane desire is often all too real. A desire the neurotic suffers from and tries to repress is insane because it is anomalous. It is insane because it is insistently present in consciousness even as it is stubbornly and irreconcilably contradicting other, more habitual, familiar, and preferred elements of consciousness and their inertia.

Incoherence: Responsibility without Biography

So Freud criticizes the idea that conscious psychological life is and should always and everywhere be "sane," in either content or form or both. The kind of sanity the neurotic tries to sustain is a destructive fantasy. We might say that what is insane is the neurotic's insistence upon this kind of unreachable sanity.

The next question is Can the neurotic find a way out of their stymied position? The answer is: yes and no. In something of a paradox, Freud thinks that the way for the neurotic to escape the insanity they face is to enter more deeply into it. The neurotic needs to embrace the insane upsurges of desire they find coming over them, resist the temptation to eliminate those urges, and thus restore what they think is their ordinary sanity. While Freud's analytic treatment could have aimed to eliminate or minimize madness in the psyche—a goal that, in many ways nobly, defines modern clinical psychology and psychiatry—that was in fact not Freud's goal. Rather than aiming to dissolve the neurotic's mad desires, Freud's goal was to assist the neurotic in taking responsibility for them by accepting them.

We have already seen something like this process at work in the nature of symptom relief. The neurotic has become hysterically symptomatic in the first place because of their fear that if they allowed themselves to experience their frightening feeling directly, then they would lose control; the desire would overwhelm and destroy them. But through abreaction, the neurotic discovers that the truth is the opposite. When they experience feeling directly as feeling, and desire directly as a desire, they find that the painful phenomenon loses much of its force and insistence. The paradox is that the surest way for an individual to guarantee that they will stay within the grip of a difficult psychological experience is to refuse to entertain it directly.

To regain health (or to gain it for the first time), Elisabeth must give up the project of repressing her insanity; she must, instead, directly experience her insanity. She needs, to begin, to un-repress and abreact her individual "insane" desires. For, at one level, it is an insane desire, which Elisabeth made unconscious by repression, that has returned in a disguised way as a psychosomatic symptom. The renegade moment of consciousness has become differently and abnormally conscious through conversion.[27] The psychological has become physical.[28] She suffers in her lived body what she has refused to suffer in her psychological life. Thus Elisabeth's cure, when it happens, will involve abreaction. The unconscious—the indirectly conscious insanity—will become directly conscious insanity. Freud writes, "I declared that I knew very well that something *had* occurred to her and that she was concealing it from me; but she would never be free of her pains so long as she concealed anything"—from Freud and from herself (154; original italics). The original moment of immediate psychological experience—in its insanity—will be able to unfold in the process of psychological reaction that it initially demanded, once Elisabeth decreases her resistance and welcomes that moment more intentionally and explicitly, even as it conflicts with what she takes to be her habitual pattern of desire and even as it flagrantly refuses to be at one with the whole, as it disturbs the peace.

But Freud thinks that the process also involves something more. The neurotic individual must not only accept and appropriate specific insane psychological moments of content; they also need to accept the sometimes insane logic of the psyche in its immediate experience. The problem the neurotic needs to address is not only the presence of discrete moments of immediate psychological experience that disturb the peace; the problem they need to reckon with is also that peace is an inappropriate ideal and aspiration for the psyche in the first place. The individual needs to accept the broader syntax of their desiring life—how the parts relate to one another—as unavoidably insane. Psychological life never has a total integrated wholeness without remainder, never has all its dimensions reconciled. Psychological existence is always shot through with agonistic conflict between parts that do not and cannot make up a whole.

To accept what appears as one insane moment in her conscious life, Elisabeth has to accept the sometimes insane character of her psyche, in the sense of "insanity" as laid out above. Elisabeth's desire to murder her sister and steal her brother-in-law can and does exist alongside her love for and loyalty to her sister and brother-in-law. What is insane is the individual moment of lust and the death wish along with the coexistence of lust and death wish in the same psychological life as love and loyalty. To echo the classical Aristotelian language of logic, Elisabeth does not love and hate her sister in successive moments; she loves and hates her sister and brother-in-law simultaneously—that is, at the same time and in the same respect. And it is not just a moment that is separated from the rest; it is Elisabeth who is separated from herself. The logic of her immediate experience is such that her psychological subjectivity is occasionally and frequently, not only contingently but essentially, fragmented, contradictory, plural, unreconciled, and irreconcilable—incoherent in the sense that it does not cohere.

Adam Phillips eloquently articulates Freud's neurotic's situation in his own words. He contends that "we are always, in Freud's views, trying to contain the uncontainable.... We fear the immediacy of experience."[29] For Phillips, many immediate desires and emotions feel traumatic because they conflict with an individual's psychological autobiography, their self-avowed psychological identity. This autobiography is a story that defines who someone is and wants to be psychologically: their specific likes and dislikes, loves and hates, feelings and wishes, hopes and fears, and so on. It also defines who someone is not and does not want to be. We know that the temptation is to repress any emergent psychological phenomenon that the self believes will challenge the truth and legitimacy of the individual's autobiography by transmogrifying it into something different, viz., the hysterical symptom. This autobiography thus rigidly constricts psychological identity.

Relief from a symptom, for Phillips, requires unsettling the psychological autobiography that is creating the need for the symptom. The hysteric needs freedom from the pressure of the specific mind narrative that forces them to repress something, to desire it only unconsciously, differently consciously, and indirectly. Only by abandoning this restrictive mind narrative can the neurotic begin to enjoy some measure of symptom relief.[30]

In addition, Phillips believes the neurotic will not be cured by trading one psychological autobiography for another one.[31] Instead, in his opinion, Freud's work shows that the neurotic must abandon the project of autobiography altogether. Phillips writes: "Psychoanalysis would one day be Freud's proof that biography is the worst kind of fiction, biography is what we suffer from; that we need to cure ourselves of the wish for biography, and our belief in it" (21). The neurotic does not need to replace a false biography of their psyche with a more truthful one; they need to replace an autobiographical form of psychological life with a less biographical form of it as such.

Phillips's Freud thinks the neurotic needs relief from the pressure of autobiography because biography all too frequently insists that the story of an individual's life, and even their psychological life and its immediate contents, must be marked by unity and coherence. But absolute unity and coherence, Phillips thinks Freud shows, are misplaced ideals regarding psychological identity and existence.[32] Psychological existence, on the contrary, is often constituted by "competing (inner) voices" (33). The contents of the psyche's desires are often incoherent in the literal sense of the word: they do not cohere. The psyche regularly experiences inconsistent and incompatible desires and feelings. Its contents are repeatedly in conflict. Immediate psychological experience is often defined by irresolvable contradiction. Contradiction is part of the essence of consciousness, a sine qua non for it.

The contradictory character of psychological life is experienced through the psyche's experience of the continually diverting and deviating nature of its desiring life. Here Phillips speaks of "the waywardness of ... desires" (67). In Latin, *divertere* means "to turn aside," and *deviare* means "to go away from the way," or "to deviate from the path." If diversion and deviation are essential to the definition of consciousness, then immediate psychological experience is constantly going awry and changing course in internally contradictory ways. Its anomalies are repeatedly departing from the appropriate, the planned, the expected, and the gratifying—and from what seems to be the reasonable and the moral.[33]

Hence if the psyche's first-order feelings, desires, and beliefs are inevitably spinning off in contradictory directions in a process that takes no account of the psyche's intentions, preferences, settled horizons, or established patterns, in a process that seems to give no regard to logic or rationality at all, then the biographer's demand that the various moments of psychological life be knitted together into one story of one life is inappropriate and unhelpful. The ideal of a mind unified in a coherent psychological drama, in which each moment exists in consistent harmony with the others, is a false and illusory ideal.[34] Insisting upon this false ideal does violence to the actual existence of psychological life. As Phillips writes: "What modern people suffered from, in what became Freud's view as a psychoanalyst, were spurious forms of internal consensus" (33). The pressures of these spurious forms of consensus can only lead to hysterical neurosis in the pattern that we have seen.

Here, we need to say another word about virtue. Here we see again that Elisabeth, and any neurotic, is tempted to let the terms of her established psychological content and patterns determine the conditions of possibility for any future psychological life. Hence the ultimate issue is not so much the immoral or amoral content of Elisabeth's desire but the fact that her desire is incoherent vis-à-vis what it has been. We might even say that her desire's incoherence is indeed what is ultimately its immorality, at least at a descriptive level. Elisabeth's implicit idea that something like a perfectly coherent, consistent, and unified psychological existence is a worthy or attainable ideal needs to be diagnostically unmasked as generated by fear of the anomalies of immediate psychological experience—even as this ideal then furthers just this fear. Freud aims to help her, and the neurotic in general, see the incoherence of her desire. And diagnosis is not enough; Elisabeth also needs to be liberated from the desire to make her psychological life measure up to this imaginary ideal; the ideal needs to be therapeutically dismantled at an experiential level for the neurotic to find healing; the neurotic needs to develop the ability to live within the incoherence of their desire.

We do not have to say that Freud endeavored to eliminate every experience of psychological conflict. In a certain way, Freud sought to increase such conflict. The healthy psyche, to Freud, can consciously entertain and tolerate its inevitable contradictions, inconsistencies, and illogicalities in both form and content.

This position is what Phillips believes Freud was endorsing when he thought that healing happens only when the neurotic can stop trying to make as much sense—that is, as much coherent and unified sense—of their psychological life as they have been trying to do. Freud's work opened up, Phillips thinks, not only "new stories" of the psychological self—that is, new ways of making sense of one's mind, such as letting it be less inhibited, more affective, and so on. Psychoanalysis also opened up "new ways of telling stories—even the ways of not telling stories, of finding alternatives to narrative coherence" (18–19). The psychoanalyst asked, "what kind of sense was now possible, and whether it was sense that now needed to be made" (19–20). The psyche works best, with less neurotic pain, when it can tolerate an ongoing level of nonsense within itself.

We need to be clear about one thing, however. What Freud is proposing is not a blanket celebration of insanity; we are not in a Dionysian realm of emotional and libidinal abandon. Instead, the point is that, amid the settled and habitual trajectories of psychological existence that individuals cannot but inhabit, they need to see that not every disintegrating or incoherent moment in psychological life is pathological, at least not for neurotics. In Phillips's reading, Freud came to see that the healthy mind will be open to and will accept the moments of psychological life that cannot be integrated into the settled and habitual trajectories that have stably defined it up to a specific time. The neurotic realizes that contradiction, diversion, conflict, deviation, and nonsense are dimensions of psychological life as intrinsic as settledness and habituality. Since the possibility of a coherent, consistent, or unified mind narrative is foreclosed (since plausible logics and pathways for thinking, wishing, and feeling are constantly being upended and contradicted), individuals should abandon attempts to recover a wholly unified and coherent psychological life. Instead, they should directly and deliberately embrace moments of incoherence, discontinuity, and fragmentation in their psychological life.[35]

Freud does not mandate abandoning all commitments to ideals of self-coherence, self-consistency, or self-integration. In certain areas of life—romance, family, friendship, work—these qualities can be beneficial and necessary ideals.[36] Phillips's Freud thought only that these ideals could not be normative for psychological life. Once these unattainable and masochistic ideals have been deflated, the psyche can embrace its psychological incoherence, disunity, inconsistency, and fragmentation along with its coherence, unity, consistency, and wholeness in an explicit, truthful, and self-aware way. The mind can more consciously and intentionally participate in the contradictory flow of consciousness—to participate directly in its own difficult nonsense—in the difficult insane form of psychological existence alongside the difficult insane contents. The ultimate point is that an individual can be symptomatically psychotic, neurotically psychotic, or post-neurotically psychotic, but no one can eliminate the elements of insanity that permeate the form and content of psychological existence.[37] Yet there are still different forms of psychosis—*psychotic* psychosis and *neurotic* psychosis. Freud's interest in his early work was in what we can call neurotic insanity—how this insanity afflicts human life and how the individual can and must learn to live with it.

The neurotic, to go beyond neurosis, has to take a specific step in the direction of responsibility. In fact, in another paradox, they have to accept responsibility for what they are not responsible for. Freud writes, "we are not responsible for our feelings" (157). The form and content of immediate psychological experience *subjects* the subject of these feelings and desires. Yet Freud believed that neurotics, to go beyond neurosis, are nevertheless responsible for feeling their emotions and wishing their desires. They are responsible for directly undergoing their immediate psychological experience, however hazardous and hard to handle this may initially seem to be. The insane elements of psychological life have to be reckoned with—either indirectly or directly. Freud invites the neurotic to follow the latter path, the path of responsibility, the path of voluntarily chosen and embraced anomaly, fragmentation, and incoherence in psychological life.

Elisabeth finds herself in a situation where she must make a choice. Her neurosis, after all, did not happen by chance. She is not simply a passive victim; she is also an agent in her misery. She could not ward off the advent of her sexual and aggressive desire, but she did have a measure of agency in deciding how to engage this desire once it was on the scene. Freud said that it was by "an act of will" that she engaged in "fending off" her immediate experience (157) via repression and conversion.[38] She made the choice to repress the threatening, insane content from her psychological consciousness, which resulted in her having an indirect experience of it instead.

For Elisabeth to heal, she needs now to make another choice, another act of will. She needs to choose not to fend off her insane desires. She needs to voluntarily embrace as much of her immediate psychological experience as possible, even when such an embrace seems at first an insane prospect. And this point does arrive: Freud and Elisabeth discover together "the girl's wish, of which she was now conscious" (159). Her emergent desire to have her sister out of the way so she could possess the affections of her brother-in-law, the desire that spontaneously came into her awareness before any reflection or evaluation on her part, she now embraces as her desire in a direct, authentic, truthful way. Elisabeth has begun to develop the ability to be crazy enough to stay close to that which is closest to her—her dangerous immediate experience—just where she used to give in to the temptation to keep herself distant from it.

There is a happy result. Freud writes, "During this period of 'abreaction' the patient's condition ... made ... a striking improvement" (148). And: "Two months later ... Elisabeth felt perfectly well and was behaving as though there was nothing wrong with her, though she still suffered occasionally from slight pains" (160). Elisabeth has made something unconscious, differently conscious, or physically conscious into something psychologically conscious. Having surrendered her insistence on keeping up a unified and consistent psychological consciousness, she is now taking responsibility for her desires just as they originally, pre-reflectively, pre-evaluatively, come into mind, no matter how anomalous they may be. Having chosen to consciously dwell within this new state of mind, Elisabeth finds she no longer has any need for her hysterical symptom, so she is free of its grip. Having taken responsibility through abreaction for her desire—having subjectified the desire that originally dominated her—she has given the emergent desire the reaction it always demanded.[39] She is free because she has owned her insane desire as her own within her consciousness. She has come to know that her desire to murder her sister and steal her brother-in-law is not an alien intrusion into her psyche; it is a dimension of her desiring life through and through. By making this inchoately conscious desire entirely, directly, and completely conscious, by owning this desire that she initially could not conceive of as being her own, she has made it possible for herself to walk again.

Embracing Pain: Suffering Virtue Again

When we listen to Freud describe the process of consciously owning mad desires, something interesting comes into focus. For Freud, the difficulty in holding these desires is not only with their madness but also with the emotional pain involved in owning them. And this emotional pain is bound up, again, with the issue of neurosis and the ethics of experience. Because of the imperatives of virtue, the neurotic's work of taking responsibility for their desires is a painful process.

Some readers of Freud have interpreted this kind of moment of abreaction as a joyful liberation. As Nancy McWilliams has suggested, someone like Elisabeth could come to enjoy her hitherto forbidden desires. Others, like Norman Brown, would take the motif of a celebratory liberation of the drives even farther.[40] In this picture, Freud was trying to dismantle—or at least, loosen the grip of—the unrealistic and punitive ideals for her psychological life that permitted Elisabeth to experience only desires that were, to her mind, moral.[41] Once these ideals lost power, Elisabeth could better tolerate her immediate psychological experience of sexual and aggressive desire and resist the temptation to repress it. She could even come to experience such desire as gratifying, even if only in her imagination. Such a change would be of a piece with our discussion of the amorality of psychological life: Elisabeth could enjoy a sadistic desire as a psychological desire without morally condemning herself. But did Freud think of abreaction in this celebratory, affirmative way?

Here we need to nuance our earlier discussion of the amorality of psychological life. On one level, Freud's psychoanalysis does think that psychological life is a region where moral concepts do not have to apply. At another level, however, Freud knows that convincing human beings to drop their moral interpretations of psychological phenomena is impossible. Some desires seem forbidden because, for the neurotic, they can never be enjoyed. With her loyal love for her sister and brother-in-law, Elisabeth will never arrive at a point where her unsummoned lust and death wish will be gratifying.

Hence, although it is true that Elisabeth refused to allow something traumatic to gain a "reaction" in consciousness, it does not seem to be only her disturbing sexual or aggressive wishing that she has repressed. It is also, in fact, the psychological, emotional, and moral pain that these forbidden wishes bring in their wake that she has been unable to accept and has therefore repressed. "She succeeded in sparing herself the painful conviction that she loved her sister's husband by inducing physical pains in herself instead ... her pains had come on, thanks to successful conversion" (157). It is not, that is, only the specific disturbing sexual or aggressive desires that Elisabeth is choosing to engage indirectly and symptomatically in her lived body. She is also, and just as preeminently, undergoing as physical suffering the mental suffering of guilt and shame that she feels crashing down upon her for having these sexual and aggressive desires. While Elisabeth indeed repressed her sexuality and aggression, Freud's focus was not exclusively on the sexuality or the aggression by themselves but also on the "mental pains" of shame and guilt that she also repressed.

What is interesting here is Freud's counterintuitive insight about the pain of neurosis. He writes:

> the motive for the splitting of consciousness ... was that of defence, the refusal on the part of the patient's whole ego to come to terms with this ideational group. The mechanism was that of conversion: i.e. in place of the mental pains which she avoided, physical pains made their appearance. In this way, a transformation was effected which had the advantage that the patient escaped from an intolerable mental condition.
>
> (166)

No matter how physically painful it is, the hysterical symptom is effected by the neurotic so as to avoid the even more intense emotional pain that the symptom converts psychosomatically. She resists direct consciousness of her feelings as feelings so as to experience them as something different. She does so because she can tolerate the leg pains of somatic conversion more easily than the feelings they displace. Freud thinks that the symptom, no matter how painful, always seems safer than what it replaces or displaces: the intense, immediate psychological experience that seems too disturbing and dangerous to handle on its own terms. Indirect, disguised, and distorted experience—which we could also call symbolic or metaphorical experience—in the form of leg pains in the lived body seems more manageable for Elisabeth to handle than the direct and authentic experience, which we might also call literal experience, of emotional pain in the psyche (which is not to say that the symptom is ever easy).[42]

Thus, Elisabeth's psychosomatic pain could only be relieved by her decision to experience the psychological pain of her disturbing emotions directly. When she does so, Freud writes,

> the recovery of this repressed idea had a shattering effect on the poor girl. She cried aloud when I put the situation drily before her with the words: So for a long time you had been in love with your brother-in-law. She complained at this moment of the most frightful pains, and made one last desperate effort to reject the explanation: it was not true, I had talked her into it, it *could* not be true, she was incapable of such wickedness, she could never forgive herself for it.
>
> (157)

That is, Elisabeth dissolves her leg pains not only by abreacting her hitherto repressed forbidden sexual and aggressive desires; she does so also, and perhaps even more importantly, by feeling, in a direct way for the first time, her awful and powerful emotions of guilt and shame at having what she takes to be those wicked desires.[43] The paradox is that Elisabeth came to Freud for treatment so that she could feel less pain, but his treatment promises her relief only if she is first willing to feel more pain.

Freud's point is that when the mind experiences the disturbing themes and logics of immediate psychological experience, it needs to experience them as disturbing. When disturbing wishes elicit painful emotions like shame and guilt, the first task is not to modulate the pain by showing the analysand that they do not have any real reason to be pained. We remember that Elisabeth's goal is the same as every recovering neurotic's goal: to desire and feel desires and feelings in as conscious and direct a way as possible. Freud's task was to help Elisabeth embrace her disturbing immediate psychological experiences *as* disturbing. To become less psychologically defended, less tempted to repression, Elisabeth needs to live more deeply into her first-order psychological experience, in content and form, precisely as it comes, no matter what it is. The point is to desire the difficult desires and feel the difficult feelings as they are and as they come up.

Thus, the overall goal of Freud's strategy with Elisabeth is not, perhaps surprisingly, to remove all her guilt and shame or feelings of self-contradiction. In contrast, Freud offers his treatment as a way to help her feel all her guilt and shame and incoherence simply because these are the feelings that her wishing has elicited in her conscious psychological life. The real issue is, again, whether Elisabeth can develop the capacity to give a "reaction" to whatever becomes conscious—including disturbing desires, guilty and shameful reactions to these disturbing desires, and feelings of biographical incoherence—and whether she can keep all this material in consciousness by directly embracing it as her own. Doing so is, for Freud, the only way that she will move beyond hysterical suffering. She has to be liberated into her sexuality and aggression, guilt and shame, self-contradictoriness, and self-fragmentation—having this experience directly and truthfully for the first time.

The direct experience of her immediate psychological experience will always involve suffering for Elisabeth. She will always have unpredicted and unsummoned sexual and aggressive wishes. She needs to develop a psychological identity that allows her to wish these wishes directly and also tolerate the feelings that arise in response to these wishes. She has to accept both that she is an individual who has the wishes she has and that she is an individual who feels guilty and ashamed of just these wishes. She has to recognize that she can handle incompatible emotions and wishes simultaneously. What demands abreaction is not only the repressed dangerous desires but also the painful shame and guilt and feeling of incoherence that have resulted from these desires. We are not speaking of liberation from guilt and shame or incoherence; if anything, we are talking about liberation into the guilt and shame and incoherence, perhaps fully for the first time. If Elisabeth is committed to the preeminence of virtue and its rights over psychological life, and Freud does not tell her she should not be, she has to suffer for it. Freud invites her to do so in a direct and authentic way rather than an indirect and distorted way.

We can see how Freud is again, perhaps surprisingly, defending the rights of virtue. Although he believed that a good analysis would reduce the neurotic individual's guilt, shame, and self-fragmentation, he did not necessarily endorse or promise a complete liberation. At least in his study of Elisabeth, he seems to accept that certain desires will inevitably elicit guilt, shame, and self-fragmentation, and the goal of analytic treatment is not to eliminate these feelings but to experience them as directly as possible, even as the individual continues to own the desire that elicited those feelings as directly as possible. Freud is not a revisionary moralist in this discussion. Elisabeth's problem is not primarily her strict commitment to having a virtuous psyche; her problem is primarily her refusal to accept the full emotional consequences of this relentless commitment. Her morality remains the same. Freud is inviting Elisabeth not to undergo a moral transformation but an ethical one (ethical in the sense of an overall way of psychological life). She needs to embrace the ethics of immediacy and experience the full range of her consciousness in both its content and its logic for the first time.

Learning to Dance: The Possibility of Joy

Yet Elisabeth's story, and the story of the neurotic as such, is not a Stoic story. That story would say that the neurotic has only two options: either to indirectly and cowardly flee from the dangers of conscious immediate psychological experience or to directly and courageously face up to its terrors. The unfortunate result of having only these two options would be that, whether Elisabeth took the former approach of experiencing her pain in a distorted and false way or the latter approach of feeling it authentically and truthfully, she is trapped in conscious pain. It is not much comfort to know that the only options available are different ways to consciously feel horrible amounts of pain.

The happy news is that Freud's story of Elisabeth and hysterical neurosis is not only a story of unceasing and inescapable suffering. He believes there is a benefit to experiencing emotional suffering directly and authentically: the suffering can then depart. Freud proudly concludes his account of Elisabeth's neurotic travails with a vignette of Elisabeth's experiencing something beyond her neurotic travails: "In the Spring of 1894 I heard that she was going to a private ball for which I was able to get an invitation, and I did not allow the opportunity to escape me of seeing my former patient whirl past in a lively dance" (160). After her work of abreaction with Freud, Elisabeth now can not only walk but also dance. She can not only function in ordinary life but enjoy festivity.

We see that, by taking responsibility for the content and logic of her desiring and emotional life, Elisabeth does not only relieve her hysterical symptom; she does not just substitute mental pain where physical pain once reigned; she did not just restore her ability to walk. Abreaction accomplished all these things for her, but it also dissolved mental pain now that it had been felt. Abreaction provided Elisabeth, at some level, with a way out of being trapped in the moments of lust, death wish, guilt, and shame that she had found so traumatic. Freud's explanation for this liberation is this: "*the ideas which have become pathological have persisted with such freshness and affective strength because they have been denied the normal wearing-away processes by means of abreaction*" (11; original italics). First, directly and authentically experiencing immediate psychological experience dissolves the hysterical symptom and replaces its physical pain with actual emotional pain; but then, second, it allows the emotional pain, once it is experienced directly and authentically, to dissolve, to give up the room it was colonizing in the psyche so that other emotional experiences can enjoy centrality, experiences that may not always be painful—that may sometimes, in fact, be joyful.

The logic of this process can seem odd. As in the case of our angry young man, only when Elisabeth embraces her painful moment of desire and all the emotional suffering it has entailed in a truthful and direct way does it cease to dominate her conscious life. Only when she accepts her self-incoherence can she begin to live more coherently. For it is, we remember, the neurotic's refusal to embrace the content and logic of their painful experiences—dangerous, disturbing, and difficult guilt, shame, anxiety, sadness, despair, rage, shame, incoherence, and more—that makes these painful experiences persist in colonizing the mind. Thus, by immersing herself not less but more deeply in her painful immediate experience through abreaction, she will find freedom from its death grip on her mind.

The reason is that a wish or feeling demands to be embraced—wished as a wish, or felt as a feeling. And, at some level, this is all it demands. When each painful moment of her immediate psychological experience gets the space and time to be the intense focus of her consciousness, it relinquishes its demand. It becomes only one moment in a diverse flow of moments, both painful and joyful.

Abreaction does not guarantee that joy will always follow pain. Freud, after all, wrote elsewhere in *Studies in Hysteria* that "much will be gained if we succeed in transforming ... hysterical misery into common unhappiness" (305). Yet what abreaction does guarantee is, in Jonathan Lear's apt phrase, "the possibility for new possibilities."[44] Abreaction allows Elisabeth to escape the necessity of repetition. Her mind now has a future with many possibilities. Her psychological existence is now able to become more dynamic and polychromatic. In this new kind of psychological life, joy beyond pain can be a possibility in her psychological life, whereas before, joy was not even a possibility at all.[45]

So, Freud thinks, by learning to respect her immediate desires and feelings and the logic of their coming and going, Elisabeth has moved into a new and more dynamic psychological identity. By experiencing pain, she can have the chance to have experiences beyond pain. Her more mobile and kaleidoscopic psychological life is now able to undergo the painful moments of difficult, dangerous, and disturbing sexuality, aggression, guilt, shame, and contradiction that deserve and require their own space and time in conscious experience. As a consequence, her mind can now also experience joyful and vitalizing moments.

Again, we see Freud's psychoanalysis did not aim only to make isolated repressed emotional moments conscious. Instead, he aimed to help human subjects imagine and progress into a form of life where the mind consciously welcomes the whole depth and breadth of immediate psychological experiences—especially initially dangerous wishes, feelings, fantasies, and reveries that come unexpected and unbidden—and the logic of their presence. For Freud, what is key is that the mind works to experience directly, honestly, and authentically as much of its immediate data and structure as it can—to own what owns it. This approach to psychological life does not eliminate all pain; Freud is not offering a "positive psychology." But this mind does enjoy emotional motion and differentiation, an ongoing dialectic of both pain and joy. This kind of psychological mind—more conscious of emotional consciousness, even emotionally conscious in an authentic way for the first time—is intensely real, truthful, and alive.

The pain and joy may never be fully integrated, nor may one or the other ever predominantly define Elisabeth's, or any individual's, life. The point is that, through catharsis, Elisabeth has enabled herself to live a profoundly different kind of conscious psychological existence than she had been living before. Her conscious thinking, feeling, and desiring life, in the vicissitudes of its joys and pains, will still be more incoherent and fragmented but also significantly richer and broader—we might say her psychological life will become more real because her consciousness is more conscious.

Ethics and the Case Study: Reading as Free Association

Freud's account of therapeutic action in psychoanalysis is action centered on the practice of free association. The "fundamental rule" that analytic treatment demands—its ethics, if you will, as Freud will describe it a little later, in 1913—placed the neurotic "under an obligation to remain completely objective and say what had come into [their] head, whether it was appropriate or not" (154).[46] Freud's analytic patient had to commit to saying out loud, in the presence of the analyst and without any kind of censorship, absolutely everything and anything that consciously comes to mind during the session—in the manner it comes to mind, no matter how offensive, immoral, unintelligible, incoherent, contradictory, or irrelevant any of it might seem.

Although the therapeutic action of psychoanalysis has often been seen by the broader culture to be located in the analyst's brilliant interpretation of their analysand's forgotten traumatic memory, this account has little basis in Freud's actual theory and practice.[47] It is, in truth, the activity of free association that heals the symptom and makes psychological life dynamic and differentiated. It is the commitment to the ethics of acknowledging and saying whatever comes to mind—to one's analyst or oneself—that heals. Freud did not think his interpretations were the primary mechanism of psychic transformation; rather, he saw them as a tool to facilitate the patient's embrace of the practice of free association. Freud wrote later that "the technique of free association [is] considered by many people the most important contribution made by psychoanalysis, the methodological key to its results."[48]

Free association is the concrete act of taking responsibility for immediate psychological experience in both theme and form. To embrace free association is to take up the ethics of immediacy, a way of life that invites and rewards broader and deeper participation in immediate psychological experience. Whereas the untreated neurotic seeks to keep immediacy at bay, the free-associating analysand commits to allow it to stay within conscious awareness and even, in a radical shift, to allow its momentums, deliverances, and logics to make up the ground that shapes their most fundamental psychological identity and possibilities.[49]

Embracing free association is itself the healing process. As one of Freud's early colleagues, Sándor Ferenczi, famously said: "The patient is not cured by free-associating, he is cured when he can free-associate."[50] Living according to the ethics of immediacy in free association, a hysteric such as Elisabeth can enter a new pattern of lived experience, develop a new qualitative feel to her subjectivity across all its dimensions, build a new sense of being a person and having a world.

Thus, Freud's judgment about psychoanalysis and free association seems right: "our method ... is a radical one" (17). A commitment to free association as a practice touches and transforms a person's existence down to their roots. This ethics of immediacy invites us to own our dangerous experience, our sufferings and joys (which always already own our human life). More to the point, the ethics of immediacy in free association invites the individual to hold not only isolated pieces of repressed content by bringing them back into consciousness—for the first time, so to speak—but to constantly work to own the whole region of their immediate psychological experience in both contents and logics.[51] It is an ethics that allows the patient to embrace a new form of existence in which they are attuned to the reality, drives, and logics of their immediate psychological experience in a pervasive and enduring way. Always concerned with the whole identity of the psychological person, Freud offered an ethics to assist Elisabeth in the work of self-transformation that she needed, in the work of revolutionizing her total experience of herself as a psychological subject that she, quite unknown to her at the beginning of the process, desired.

Now up to this point, Freud the therapist has been our focus, and rightly so. But what about Freud as a writer? Did he write only to communicate ideas about the structure of the mind, its sicknesses, and its treatment, to inform his analytic friends about his thinking, and to try to persuade his skeptical medical colleagues of his theories?

Freud did write for these reasons, but he may also have had other motivations.[52] It is possible that, although Freud would have believed that an actual psychoanalytic treatment best facilitated psychological healing, he also wanted to offer his writings as a therapeutic resource to invite individuals into the new ethics of immediacy. His writings gave readers the chance of a new way to experience themselves as psychological beings. In this sense, Freud offered his readers what the philosopher Pierre Hadot has described as a spiritual exercise.[53] Although the idea of Freud promoting spirituality may sound odd, the spirituality Freud's texts would be encouraging in this reading has nothing to do with anything like a transcendent God or an immaterial soul. Instead, in the sense intended here, a spiritual exercise is any kind of ongoing personal practice through which a human being strives to transform the ethos of their thinking, feeling, sensing, and desiring in a more satisfying direction.

In this interpretation, Freud's case studies—the collaborative creations of Freud and his patients—aimed at more than scientific description. Through them, Freud sought to offer the reader an ethics of immediacy, to open up for them the practice of free association. He believed that his texts, especially his case studies, could foster an embrace of immediate psychological experience and invite some of the same subjective transformations that could take place in actual in-person analysis. Attending to Elisabeth's newfound commitment to embrace the flow of her immediate psychological experience elicits the reader's own commitment to do the same. Freud's readers could begin to experience free association themselves, to recognize and participate more deliberately and deeply in the reality of their own psychological immediacy, their own anomalous and insane feeling and desiring life. Readers could enter into their own self-transformation by making the stories within his pages their own. They could begin to enter conscious life—with a less neurotic, more dynamic and polychromatic, emotional and desiring form of psychological existence.

It is essential to clarify what this ethics or spiritual exercise is and what it is not. Freud's text does not primarily aim to give the reader new information about the nature of their mental life—for example, that it is permeated with sex, aggression, and contradiction. Instead, Freud's text invites the reader to embrace an experiential practice and process of noticing, acknowledging, and embracing the emergent anomalous moments of immediate psychological experience in a self-aware way, whether these moments are aggressive, sexual, contradictory, or something else entirely.

Thus, Freud never intended his writings only to convince the reader to cognitively acknowledge the presence of sexuality or aggression in the psyche. Instead, Freud wanted those who read him to embrace an ethics of immediacy that would transform their ongoing conscious existence—so that they could better negotiate the constant interference of strange desires and feelings with their eyes wide open, to stop fighting, to stop constricting psychological life and self-understanding, to move from a psychological existence hell-bent on preserving psychological order and stability to one that lets psychological stability be unsettled by the anomalies and contradictions within conscious life, difficult and dangerous though they seem. Reading Freud would be a practice in which readers could develop their ability to live a more conscious life and cultivate a more fine-grained awareness of the true nature of their psychological life. Through this more intentional awareness of the immediacies of their emotions and desires, the reader can begin to escape a psychological existence that is too often traumatized, symptomatic, constricted, and static to enter one that can be more healthy, authentic, capacious, and mobile. Elisabeth's journey to more conscious life, mutatis mutandis, has the potential to become the reader's.

Conclusion: Danger and Salvation

Looking at early Freud's account of *immediate experience*, we saw how this type of experience puts human life in a quandary. On the one hand, the individual seemingly cannot live with a direct engagement of it, but on the other, immediate experience seemingly does not allow human life to take place without immediate experience getting its rights one way or another. Yet, Freud may have discovered a way out of the dilemma: embracing an ethics of living a more conscious life.

In his early texts, Freud promoted the value of directly accepting and embracing conscious immediate psychological experience even when its moments are insane and anomalous. The neurotic needs to realize that escaping the grip of profoundly unsettling emotions that interfere with the settled trajectories of their psychological life requires that they not succumb to the temptation to avoid and eliminate these emotions outright, to quash their interference, to deny them a place in psychological existence. Rather than defending themselves against immediate anomalous feelings and wishes in inauthentic, untruthful, ultimately pyrrhic and futile ways, the individual needs to move beyond clinging to its psychological stability and unity. The mind needs to move toward truthfully and authentically owning the insanity, unsettledness, and incoherence that always already owns it. To do so, the mind needs to relinquish certain tightly held illusions regarding the way psychological life should work.

The neurotic individual must accept the fact that there is no completely normal, unchangeably enduring, seamlessly consistent psychological life. They discover that their psychological mind consistently exceeds and upends the usual and the typical. They learn that they can cultivate a sensibility that is open to more sudden and unexpected feelings and desires. Although a psychological subject cannot live without being grounded in past experience (experience that creates trajectories of coherence and anticipation for present and future experience), this subject will develop a more flexible attitude toward this coherence. Living in the ethics of immediacy, they discover that their psyche is not static but dynamic, its contents not immutable but continually transforming, its contents not homogenous but differentiated, its logic not always coherent or consistent but often incoherent and contradictory, its tendencies not always centripetal but often centrifugal.

In the ethics of immediacy, the neurotic individual becomes less neurotic when they see normality, stability, virtue, consistency, and sanity as illusory ideals for their psychological subjectivity. These ideals are intended to defend against having to negotiate the vicissitudes of immediate psychological experience and the attendant dangers they impose on human existence. They see that these illusory ideals and norms, in a reverse of events, are themselves the actual pathology from which they need deliverance—inappropriate evaluative ideals and norms for psychological life that lead to needless suffering. Misguided and destructive, these standards, and the futile attempts at self-protection they underwrite, are renounced and dissolved. In the ethics of experiencing experience, the pressure to live up to a punitive ideal of psychological identity, virtuous, coherent, and stable, is relieved.

In this process, the neurotic finds they can give up the illusion of control over their psychological life. They may always desire their psyche to be virtuous and coherent, but they concurrently stop trying to force their psyche to be always virtuous and coherent. They give up the pride and self-regard of seeing themselves as always and everywhere reasonable and moral. They begin to practice an ethics beyond the moral—an ethics of experience, an ethics of immediacy, and they discover within themselves a new kind of agency. This agency can subjectify that which has subjected them, and they can voluntarily accept the involuntary advents of immediate experience.

What happens to psychological life when the sometime neurotic becomes able to subjectify that which has subjected them, to own that which has owned themselves? What happens when psychological life embraces an ethics of more consciously living with the grain of immediate psychological experience rather than against it, when it lets this experience have its rights in the psyche, when it even enables this experience to lead the psyche? A conscious psychological life ensues that is perpetually unsettled, unmoored, interrupted, uncertain, and incoherent but also significantly richer in depth and breadth, more plural than uniform, more dynamic than static, more free than constrained.

In these ways, Freud called human psychological life to embrace neurotic insanity. This affirmation of insanity is important because, etymologically, the Attic Greek *psúkhōsis* could indicate not only an abnormality and disease in the soul. It could also mean an increase of soul, an animation to life. Freud's work, in his discussion of neurosis, resonates with this latter possibility: to get in touch with conscious immediate psychological experience is to come fully into psychological life or, paradoxically, to come back to psychological life, dynamic and polychromatic psychological life, for the first time.[54] The ethics of immediacy enriches human life.

Thus, beyond describing and acknowledging them, Freud championed the reality, significance, value, and power of the mind's most immediate conscious wishes, fantasies, thoughts, and feelings as they are and as they come. He created an ethics of immediacy. This ethics of embracing immediate conscious psychological experience would help conscious psychological life become more alive in an existence that includes both joy and pain.

Freud believed that we become more alive by becoming more conscious. Yet it is not precisely accurate to say that Freud's therapeutic ethics makes the unconscious conscious; instead, paradoxically, it is an ethics of trying to make consciousness conscious for the first time. The difference is subtle but essential. Freud shows that a genuinely conscious psychological life is not a given; it is a possibility that may or may not be achieved, whether through an analytic treatment or through reading.

Freud knew that embracing immediate psychological experience—this ethics of making consciousness conscious, of letting sanity be insane—is difficult. But he also would have said that this ethics is salutary. Freud's work showed that what can begin as neurotic nausea or leg pains can, if engaged with the right kind of ethics, become the gateway to a profoundly new kind of subjectivity, a new, more vital, more authentic self-experience. Paradoxically and counterintuitively, Freud shows that what at first seems like a curse can turn into a blessing. A temptation to become less conscious is an invitation to become more conscious. By accepting this invitation, the individual trades an avoidance of conscious life for a more deliberate entrance into conscious life. Immediate experience is dangerous experience, but as Friedrich Hölderlin famously said, where the danger lies, there too is salvation.[55] Or, as we might say, where the danger lies—the ostensible immorality, the neurotic insanity, the emotional, desiderative, cognitive incoherence—there too is the dancing—at least sometimes.

Part II

Freudians Beyond Freud

Chapter 3

Toward Creative Life: Recalcitrance and Futurity in Woolf

Introduction: Was Woolf a Freudian?

Was Virginia Woolf a Freudian? It seems not, if we listen to her own words from 1920 in the book review "Freudian Fiction."[1] Relying on Freudian concepts as one creates or interprets fictional narratives, Woolf believed, is reductive and homogenizing: "characters have become cases," and by "becoming cases they have ceased to be individuals" (3:197).

The individual disappears, specifically, because of how psychoanalytic concepts function, as Woolf understood them. She writes, "Yes, says the scientific side of the brain, that is interesting; that explains a great deal. No, says the artistic side of the brain, that is dull and has no human significance whatever" (3:197). To her mind, psychoanalysis explains: it theorizes causes beneath and behind a character's lived experience; its concepts do not explore the quality and meaning that are intrinsic within that experience in its own right.

In addition, Woolf thought that Freudian notions could straitjacket a character's experiential possibilities. Such concepts diagnostically provide "a patent key that opens every door ... [that] simplifies rather than complicates, detracts rather than enriches" (3:197). The character who is constantly wrestling with oedipal issues is a character who is always and only wrestling with oedipal issues; they lack the opportunity to wrestle with anything else.

Woolf's criticisms no doubt hit the mark concerning some reductionist and homogenizing "Freudian fiction," but it seems she may not have recognized that the fiction she disliked in fact did not exhaust all possibilities for literature that is Freudian in spirit—especially if we appreciate that Freud focused on understanding and transforming conscious experience more than on theoretically explaining or manipulating its underlying causes, that he affirmed how we thrive best when this experience is dynamic and plural rather than self-reiterating and uniform. Woolf may also not have recognized the way that her work actually constituted a kind of "Freudian fiction" (if Freud's field of thought and practice is considered the way we have outlined). So, if Adam Phillips is correct in seeing Freud as a modernist, then we are correct in seeing Woolf's modernism as Freudian, but only if we see her connection to Freud as a subtle, implicit one.[2]

To say as much, however, is not to say that Woolf merely reiterated Freudian ideas—not even when they are understood as experientially focused. Far from it. Rather, she seems to have been influenced by Freudian concepts (or more precisely, a Freudian atmosphere), only as she in turn influenced Freudianism. A Freudian grammar defined her literature only as she redefined the nature and scope of that grammar— that is, rather than slavishly repeating or applying Freud's work, Woolf critically and creatively developed that work beyond Freud's own understanding of its nature and relevance. Woolf was, brilliantly, a non-Freudian, more-than-Freudian, Freudian.

Why Write Fiction? Charting Human Nature

What is the point of fiction? Woolf gives an intriguing answer in a series of essays written between 1920 and 1925 on the nature of literary character. Why, she asks, should authors invent characters? What is the meaning of their "existence" in a narrative?

Woolf engages the problem of character using a vignette about a real woman—Woolf names her "Mrs. Brown"—whom she briefly encountered on a train. Woolf outlines what she takes to be the essentials of this encounter in her essay "Character in Fiction":

> I will tell you a simple story which, however pointless, has the merit of being true, of a journey from Richmond to Waterloo, in the hope that I may show you what I mean by character in itself. ... One night some weeks ago, then, I was late for the train and jumped into the first carriage I came to. As I sat down I had the strange and uncomfortable feeling that I was interrupting a conversation between two people who were already sitting there.

(3:422–3)

3. Toward Creative Life

Whatever problem of literature Woolf is going to be addressing, she is coming at it from the background of a real-life situation. The literary will arise from real life. Woolf continues:

> They were sitting opposite each other, and the man, who had been leaning over and talking emphatically to judge by his attitude and the flush on his face, sat back and became silent. I had disturbed him, and he was annoyed. The elderly lady, however, whom I will call Mrs. Brown, seemed rather relieved. … There was something pinched about her—a look of suffering, of apprehension. … Then I looked at the man. He was no relation of Mrs. Brown's I felt sure … he had an unpleasant business to settle with Mrs. Brown; a secret, perhaps sinister business, which they did not intend to discuss in my presence. … It was plain, from Mrs. Brown's silence, from the uneasy affability with which Mr. Smith spoke, that he had some power over her which he was exerting disagreeably.
>
> (3:423–4)

At this point Woolf's imagination kicks in; she begins to create a literary character and story that would, while imaginary, nonetheless have a true-to-life quality, a story that *could* express the authentic truth about Mrs. Brown or a woman like her. Again, Woolf:

> It might have been her son's downfall, or some painful episode in her past life, or her daughter's. Perhaps she was going to London to sign some document to make over some property. Obviously against her will she was in Mr. Smith's hands … Mrs. Brown and I were left alone together. She sat in her corner opposite, very clean, very small, rather queer, and suffering intensely. The impression she made was overwhelming. It came pouring out like a draught, like a smell of burning.
>
> (3:424–5)

For Woolf, this experience of a seemingly ordinary woman's life is a seed for developing a fictional character. In explicating the process of this development, Woolf envisions the meaning and purpose of fictional characters—how they do and should matter to both writer and reader.

Woolf's first point is that fictional characters are developed out of nonfictional characters: "Most novelists have the same experience. Some Brown, Smith, or Jones comes before them and says in the most seductive and charming way in the world, 'Come and catch me if you can' ... men and women write novels because they are lured on to create some character which has thus imposed itself upon them" (3:420–1). An author does not invent characters out of whole cloth; someone who exists in the world outside the text inspires them to create a character within the world of the text.³ Thus a fictional character's imagined existence will represent a real person's possible actual existence; fiction must "search out *her* real meaning," as it might be, we might say (3:387, my italics). To Woolf's mind, this characterological verisimilitude is fundamental and crucial in a work of fiction.

Woolf's ambition, however, reaches further. She wants to tell the real Mrs. Brown's possible real story. For, in Woolf's words, "Mrs. Brown is human nature" (3:430); she is "the spirit we live by, life itself" (3:436). Through the narrative of one particular individual's existence, Woolf wants to promote a more universal vision of what it means to be human. Hence the comment "In real life there is nothing that interests us more than character, that stirs us to the same extremes of love and anger, or that leads to such incessant and laborious speculations about the values, the reasons, and the meaning of existence itself" (3:387).⁴ Literature presents a fictional character to show something true about the human condition—its logic, reality, essence, and possibilities.

For Woolf, the critical point is that the real individual, the imagined character, and the existential vision are inextricably intertwined. Thus, her essays do not clarify moment by moment whether her topic is the woman on the train, the fictional "Mrs. Brown," or the human condition. Woolf was always discussing all these topics at the same time.

Literature of Death: The Road Not to Be Taken

Woolf was uneasy with the fiction of her day.⁵ To her mind, authors had massively misconceived the essence of literary character and thus the essence of human nature; they had failed to engage the meaning of an actual individual's life, of a fictional character's life, and of human life as such. There were several reasons for these failures. To anticipate the most important of them, we can say Woolf regretted that this literature separated (in ways that will become clear) what should be connected: a real individual's life, a fictional character's life, and a philosophical vision of the meaning of human life. This separation stood at the heart of her contemporaries' inability to achieve verisimilitude, their incapacity to make fiction representing the possible real meaning of an actual person's existence or the possible real meaning of existence itself.

We can start to appreciate Woolf's critique by noting her examples of different ways that national literatures often abandoned verisimilitude of character. Close to home, "The English writer would make the old lady into a 'character'; he would bring out her oddities and mannerisms; her buttons and wrinkles; her ribbons and warts" (3:426). Mrs. Brown can become a fictional character only if she stands out from the crowd or is made to do so. Her behavior and psychology must be peculiar; her life must embody a kind of theatricality.[6]

Woolf also mentions how an English writer might moralistically fictionalize the woman on the train into Mrs. Brown. Again, verisimilitude disappears: "I do not think that Mr. Wells, in his passion to make her what she ought to be, would waste a thought upon her as she is" (3:428). This writer will transform the woman on the train into Mrs. Brown only insofar as he can make her into someone morally noble, who embodies a praiseworthy ideal for what human life can and should be.

On the other hand, the French writer would abandon Mrs. Brown in a different way. "A French writer would ... sacrifice the individual Mrs. Brown to give a more general view of human nature; to make a more abstract, proportioned, and harmonious whole" (3:426). Here a philosophical vision of what it means to be human would replace most of the original concrete reality of the woman on the train.[7] What does remain of her reality will be refashioned on a procrustean bed of aesthetic ideals.

And the Russian? "The Russian would pierce through the flesh; would reveal the soul—the soul alone, wandering out into the Waterloo Road, asking of life some tremendous question which would sound on and on in our ears after the book was finished" (3:426). Here the real Mrs. Brown would be merely an inspiration to the reader to interrogate their inner depths; this self-exploration, not a specific character, is what would stay with them.

Woolf's problem was that these three approaches do violence to the actual reality of the woman on the train; they eliminate the possibility of representing her in a true-to-life way in fiction. In fact, for Woolf, these approaches abandon character; they abstract something from character; they make the woman on the train into someone or something else. The real woman on the train and any character true to her largely vanish: "character disappeared" (3:385). Rather than staying close to the woman on the train and presenting her in a fictional mode, the writer extrapolates from her: because she wears an oddly colored raincoat the writer makes her into an eccentric, because her face has a look of Stoic endurance the writer transforms her into the embodiment of a philosophy, and so on, as the writer turns her into the expression of an ideal or an encapsulation of an existential dilemma. Woolf does not deny that this method of abstraction can produce exciting results—like Dostoevsky—but these results will be distant from the reality of the woman on the train. In this respect, the fiction will lack verisimilitude.

Woolf believed that on the rare occasions her contemporaries aimed at verisimilitude in character, they failed to achieve it because they conceived character adjectivally. When this literature engages Mrs. Brown, "we are told *about* her" (3:387, my italics). Being told "about" her means: "the Edwardian novelist scarcely attempted to deal with character except in its more generalized aspects" (3:386–7). Mrs. Brown becomes a type—sad, nostalgic, resigned, pummeled by life, and so on—a generic kind of person more than a concrete, specific individual: "The Edwardian novelist … gives us a vast sense of things in general, but a very vague one of things in particular" (385–7). Here Mrs. Brown's identity will be fixed, her disposition settled, her range of emotions, thoughts, desires, and actions unchanging.

So, it is no surprise that Woolf questioned whether the literature of her time was literature at all. "Yet what odd books they are! Sometimes I wonder if we are right to call them books at all. For they leave one with so strange a feeling of incompleteness and dissatisfaction" (3:427). By abstracting from the woman on the train, by substituting something else in her place, "Edwardians were never interested in character in itself. … They were interested in something outside" (3:428). But outside what?

Here Woolf's diction is interesting. She summarizes her diagnosis of Edwardian literature's failings: "these writers are materialists … they are concerned not with the spirit but with the body" (4:158). In other words, their work offers "soulless bodies" (3:387). If Woolf was not endorsing a body-soul dualist ontology of the human being, and she was certainly not, why the metaphysical and even theological terminology?

The reason for such language, it seems, is the way it metaphorically crystallizes her belief that her contemporaries were writing morbid literature. To her mind, "their books are already a little chill"—like corpses in the morgue (3:387):

> With all his powers of observation, which are marvelous, with all his sympathy and humanity, which are great, Mr. Bennett has never once looked at Mrs. Brown in her corner. There she sits in the corner of the carriage—that carriage which is travelling, not from Richmond to Waterloo, but from one age of English literature to the next, for

Mrs. Brown is eternal, Mrs. Brown is human nature ... there she sits and not one of the Edwardian writers has so much as looked at her. They have looked very powerfully, searchingly, and sympathetically out of the window; at factories, at Utopias, even at the decoration and upholstery of the carriage; but never at her, never at life, never at human nature. And so they have developed a technique of novel-writing which suits their purpose; they have made tools and established conventions which do their business. But those tools are not our tools, and that business is not our business. For us those conventions are ruin, those tools are death.

(3:430)

The language of spirit or soul designates the "something" whose presence makes a body alive, whose absence means it is dead. In this sense, she felt that her contemporaries offered characters who were corpses; they were committing literary murder. By making the woman on the train into an oddball, a philosophical position, an aesthetic ideal, an existential question, or a generic type, their literature killed off character in itself, whether instantiated concretely in the woman on the train, literally in the character Mrs. Brown, or thematically in the vision of human nature Mrs. Brown embodies. In a not unreal sense, the woman on the train dies, the character Mrs. Brown dies, and the meaning of human existence dies. Life vanishes from life.

For all these reasons, Woolf thought her day's literature lacked something essential. If one asked of its characters "Is life like this?" the answer would be no (4:160). Human beings are not intrinsically theatrical, not primarily philosophies, aesthetic ideals, or existential quandaries, not essentially types. Thus, referring to her English Edwardian compatriots, Woolf said, "the sooner English fiction turns its back upon them ... the better for its soul" (4:158). Yet as Woolf was walking away from this English fiction, she was also walking toward a different kind of fiction with a different conception of character and life. What was it?

Literature of Life: Immediacies of Character

Woolf's frustration with Edwardian fiction, her insistence that it could not express what life is like, was founded on her belief that the Edwardians had been making a category mistake. They were treating characters like objects rather than as subjects. They were writing character from a third-person perspective, a perspective that Woolf considered inappropriate for writing character and a narrative modality that needed to shift.

The shift Woolf proposed in her criticism and carried out in her fiction, as everyone familiar with modernist literature knows, involved the embrace of stream-of-consciousness narration. Here is Woolf's description of what the true life of a character—the woman on the train, Mrs. Brown, human being as such—is like: "Examine for a moment an ordinary mind on an ordinary day. The mind receives a myriad impressions—trivial, fantastic, evanescent, or engraved with the sharpness of steel. From all sides they come, an incessant shower of innumerable atoms" (4:160) and "In one day thousands of ideas have coursed through your brains; thousands of emotions have met, collided, and disappeared in astonishing disorder" (3:436). Here we see no third-person perspective. Instead, reader and writer can know a character only within the terms, in form and content, of that character's first-person subjectivity, their lived and living experience. Stream of consciousness means stream of lived experience. The character Mrs. Brown, the woman on the train who inspired the creation of Mrs. Brown, and the meaning of human life that Mrs. Brown expresses only have what Woolf called "real meaning" when engaged from a first-person perspective. Only within the pages of literature centered in the domain of Mrs. Brown's subjective consciousness do writer and reader encounter what Woolf perceives as "life itself" and "human nature." It is precisely subjective life that constitutes "the spirit we live by." When Woolf wrote of Edwardian fiction that "sometimes, more and more often as time goes by we suspect a momentary doubt, a spasm of rebellion, as the pages fill themselves in the customary way" (4:160), it was the subjectivity of first-person life that was the insurgent rebelling against the limits of the avowed objectivity of third-person narration, that became a fly in the ointment, a spoke in the wheel, in the literature of death. This life was what stream of consciousness or stream of experience literature could embody and express.

Even as the shift from the third person to the first person in fiction—and the corollary shift in the concrete human life this fiction was presenting—was a profound one, it was not the whole story, however. Noting a turn from the third person to the first person is insufficient for a complete understanding of Woolf's achievement because first-person consciousness is not Woolf's only focus. Her ultimate focus is on one specific kind of first-person subjectivity. First-person experience is not monolithic; lived experience, in general, does not exist; subjective life contains irreducibly diverse contents, like the ideas, emotions, and impressions Woolf mentions. First-person experience also involves irreducibly different forms such as reflective, evaluative, and aesthetic intentionality (to speak in phenomenological terms).

Woolf's particular focus within the field of lived experience is immediate lived experience. First, the mind receives impressions in its cognitive, emotional, and desiderative space; consciousness is receptive to consciousness. At least initially, overt agency is lacking; the mind is passive more than active; the self undergoes more than it acts; immediate experience happens to a person more than being something they enact. In a famous discussion, Erich Auerbach captured the radical receptivity in Woolf's conception of immediate experience: "something new and elemental appeared: nothing less than the wealth of reality and depth of life in every moment to which we surrender ourselves without prejudice."[8] The impressions themselves are the nominative subjects of the experiential process: *they come*; the *ideas have coursed through the brain*; the *emotions have met, collided, and disappeared*. In this register, human subjectivity is subjected to its own impressions, ideas, and feelings; the mind finds itself rained upon by a shower of data. Last, Woolf's terminology of impressions is connected to the passive voice: the mind is impressed upon by something. Impressions also denote phenomena that precede reflection and evaluation—one has a "first impression" of someone, an impression that may or may not correlate with one's later, more studied judgment of the person's character. Impressions are given just as they are given, be they pleasant or painful, helpful or unhelpful, justifiable or baseless.

The mind's passivity and receptivity to what is given, just as it is given, seems to entail something else, which is that mind is internally differentiated. There is otherness internal to any conscious life. Mind and the experiences it undergoes do not always smoothly coincide. In mind as a subject (mind in the nominative case), the self feels at home, as it is located at the center of its own identity and intentions. But in mind as an object (mind in the accusative case), the self can feel out of place, displaced even, intruded upon by emotions and ideas that seem to arrive unsummoned from elsewhere, from a place that seems far away from the self's sense of its own identity and intention at any given moment, even as these emotional and cognitive phenomena are a dimension of its own mind. Mind both is and is not what it is; the self and its experience are both coincident and not.

So, it is not sufficient to say that Woolf was committed to first-person stream of consciousness in life and literature. Literarily and existentially, her ultimate interest was, beyond subjectivity in general, immediate subjectivity. Pericles Lewis summarizes Woolf's modernist commitment to immediacy:

The stream-of-consciousness novel offers a phenomenology of mind, an account of the contents, in Virginia Woolf's phrase, of 'an ordinary mind on an ordinary day,' without any filtering devices. Modernist writers, in particular, emphasized the attempt to capture immediate experience, 'to record the atoms as they fall upon the mind,' independent of all philosophical categories or ideas, experience as it is actually lived.[9]

Fiction and life needed to reclaim this consciousness, to be in touch with character in itself, to reflect and embody what life is really like. The woman on the train, Mrs. Brown, and human nature all needed to be immersed in this experience to touch the authentic meaning of human existence. This particular experience—passive, receptive, given, and other—is the soul and spirit that life and fiction must reach toward. This particular experience offers the source from which a literature of life can be drawn. Woolf's remark about her fellow modernist James Joyce captures her sentiment well: "Mr. Joyce is spiritual; he is concerned at all costs to reveal the flickerings of that innermost flame which flashes its messages through the brain ... its sudden lightning flashes of significance ... so close to the quick of the mind. ... If we want life itself, here surely we have it" (4:161). And, of course, she was referring not only to what Joyce's work had achieved but also to what she was trying to achieve in her own work.

Here, we can understand some of Woolf's most famous words: "on or about December 1910 *human character changed*" (3:421, my italics). The change was that the essence of human being was coming to be located first and fundamentally in the register of immediate lived experience. This register was now seen as what is "life itself" and "human nature" and "the spirit we live by." For Woolf, life is immediate experience as it is defined in all the ways we have noted so far in this chapter. For Woolf, this shift in how the nature of human nature should be understood was a radical one; it involved a change from morbidity into animation.

The Improbable: Surprise and Aberration

For Woolf, three qualities of this immediate experience come to the fore. First, she writes of Mrs. Brown: "she is an old woman of unlimited capacity and infinite variety" (3:436). Her stream of immediate consciousness unfolds without respect to any homogenizing limits or boundaries; the scope of its plural realities and potentials is unrestricted.

Next, Woolf notes the second quality of experiential immediacy. The writer of Mrs. Brown, she avers, must represent "the gleams and flashes of this flying spirit" (3:387–8). Her immediate experience is not only unlimited and infinite in content, it is also mobile, and its contents remain constantly in flux. Her immediacy's limitless pluralities and potentials come and go sequentially; a dynamic temporality defines them that resists all stasis.

But then Woolf highlights the third feature of the infinite variety of immediate experience in its fluxing. We can remember her famous words: because "thousands of emotions have met, collided, and disappeared in astonishing disorder," the stream of immediate mental contents lacks internal unity and harmony. The stream of immediacy is dissonant. So, she sets the writer's task: "Is it not the task of the novelist to convey this varying, this unknown and uncircumscribed spirit, whatever aberration or complexity it may display, with as little mixture of the alien and external as possible?" (4:160–1). The differentiated and multiple data of immediate experience can go rogue. But what is it going rogue from? What lines is it transgressing? And what form is it deviating from?

The clue may rest in the word "unknown." Listen to Woolf as she further describes her compatriot James Joyce's engagement with immediate experience: "he disregards with complete courage whatever seems to him adventitious, whether it be probability or coherence" (4:161). The plural contents and fluxes of immediate experience resist being known because they are improbable—that is, surprising. A coherent stream of such experience would stay on a given course. Moments of experience would follow one another in a consistent way; every moment would cohere with every other moment; experience would reflect an ongoing, predictable logic—in theory, at least. Yet the moments of immediacy that flash through consciousness, to which consciousness finds itself subjected, lack this consistency. This dynamic stream is often—perhaps perpetually—surprising. And not surprising in a way that will necessarily make sense retrospectively, as when someone says they could not have anticipated a development, even though it made sense as one looked back on it. No: this kind of experience is improbable and surprising in ways that, at some level, do not make sense—hence the word "aberration." These aberrations, these improbable and seemingly illogical developments, make immediate experience fundamentally an unknown register. Thus, Woolf's problem is that the literature of her time has tried to "palm off … an image of Mrs. Brown which has no likeness to that surprising apparition whatsoever" (3:436). This inability to tolerate the surprising essence of life is a moment of failure for the literature Woolf criticizes with its reliance on generalizing. Against the temptations of philosophizing, aestheticizing, and existentializing—temptations that lay down tracks of probability—literature, and the life it expresses and encourages, must remain faithful to the startling and unlikely revelations of immediate experience.

Beyond the Self: Experience and World

If we stopped now, we might think that Woolf's account of immediate experience largely paralleled Freud's account. Just as it was in Freud's work, experiential immediacy in Woolf's work is first-person, subjective; it is spontaneous, pre-evaluative, pre-reflective, and unselfconscious; its anomalies come unanticipated and unsummoned; it often follows a nonlinear path; it takes strange turns that deviate from expected, preferred, yet artificial trajectories; it is fluid, not static; it is intimate at the same time as it is alien, familiar even as it is foreign; it feels implausible and even impossible; it is given, passively undergone at least initially; it is fleeting more than enduring; it is subjecting more than chosen; it unsettles sedimentations and stabilities of psychological identity; it is continually self-differentiating, dynamically becoming other, ateleological, both in time and simultaneously; it is almost infinitely polychromatic, variegated, and plural; it is almost unlimitedly vast in scope and depth; its abundance is thematically disjointed and inconsistent; it can harbor internal conflicts; it brooks no respect for moral or psychological norms. This experience is characterized by freedom: it comes and goes when it will, in whichever form it will. All these features comprise what immediacy is like, in fiction and in real life.

Yet even accounting for these similarities, Woolf's perspective still fundamentally differs from Freud's. Woolf asserts of the writer's task: "Mrs. Brown must be rescued, expressed, and set in her high relations to the world" (3:433). Her immediate experience always remains connected to realities outside of herself: "one sees the person, one sees Mrs. Brown, in the centre of all sorts of different scenes" (3:425). Mrs. Brown—and the woman on the train and human life as such—is ever in the world; her subjectivity rests at the zero-point of an atmosphere made up of the people, places, and things surrounding her. Hence, Woolf believed that "life is a luminous halo" (4:160). Immediate experience does not terminate at the limits of the individual's body;

in some sense, it includes what is outside and around the individual. Immediacy is not only a self-related phenomenon. It is also a world-related phenomenon. The human nature it expresses is unavoidably *worlded*. We might articulate the point by saying that, in Woolf's view, immediate experience is subjective only in relation to the objective. Thus, to know a character's immediacy—and so to know the essence of human nature, the real meaning of life itself—is to know their first-person participation in situations in which they engage with other people, creatures, places, tools, events, and so on.

This focus on the worlded nature of the self's immediate experience is what Freud's work sometimes seems to lack. For Freud, the issue was interior self-relation; for Woolf, it was interior world-relation. Rather than being self-enclosed or self-contained, immediate experience is self-transcendent. All of which is not to say that Woolf abandons psychology: her focus remains on the realm of emotions, thoughts, perceptions, and desires, but now as they show themselves not only "in the head" but also as always related to the world "outside the head"; interiority and privacy remain, but interiority is never wholly interior.[10] Sue Roe's comment that, for Woolf, "what could be said seemed to be moving closer to what was actually being felt ... [to] find new languages for subjective experience; new ways of depicting the rhythms of the inner life" is valid only if the rhythms of the inner life are bound up with the rhythms of outer life—that is, immediate psychological experience exceeds the bounds of private feeling, thought, or fantasy.[11]

So, Freud's picture of immediacy was too interiorized, too self-referential to Woolf. For her, immediacy's self-reference and world-reference go together: "The important thing was to realise her character, to steep oneself in her atmosphere" (3:425). Woolf's insight into the exterior dimensions of immediate experience was her way of embracing Freud's focus on immediate psychological experience and creatively developing and expanding this focus in a unique "worlded" way.[12]

Woolf's point is easy to misunderstand. It is all too easy to imagine a world without any subjectivity to which the world appears. The Edwardians, to Woolf's mind, made this mistake, referenced in a passage already cited: "Edwardians ... were interested in something outside ... looked very powerfully, searchingly, and sympathetically out of the window; at factories, at Utopias, even at the decoration and upholstery of the carriage" (3:428–30). For Woolf, this attempt to represent the world outside by itself, the environment exterior to and different from the self without reference to the self, implies separation from life—that is, death.

And it is equally easy to make the opposite mistake: to try to conceive and represent subjectivity without a world. Here Erich Auerbach could famously say the following about consciousness in Woolf: "Most of these elements are inner processes, that is, movements within the consciousness of individual personages, and not necessarily of personages involved in the exterior occurrence."[13] Auerbach will qualify this statement, but it seems problematic if left to stand alone. We have seen that Woolf did make the outside world a dimension of primary importance within immediate experience. She did think it essential for characters—and all they derive from and point to—to be involved in exterior occurrences.

The issue has to do with the nature of Woolf's realism. This realism certainly included an attempt to reclaim the reality of interiority, but she never made the realm of interior subjectivity the only reality. Instead, she was aspiring to represent the world as it is real for human subjectivity. Pericles Lewis writes, "Modernism offered an artistic and literary response to a widespread sense that the ways of knowing and representing the world developed in the Renaissance, but going back in many ways to the ancient Greeks, distorted the actual experience of reality." The attempt to present the world without relation to the subject is unreal, and Woolf's formal innovation is to create a more real realism. Lewis continues: "The stream of consciousness, while breaking from the 'realist' convention of the omniscient narrator, in fact corresponded to another form of realism ... conventional representations were replaced not with non-representations, but with new systems of representation that acknowledged the limitations of the old conventions."[14] Woolf was not against realism, but she was against realism in the traditional, not so real, sense of the term, in which characters and their surrounding worlds are given in a disengaged, abstracted, third-person perspective. So, when Michael Whitworth comments that "Woolf is rejecting the Victorian idea of reality itself," it is reality without subjectivity that is being rejected.[15]

Qualifying himself, then, Auerbach summarizes Woolf's revolutionary mode of literary realism, a mode paralleling and embodying a revolutionary mode of conceiving the fundamental reality of the woman on the train and the ultimate truth of human existence itself:

> The writer as narrator of objective facts has almost completely vanished; almost everything stated appears by way of reflection in the consciousness of the dramatis personae. When it is a question

of the house, for example, or of the Swiss maid, we are not given the objective information which Virginia Woolf possesses regarding these objects of her creative imagination but what Mrs. Ramsay thinks or feels about them at a particular moment ... there actually seems to be no viewpoint at all outside the novel from which the people and events with it are observed, any more than there seems to be an objective reality apart from what is in the consciousness of the characters.[16]

In Woolf's more authentic realism, objectivity is never only objective, and subjectivity is never solely subjective. The true meaning of character—whether of the woman on the train, the character Mrs. Brown, or human existence itself—is found in the character's engagement with the world. Woolf thought much of the fiction of her day remained morbidly outside of such realism, and she wanted the fiction she wrote to stay alive inside of it.

So, it is clear why Woolf uses the language of Mrs. Brown's "atmosphere." When immediate experience gives a self in a world (a subject in an atmosphere), then "atmosphere" indicates something that envelops something else, but it does so only in relation to what it envelops. It differs from whatever it surrounds yet exists relative to what it surrounds. Correlatively, every entity is surrounded by and exists relative to an atmosphere that is different from yet essential to it. Thus, the reality of immediate experience encompasses subject and object, interiority and exteriority, each co-constituting the other. Character and atmosphere, self and world, are distinct but not independent of one another. The atmosphere is the home without which the character does not exist, even as the home does not exist without the character inhabiting it. An atmosphere is meaningful only in relation to the life of the one who inhabits the atmosphere, the one whose life is meaningful only in relation to that atmosphere.

Creative Immediacy: Freedom to Upset the Given

A stream of consciousness form, then, is not always solipsistic; it is frequently worlded. Here is Woolf: "If ... you think of the novels which seem to you great novels ... you do at once think of some character who has seemed to you so real ... that it has the power to make you think not merely of it itself, but of all sorts of things through its eyes" (3:426). Yet if the atoms in the mind are often more than just internal psychological events, if they as often as not make up the substance of the various ways that a self dwells in a world, what defines these atoms functioning in these ways? If, as Woolf writes, "Mrs. Brown must be rescued, expressed, and set in her high relations to the world" (3:433), if Mrs. Brown is much of the time a zero-point in, of, and for a world encircling her from above and below, to the left and right, from before her and behind her, if she is repeatedly a center of scenes, what precisely is the relationship between her as a center and the scenes that surround her? If she is regularly positioned within an array of phenomena that afford themselves meaningfully to her in relation to her desires, thoughts, and feelings, what are the overall patterns and textures of being so positioned?[17]

To begin to answer these questions, we need to recognize that Woolf sees the truth of the self and world as perpetually open to question. Reality gives in such a way that the ones who experience it enjoy a large amount of freedom in how they experience it. She remarks, "I ask myself, what is reality? And who are the judges of reality?" (3:426). Woolf was not necessarily promoting a full-blown relativism here, but she was implying that reality's evident givenness in immediate experience is always underdetermined.[18] The meaning of self and world in immediate experience always remains ambiguous and requires interpretation; meaning is mutable. The world's "reality" is never conclusive or fixed; its data are ambiguous and open to multiple understandings. Within immediate experience, the nature of self-in-the-world is to lack a fully determined, irrevocably enduring character. Any present meaning of self and world, at least within the realm of immediacy, is thus haunted by its own contingency. Other judgments about the meaning of reality necessarily remain on the table, and they contest any complacent confidence in the absolute validity of any current account of such meaning.

Woolf then makes an additional point. More than simply affirming that the meaning of reality within immediate experience always remains open to the possibility of different interpretations, she posits that this kind of experience continuously performs new readings of reality and freely offers novel interpretations of the meaning of self and world. The meaning of reality is essentially mutable and is, in fact, in motion. For Woolf, we know, "life is a luminous halo, a semi-transparent envelope surrounding us from the beginning of consciousness to the end" (4:160). In immediacy, self and world are illuminated in specific ways and are allowed to appear in certain ways. And new ways of presenting self and world consistently undermine and upset the order of past and current ways. We can return to words quoted above: "In one day thousands of ideas have coursed through your brains; thousands of emotions have met, collided, and disappeared in astonishing disorder" (3:436). This "disorder" does not only define the coming and going of interior psychological data; it also defines how the whole self-in-the-world reality as it is given in immediacy finds itself constantly being disordered. In virtue of its logic, immediate experience is always capable of unfolding a new and different constellation of self-world meaning. In this register, any established meaning of self-in-the-world is also a canvass on which human life is at work deconstructing and re-creating this meaning. This process does not have to be willed deliberately. On the contrary, this making different, this reconceiving, spontaneously happens, willed or not, as an aspect of the intrinsic logic of immediacy, a logic in which human life forever participates whether it affirms its participation or not. Hence Woolf names Mrs. Brown a "flying spirit"—her self-in-the-world meaning, that of the woman on the train, and that of life itself, will not remain still (3:388).

So, the meaning of self-in-world existence remains always unfinished and incomplete; it cannot stop itself from being taken up and constituted in more than one way. So, what is the particular way that Woolf thinks immediate experience exercises its freedom to take self and world up in different ways? We can return to the words explored above—"The mind receives a myriad impressions ... fantastic"—and now accent the reference to fantasy.

In the field of immediate experience, human life fantasizes. Fantasy, at a minimum, means the modification, the re-creation in imagination, of some reality. Thus, it entails the significant transformation, more or less radical, of one vision of the character of self-in-the-world existence into another.[19] Sue Roe's insights are helpful here. She notes that Woolf attends to "the mystery of the connection between the organic external world, and interiors ... of the heart, the mind, and one of the mind's most vibrant manifestations: the imagination."[20] Rather than denying the reality and significance of the world, again, Woolf affirms the self-in-the-world—as human life creatively, imaginatively encounters it through the immediacies of experience.

And since Mrs. Brown is, as we saw above, a "surprising apparition," we should expect the creative and fantastic re-creations of self and other that are found in her immediate experience (for self and world never exist as simply given, in a way that preexists the re-creating operations of this experience) to be surprising and improbable. And they are:

> She becomes a will-o'-the-wisp, a dancing light, an illumination gliding up the wall and out of the window, lighting now in freakish malice upon the nose of an archbishop, now in sudden splendor upon the mahogany of the wardrobe. The most solemn sights she turns to ridicule; the most ordinary she invests with beauty. She changes the shape, shifts the accent, of every scene in which she plays her part.
>
> (3:387–8)

These rich words demand our close attention.

One idea here is familiar—namely, that Woolf conceives of Mrs. Brown as an agent of illumination. She casts light on self and world in various ways so that self and world are meaningful in multiple ways. Her so-called objective reality—of self or world—is what it is in relation to the so-called subjective desires, feelings, ideas, and purposes in her immediate experience that enable reality to appear in the way it does.[21]

Beyond this kind of idealism, the less familiar idea that Woolf is promoting concerns the striking way in which Mrs. Brown's immediate experience lights up the reality of self and world in creative and improbable forms. In this experience, Mrs. Brown enjoys a broad measure of freedom in how she perceives self and world, which, again, are semantically underdetermined, which lack an absolute or final givenness, which need their meaning to be completed and finished within immediate experience. Woolf's comment about Mrs. Brown's perception of the church prelate and the armoire shows that Mrs. Brown rewrites the reality of self and world in counterintuitive, contrary ways. Within her immediacy, without even trying, she is a virtuoso of counternarrative. Her rewriting cuts against the grain of standard, authoritative accounts of this reality. She dethrones the ostensibly noble and elevates the seemingly ordinary; she denigrates the bishop's presumptive and usually revered prestige and transfigures the unassuming and usually overlooked appearance of the armoire. The once beautiful can come to appear ugly, the once unattractive become attractive. So, Mrs. Brown's rewritings of reality can do more than just ateleologically deviate from settled teleologies and habitual trajectories; they can deviate rebelliously. They can be the acts of fugitives battling and upsetting inherited traditions of regard and sedimented forms of evaluation. In religious terms, which Woolf's words imply, the deliverances of immediate experience can damn the holy and redeem the secular by deconsecrating and enchanting whatever they engage.

We see how Mrs. Brown's immediate experience, simply in virtue of being what it is, claims its own interpretive authority. The bishop appears as he does (and in Woolf's time, a bishop was a "he") from immediacy's own perspective. Through her immediate experience, Mrs. Brown enjoys agency in the process of meaning-making. This agency is ineliminable in human existence, whether this agency is later given any broader practical authority in human life.

Mrs. Brown's immediate experience claims interpretive authority in precisely those situations in which it might be considered lacking. Most often (especially in Woolf's time), it would have been the bishop whose experience would be thought to enjoy the power to define the meanings of self and world, not Mrs. Brown. But now, Mrs. Brown possesses the power to perceive the meanings of self, other, and world for herself, in line with her own purposes. Her immediate interpretations are given their rights to operate in revolutionary ways. For self and world are always given in multiple and competing ways, Woolf seems to say: they are given, on the one hand, with their socially normative meanings and, on the other, with the perhaps anomalous but nevertheless significant meanings they spontaneously display within the theater of immediate experience. These latter meanings give human life a measure of freedom from simply taking socially normative meanings of self and world as given finalities, as absolutes. In addition, rather radically, Woolf does not only think that the immediate meanings of self and world can and do often complicate and challenge the coherence of socially normative meanings of them, and these meanings' claim to be unquestionable. Rather than society's normative modes, it is the immediate modes of finding self and world that present any absolute givenness that demands recognition.

Some of Woolf's words, explored in part above, sum up the situation. Against Edwardian fiction's "air of probability embalming the whole ... sometimes, more and more often as time goes by we suspect a momentary doubt, a spasm of rebellion, as the pages fill themselves in the customary way" (4:160). A rebellion is breaking out, which is the ascendence of the value of immediate experience and of the meanings of self and world that immediate experience contains. These meanings often enjoy freedom and distance from the socially normative but morbid meanings of self and other in which life can find itself uncomfortably situated. Chafing against the inherited normative meanings that society claims belong to reality, immediate experience offers new revelations of the meanings of self and world.

Social Existence: Intersubjective Immediacy

Woolf's insistence that immediate experience is often worlded was part of a further insistence. Here we can listen to Woolf's words about human character changing in a fuller context: "On or about December 1910 human character changed ... *All human relations have shifted*" (3:421–2, my italics). For Woolf, making immediate experience newly central in literature and human life was closely correlated with creating new forms of human sociality. Why and how did she think so?

Here we can consider a moment in Woolf's fictional masterpiece *To the Lighthouse*, where she narrates a social pattern between a paterfamilias, the philosopher Mr. Ramsay, and his children. While on vacation with his family, Mr. Ramsay insists that his children accompany him on a sailing excursion despite their reluctance to do so: "He had made them come. He had forced them to come."[22] While it might seem that this specific demand is not particularly cruel or unreasonable, Woolf reveals that this kind of demand was not an isolated instance in this kind of situation. For Mr. Ramsay's daughter Cam, her father's insistence that she go sailing with him exemplifies a pattern of despotism: her life and the lives of her mother and siblings are always subject to "some command of his; some insolence: 'Do this,' 'Do that'; his dominance: his 'Submit to me'" (229). For many people (perhaps most people) in Edwardian England, such patriarchal power, enacted and obeyed, was a norm of family life—a norm, it was claimed, that was in the best interest of all parties involved.[23]

Yet Woolf indicts Mr. Ramsay's autocratic patriarchy for a particular reason, viz. the way it affects Cam: "that crass blindness and tyranny of his which had poisoned her childhood and raised bitter storms, so that even now she woke in the night trembling with rage" (229). So we are in the realm of immediate experience: an experience wrests her from her slumber; it spontaneously comes upon her unsummoned before any reflection or evaluation comes into play; she is passively subjected to its imposing givenness. But we also see that self-experience and other-experience frequently go together in immediacy.

Immediate experience is often nested within contexts of intersubjective life, dyadic self-other contexts, and the social practices of family, work, and education that are located within it. Human subjectivity is continually immersed in a contradictory and anomalous stream of *intersubjective* thoughts, feelings, desires, perceptions, impulses, and dispositions that come unexpectedly and suddenly, all of which fall on the mind like atoms. For Woolf, immediate experience is often immediate intersubjective experience. Thus, Cam is not subjectivist nor solipsistic; she is profoundly engaged with the other, the other as they are immediately experienced, the other as known and perceived, felt, enjoyed, and suffered, whose identity is never just a given that preexists the operations of immediate intersubjective experience.

We can see Woolf's innovative focus when we contrast it with Freud's focus on immediate psychological experience. He affirmed the reality and value of this experience as an interior phenomenon—one of self-relation where the individual engaged with their internal world of secret fantasies, private dramas, hidden feelings, and unrevealed desires. The angry young man suffered from a private desire to tell his dad off. His immediate experience, as Freud considered it, was "in the head," interiorly existing in its own isolated sphere, largely disconnected from public, shared, interpersonal exchange, with any connection between interiority and exteriority being extrinsic and contingent.[24]

Yet, for Woolf, interiority was often unthinkable without exteriority. Immediate psychological experience has an intrinsic connection to extra-psychological life with others. Anger is a social phenomenon, not just an intrapsychic one. For character, for human life, to be defined by immediate experience meant for Woolf that it was defined by immediate intersubjective experience, by the individual self's feelings toward actual other individuals. Emotions are part of the halo that comprises human subjectivity; they denote the self's pre-evaluative and pre-reflective experience of the presence of the other in their negotiation of existence alongside and before the other, who is felt immediately as a gift, burden, threat, and so on. Woolf's revolution is to see the human person as a subject of immediate intersubjective experience: the spontaneous data of their mind frequently take place in the context of real intersubjective relations in the shared world. To her mind, all the self's social encounters carry a variety of immediate experiential content connected to exactly this sociality. Immediate psychological experience as immediate intersubjective experience is intertwined with social existence; it takes place not in a private, self-related world but in a shared, interpersonal world.

Returning to something quoted earlier, we see why it makes sense that Woolf's description of the immediate experience of the woman on the train was focused on this woman's, and her literary avatar Mrs. Brown's, experience of an aggressive companion: "It was plain, from Mrs. Brown's silence, from the uneasy affability with which Mr. Smith spoke, that he had some power over her which he was asserting disagreeably. ... Obviously against her will she was in Mr. Smith's hands"

(3:424). Whether it is the woman on the train, Mrs. Brown, or anyone, human beings are subjects of immediate intersubjective experience. When Woolf said that human character changed around 1910, and when she said that this change was a change in human relations, she may have been indicating that human life was changing in these ways because life was beginning to take account of the place of immediate intersubjective experience in the self's work of inhabiting and negotiating social existence. She uses stream-of-consciousness literary form to express the realities of immediate intersubjective experience.

Identity and Conflict: Recalcitrance and Futurity

Woolf's work not only showed that immediate intersubjective experience exists; it also envisioned how it exists. A passage from *To the Lighthouse* illuminates Woolf's perspective on the structure of this kind of experience as it often presents itself. Remember Cam's words about her dad: "that crass blindness and tyranny of his which had poisoned her childhood and raised bitter storms, so that even now she woke in the night trembling with rage" (229). On the boating trip, Cam and her siblings feel this way toward him: "In their anger they hoped that the breeze would never rise, that he might be thwarted in every possible way, since he had forced them to come against their wills" (220). Several things are happening here, experientially speaking.

The first is that Cam—and she can stand in for her siblings too—experiences herself as having a social identity, as being in a particular social location that she did not choose. This social identity is being-a-child. Experiencing herself as having this social identity entails experiencing herself as subject to certain expectations for behavior specific to this social identity. This identity bestows on her a vision of the shape of her own self and the shape of her social existence with others in her world to whom she must relate in specific, appropriate, even socially mandated, ostensibly morally normative ways. In Cam's case, within her traditional and patriarchal society, she experiences the weight of a social identity—dutiful daughter—that demands obedience to her father's wishes and demands.

In this social identity and its expectations, Cam feels oppressed. Woolf uses Cam's discontent to show how human life is often suffered as discontent in the social forms and institutions in which it finds itself, forms that feel toxically stifling of any chance to enjoy a vital existence. A social identity can stifle the movement of desire, the potential for desire to unfold in a person's life; it murders a person's possibility of satisfaction in the present moment of life. In her social identity as daughter, Cam has to fit a predetermined idea of who she is and how she should act toward the other. But the other, whether they are Cam's father or someone else, can often be a curse. This ostensibly morally and socially authoritative other pins on a person such as Cam an idea of who they are and should be if they are to be morally good and, ultimately, emotionally satisfied. Yet life in this idea—this social identity—generates for Cam, in the register of her immediate experience, only anger and resentment toward her father and his demands for her to live in a certain way.

In essence, we see a conflict between the demands of social identity and the givens of immediate intersubjective experience, between Cam's role as a daughter vis-à-vis her father and her immediate feelings toward him. Woolf's concern is always with what she calls "one's body feeling, not one's mind" (178). Here mind might be in touch with social norms, reflectively evaluated, embraced, or contested, but the body with feelings and emotion is in touch with immediate experiences like the flashes of indignation and hatred that come onto the scene of social existence before any reflection or evaluation ever takes place.

In Cam's "body feeling," we see how immediate intersubjective experience, when it is defined by rage and spite, pushes against the painful, albeit expected and ostensibly normative social contexts and identities it suffers. Her body's feelings refuse to be oriented to her father in a way that would go with the grain of her identity as a dutiful daughter. Her experience fails to coordinate with the ideals that should define her behavior and even her desires if and when they are what they should be.

In short, Cam's immediate intersubjective experience is recalcitrant. Immediate feelings and wishes that are nested within forms of social identity and practice often chafe against the limits of these forms with their normative expectations. Cam's anger and resentment, then, are not passive emotions; this pain does not signal a situation of resignation; she is not simply a forbearing victim in her suffering. Rather, her emotions are recalcitrant signs of resistance. They push back against the situation that elicits them; they indicate her refusal of fatalistic surrender to having her desire denied and the quality of her feelings poisoned. So although a social identity can demand one's submission to an other, one's immediate intersubjective experience can and often will refuse to be content in this submission. Even though life can feel harmfully pressed down in a social identity, when rage and resentment make themselves felt, their presence is a testimony that life often does not just passively "take it." Thus, rather than stoically accept having to go on the boating trip, Cam calls on the wind and waves to come to her aid to foil the wishes of her autocratic father, who has made no effort to empathize with the desires of those over whom he feels entitled to lord.

Because the self-other relationship is recalcitrant, another notable quality of the immediate intersubjective experience of "body feeling" is its futurity. Cam's wish that a change in weather would undermine her father's plans contains her wish that her relationship with her father would have a different shape, one with less pain and bitterness, where her own satisfaction, not only that of her father, carried more weight. Her immediate experience contains not only her suffering in the present arrangement but also the desire for, and the possibility of, a different future form of social existence where there would be more room for the intrinsic momentum of her wishes. Cam's unpremeditated anger is temporally constituted so that she has more than one perspective on her social situation—what it is, what it should be, what it can be (with the accompanying feelings toward her father as they have been in the past) are in the present and could and should be in the future. Her life is connected to her past and present even as it disconnects from them. Her anger shows Cam imagining a future in a newly shaped relationship, a future she is already proleptically living. So, when Woolf speaks of fiction that needs to attend to the "dark places of human psychology," she is not necessarily talking about forbidden sexuality or aggression; she is speaking about any desires that have not yet been allowed expression in the present structures of social existence, the future that has not yet been allowed to breathe (4:162). The reason Cam seethes at her father's behavior is that she is already experiencing freedom from his tyranny; she is already undertaking, within her immediate intersubjective experience, the work of liberating herself into a differently structured social world—one with a different relationship with her father in which the momentum of her desire will be allowed expression.

This futurity is what distinguishes anger from despair or resignation, which would involve a feeling of suffering in relationship with the other—being oppressed, ignored, neglected, and so forth—but would not involve a sense of alternate possibility in the present or future; one would see one's suffering as inevitable and inescapable. So, if Cam were resigned to her fate, she would foresee no future with a different social possibility. She would see her only options as acquiescent endurance or hopeless resignation, but she would not be angry and resentful.

Yet, against any acceptance of a cruel but unchangeable and inescapable fate, in her resentment Cam refuses to see the necessity of her suffering. Her rage shows that she believes a different future is possible. Her immediate intersubjective experience is defined by a dissatisfaction that makes sense only when it is seen as contingent and unnecessary. Her feelings reveal that her pain does not need to be, could not be, and should not be. Her immediate anger reveals her freedom vis-à-vis a present regrettable social dynamic. Resentment makes sense only in a horizon of imagined and desired satisfaction, in a horizon of freedom from the given or of freedom to remake the given. Anger and resignation are mutually exclusive, as are resentment and despair. Cam thinks she is being mistreated, that she is not getting something she deserves, which shows she already has a taste of a greater satisfaction and vitality in a differently structured self-other relationship. Her immediate intersubjective experience allows her to imagine and posit the possibility of freedom from an oppressive social dynamic, to imagine a different future with her father, and actually to touch the edges of this future. So, recalcitrance indicates freedom, and freedom flows into futurity. Her experience is not only rage but fugitive hope that is beginning to escape the painful form of life that imprisons it. In this way, the immediacies of intersubjective experience can be therapeutic and ameliorating because they offer the possibility of rewriting the logic and meanings of self and other in social relationships such as that of parent and child.

This desired transformation in the self-other relation, it bears saying, affects more than the self; it affects the meaning—or at least the possible meaning—of the other in the self-other relation. The other can shift from being a curse, a burden, a jailer, an affliction, a violation, or a threat to being a blessing, a gift, a liberator, a delight, an affirmation, a promise vis-à-vis the self. To contrast anger to resignation again, we might say that in resignation one feels there is no chance the other who is causing one's pain will change their behavior, whereas rage holds out the possibility that the other can indeed change. The field of immediate intersubjective experience affects the self and the self-other relation: it anticipates a future between self and other in which self and other both change. When Michael Lackey notes that "Mr. Ramsay has the tendency to dismiss the inner life of others as insignificant," Cam's anger shows that Mr. Ramsay is not trapped in his inability to empathize; he can become different, and he is different already in the future that Cam's immediate intersubjective experience is giving him.[25] Cam's experience here is a spoke in the wheel, a fly in the ointment, not only of her own social identity but of her father's as well.

Leaving and Coming Home: Immediacy and Relocation

For Woolf, Mrs. Brown—the woman on the train who inspired her and the human life the literary character was meant to illuminate and inspire—is always creatively reinterpreting the world. At least to some degree, she is free to shape how her world and self meaningfully appear. One way this freedom was exercised was in Mrs. Brown's social existence.

Here we remember that the woman on the train was a woman in a relationship with an unpleasant companion who was bullying her to submit to his wishes on some matter. In immediate intersubjective experience, Mrs. Brown can re-create the situation. We can listen again to Woolf's description of Mrs. Brown:

> She becomes a will-o'-the-wisp, a dancing light, an illumination gliding up the wall and out of the window, lighting now in freakish malice upon the nose of an archbishop, now in sudden splendor upon the mahogany of the wardrobe. The most solemn sights she turns to ridicule; the most ordinary she invests with beauty. She changed the shape, shifts the accent, of every scene in which she plays her part.
>
> (3:387–8)

Woolf is not only being cute; she is well aware that bishops are in a social relationship with women like Mrs. Brown, a relation that is not always to such women's benefit, a relation that will generate recalcitrant feelings, wishes, and thoughts in immediate intersubjective experience. Woolf sees Mrs. Brown's immediate intersubjective experience disrupting the status quo and parodying the bishop's identity.

In her immediate fantastic and revisionary sense-making, she takes up the givenness of social identities, relations, and power dynamics and subversively disorders and transforms them. By creating new meanings for the self vis-à-vis the other and the other vis-à-vis the self in her immediate intersubjective experience, she allows the subject to defect from the grip of a historically influential social structure that hitherto has pinned the subject down, to start to have the power to flee an often powerless social identity, to take the first steps to imagine and enter a different interpersonal future where they possess the authority to bestow meaning on the ones who have always presumed to have the right to confer meaning on them.

Woolf frames this insurrection in terms of Mrs. Brown's location and dress. She wrote: "You should insist that she is an old woman of unlimited capacity and infinite variety; capable of appearing in any place; wearing any dress; saying anything and doing heaven knows what" (3:436). Mrs. Brown has the potential to be anyone and anywhere, no matter how high or low on the social hierarchy. Mrs. Brown is a subject of immediacy and, as such, is a subject already living in the future. Rather than being imprisoned in her past and present suffering, she is already participating in a new time with a new social identity in a new social situation and relation.

We are arriving at a constructive way to read Woolf's critical essays on the nature of fiction. She defined the purpose of fictional representation this way: "Let us record the atoms as they fall upon the mind in the order in which they fall, let us trace the pattern, however disconnected and incoherent in appearance, which each sight or incident scores upon the consciousness" (4:161). Now we know that the atoms that fall on the mind are the thoughts, emotions, desires, and perceptions of immediate intersubjective experience; these atoms are disconnected from what society holds up as the right thoughts, feelings, wishes, and perceptions befitting someone like Mrs. Brown; these atoms, which appear incoherent from established society's perspective, offer a new pattern of social identity and existence that will disrupt and renew the patterns that Mrs. Brown has inherited vis-à-vis someone like the bishop.

Woolf thus disavows any stream of consciousness in literature or life that would remain within a realm of pure self-related interiority. Stream of consciousness concerns the subject's relocation of themselves in social space. Woolf would say that the man bullying the woman on the train should not underestimate the resources the woman may find within her immediate experience to renegotiate her relationship with him. And Woolf would say that truthful literature will express the reality of those resources that have the potential to relocate Mrs. Brown to a new social space.

Wives and Cooks: Experience and Social Revolutions

Paralleling Mrs. Brown's escape from normative social identities through her immediate intersubjective experience were a broader set of defections Woolf perceived in European life. We now can listen to Woolf describe the transformation in human character in an even fuller context: "On or about December 1910 human character changed ... All human relations have shifted, *those between masters and servants, husbands and wives, parents and children"* (3:421–2, my italics). Within the contexts of work and family life, a wife has always had immediate experiences vis-à-vis her husband, just as a worker has had them vis-à-vis their boss, and a child has had them vis-à-vis their parents. But now, the recalcitrance and futurity that often saturate this immediacy have begun to receive their rights—that is, social relations have shifted—because servants, wives, and children have started to listen to and follow the lead of their immediate intersubjective experience in its moments of recalcitrance and futurity as they go about deciding how to fulfill their social roles and perform their social identities in work and family. Doing so, it is not surprising that these constituencies change how they perform their social identities in surprising ways.

We can parse the situation as follows. Social forms and identities like being-a-wife or being-a-worker and the authority they claim are unavoidable in human life. When someone grows up in a particular culture, they are expected and encouraged to embody pre-given social roles and identities in areas such as family and labor—sometimes suffering painful consequences if they do not. Moreover, individuals are told that if they want to be happy they must try to shape their interiority in ways that align with the smooth performance of these roles.

The problem arises when women, children, and workers find themselves interiorly suffering as they try to embody their social roles and identities of family and labor as their culture expects. This suffering is precisely what Woolf presented in her vivid example of "the horrible domestic tradition which made it seemly for a woman of genius to spend her time chasing beetles, scouring saucepans, instead of writing books" (3:422). A woman's desire to make art, for example, would get painfully crushed under the weight of housekeeping duties and the weight of the expectation that keeping house would be fulfilling. While performing the role of wife in this way was supposed to make a woman happy—perhaps because she was then fulfilling her God-given nature and destiny—the truth was that many women felt oppressed and stifled in this way of being-a-wife. Many a woman found herself shot through with immediate intersubjective experiences of recalcitrance and futurity vis-à-vis her husband and children who expected them to be homemakers, mothers, romantic partners, and nothing else. Her immediate feelings while being a wife contradicted the feelings that her society, and perhaps she herself, had told her she was supposed to have while being a wife. Her immediacy chafes at her participation in inherited and authoritative social identities and forms to which she is expected to conform. Anger and resentment ensue.

3. Toward Creative Life

However, the development Woolf sees in European life is that such anger and resentment are no longer the last words in social life; the pain involved in the traditional way of being-a-servant, for example, was a recalcitrant pain that was imagining and enacting a different future. About human character changing in this situation, she writes:

> In life one can see the change, if I may use a homely illustration, in the character of one's cook. The Victorian cook lived like a leviathan in the lower depths, formidable, silent, obscure, inscrutable; the Georgian cook is a creature of sunshine and fresh air; in and out of the drawing room, now to borrow the Daily Herald, now to ask advice about a hat. Do you ask for more solemn instances of the power of the human race to change?
>
> (3:422)

When intersubjective immediacy gets its rights, human nature will creatively reconfigure the shape of the social forms it indwells. The social role of being-a-servant is not eliminated, but its inherited form is shown to be contingent, vincible, and malleable. Now that the Victorian cook lives in the parlor and not only the basement, she is seen by her employer in a new way; she has gained power and agency in a relationship that used to be defined only by her invisibility and obedience. She becomes a freer individual. Her world is larger. She can now enact and shape her reality more according to her desire. She comes to have a voice, to have an agency and curiosity that are more respected by her employer, to have a more equal meaningful concord with her employer in a world they share in common, to enjoy a newfound mutuality with her employer that enables her to make requests of them and not just fulfill theirs of her. In sum, through listening to and following the recalcitrance and futurity of her immediate experience, the cook's life as a cook has taken on a vastly different shape—a surprising new shape that, Woolf thinks, would have been unthinkable a generation earlier when immediacy did not have as much influence.

Woolf's conviction, then, to which her words cumulatively gesture seems to have been that such shifts in how social identities like being-a-wife or being-a-cook were performed followed from a major shift in how human character and human life were conceived. In this shift, immediate intersubjective experience was now seen as constitutive of human existence. This kind of experience now had the leverage to resist the constraining painful social identities and roles in which it comes to consciousness and to rework them into less constraining and painful forms. For Woolf, the shape of social identities such as being-a-wife and being-a-cook were now lived out in surprising new ways; immediacy's recalcitrance in these identities was now taken seriously because its surprising futurity was now recognized as valid and worthy of expression. In Woolf's mind, feminist and labor revolutions in social practices and identities were dimensions of a broad and powerful existential revolution—the revolution in which Europeans were beginning to value more highly and live more deeply and explicitly the momentums and materials of immediate intersubjective experience.

Reading the Literature of Life: Representation and Sociality

Now we can most clearly articulate the meaning of Woolf's literary project. For her, we remember, literature embodied human life, and human life was embodied in literature. It was the stream-of-consciousness form and content of Woolf's literature that she used to express, signal, and advance the existential transformation into a new form of life immersed in immediate intersubjective experience. Reimagining literature as she reimagined life, Woolf's literary representation, by focusing on experiential immediacy, re-presented anew the possibilities of social life; she presented a different vision of what human life in common might mean when human life orients itself from this new center. Hence her remark: "The novel is a very remarkable machine for the creation of human character" (3:384). This remark refers not only to how literary characters could be created within the world of the text but also to how actual human individuals, when Woolf's literature inspired them to follow their immediate experience, could become new characters living in new forms of social existence in the world outside the text (just as individuals who read Freud's case studies could find themselves inspired to live a new kind of psychological existence). So when Michael Rosenthal says that *To the Lighthouse* does much "to produce for the reader an almost tactile sense of felt experience," we should know that it is immediate intersubjective experience, in its recalcitrance and futurity, that she is discussing, that she wants her reader to feel in a tactile sense—and not only this kind of experience that belongs to the literary character but the reader's own immediate intersubjective experience too.[26] By conveying Mrs. Brown's or Cam's immediacy as that character lives it firsthand, Woolf could draw the reader into their own felt current of immediacy, a current that could become a resource to them for redefining the terms and ideals of their social existence.

Thus, we can see the logic of Woolf's surprising conviction that the choice of a literary form—and the content that could or could not be presented within any given form—could be a matter of life or death. Since forms of literature correlate with forms of social intercourse, fiction could express and inculcate either social death or social life. By writing in a stream-of-consciousness form that cultivates the reader's attunement to their immediacy in their social exchanges (and, one hopes, to the immediacy of others in theirs), Woolf's writing helps readers confront themselves as subjects of immediate intersubjective experience whose force can be a lever for shaping and reshaping their social existence in less painful ways. Woolf's fictions were therapeutic works. They were performative: they were ushering readers into a form of life with fewer defenses against immediacy, provoking within them a state of life that would risk allowing immediacy's energies to loosen the grip of inherited social identities and expectations that felt rigid and self-vitiating.

So, if Whitworth is correct when he writes that for "the New Criticism ... modernism was understood primarily in terms of experiments in form and style; reference to the outside world was of secondary importance," then we see how incorrect the New Criticism's interpretation was, at least as it relates to Woolf's modernism. Woolf never intended to offer only a self-contained literary artifact. Indeed, almost nothing was more important to her than creating literature that contained powerful reference to life in the outside, social world.[27]

Her literature inspired her readers to follow the lead of immediate intersubjective experience's insurrectionary force in the interpersonal, public world because, for her, changes in human character, shifts in social relations, and transformations in literary form and content all went together—as we see when we return to a passage we have cited before, but now it is emphasized for a final time in an even larger context: "On or about December 1910 human character changed. ... All human relations have shifted, those between masters and servants, husbands and wives, parents and children. *And when human relations change there is at the same time a change in religion, conduct, politics, and literature*" (3:421–2, my italics). The turn in fiction to focus on stream-of-consciousness narration, the turn in social existence to privilege immediate intersubjective experience, and the turn in marriage, child-rearing, and labor toward more egalitarian and mutual forms of relating all evoke and reinforce each other because they all rest on a picture of human life in which immediate intersubjective experience stands at the heart of social identity and existence. The form and content of literature, the existential revolution to embrace immediacy, and the feminist, family, and labor revolutions were all correlating and mutually reinforcing dimensions of the move in the Freudian age in the Europe of Woolf's day to bestow prestige on immediate experience as the new truth at the center of the human being as a social creature. Reading Woolf's fiction was an entrance to this new and complex reality.

A Freudian Beyond Freud: Woolf's Radical Reversal

There is an interesting point to be noted here too. We respect Woolf's aversion to a particular kind of theory-heavy "Freudian literature," but it should be clear that she was a Freudian in another sense. In Woolf's turn to express and advocate for the place of immediate intersubjective experience in literature and life, in her call to human beings to ground social existence in it, Woolf's work did develop within a deeply Freudian horizon and did possess a profoundly Freudian spirit, however much she was aware of these facts.

The way she developed her version of the Freudian ethics of immediacy was creative and critical. Individuals, as they were already doing, needed to recognize the rights not only of immediate psychological experience but also of immediate intersubjective experience. While working in the new existential atmosphere that Freud had helped to uncover and name, in which human life was taking on a new feel, Woolf's work was far from merely reiterating that of Freud. She was expanding this atmosphere's depth and scope beyond the domain of secret fantasy and private drama and taking it into the social environment. She was a Freudian after, beyond, and perhaps against Freud.

When I tease out the possibility that she was a Freudian against Freud, I mean to highlight the way in which she did inherit and rework Freud's ethics of immediacy, in a manner both radical and possibly inconsistent with Freud's own understanding of the experiential revolution he was trying to incite. A few comments by Adam Phillips can crystallize the issue for us. Phillips has written that Freud's neurotic is "a figure traumatized by sociability. A person whose desires don't easily fit into the world as she finds it," a person who has had "to adapt (i.e., to assimilate and conform) at the cost of vitality." For Phillips, "Modern people [were] left with a surplus of themselves that they could do nothing with. Freud's words for the individual's alternative to culture, for his inevitable protest about assimilation, were to be 'sexuality' and 'wishing' and psychopathology and the 'death-instinct,' the private utopianisms of everyday life. The individual's cry of the heart against the necessity of civilization, of acculturation."[28]

In our previous discussion of Freud, I contended that healing from neurotic suffering is made possible when the mind becomes able to directly experience its sexuality and aggression in ongoing, consciously conscious awareness rather than insisting on experiencing them indirectly in repressed symptomatic forms. But, for Freud, going beyond repression and symptom seems as if it can take place without any rearrangement of the social surround that motivated the repression and symptom. Freud gives the impression that the psychological subject can resolve their neurosis within the privacy of mind by feeling their feelings, desiring their desires, and thinking their thoughts in a new, different, and healthier way, even if the surrounding atmosphere does not change. The important thing is to feel one's anger, even if the situation eliciting the anger does not change.

Woolf thought differently. She did not believe, as Freud seemed to (at least at times), that the realm of relevance of immediate experience is only interior. She did not see abreaction as the only option when individual desire conflicted with social definition and expectation. Instead, she believed that immediate intersubjective experience should be given the authority to reconfigure the social atmosphere causing the pain along with its recalcitrance and futurity. There is a third option beyond being psychologically more or less neurotic: changing the terms and ideals of the social situation that is causing the neurosis in the first place. Within a form of life guided by the ethics of immediacy, life does not have to sacrifice inner vitality for sociability. Instead, inherited forms of sociability could be sacrificed for the sake of sustaining and advancing inner vitality. At least sometimes, humans are permitted to own, rather than repress, contra-social experiences, to embrace those experiences as levers so that the individual can rebel against the inherited forms of sociability demanding that they repress their immediate experiences, whether psychological or intersubjective, in the first place.

The Morality of the Ethics: Goodness and Thriving

Before we leave Woolf, one more question needs attention, a question that was important in the discussion of Freud as well: what of the morality of the ethics of immediacy? Is the ethics of immediacy itself moral? It is one thing to make the descriptive claim Woolf makes: "Thus it is that we hear all around us, in poems and novels and biographies, even in newspaper articles and essays, the sound of breaking and falling, crashing and destruction. It is the prevailing sound of the Georgian age" (3:433–4)—that is, that European humanity was being transformed (its character changing, in Woolf's terms) through a new commitment to the superior value of immediate intersubjective experience in its recalcitrance and futurity, to let it have a more significant purchase in life just as it appears in consciousness, whatever its friction with inherited norms of social identity. But it is another thing to make a normative claim that European humanity made the right decision in making immediate intersubjective experience the privileged source for determining the goals and structures of social life. Since this register was often seen in European history as a realm of unruly desires and impulses, inappropriate and unholy feelings and thoughts, it seems fitting to ask whether the decision to live more intentionally with the grain of immediacy—to allow its data and pressures to radically refashion the shape of social identities like being-a-wife or being-a-child or being-a-worker—is indeed a good decision? Did the new ethics lead to virtue or vice?

Although no absolute answer may be possible, Woolf would say the new ethics was moral; it led to virtue. Given the choice to fight against the advents of immediate intersubjective experience or to live into them, Woolf clearly thought it was often the appropriate choice to live into them. Here I will extrapolate from Woolf's own words to discern the existential atmosphere her words were manifesting and creating, the swirl of European life and lived experience that was the home her words indwelled and helped build.

To begin, the ethics of immediacy expressed in Woolf's work brings satisfaction. Living with the grain of immediate intersubjective experience is more satisfying than living against it. Mrs. Brown does not enjoy suffering her painful obligation to her companion on the train; Cam does not enjoy her rage at her father. Feeling freedom, having one's agency respected, and pursuing goals that one is intrinsically motivated to pursue are all forms of satisfaction that are being withheld from Mrs. Brown and Cam. For Woolf, as the way she paints these characters shows, satisfaction is a good. Human beings deserve satisfaction, pleasure, and joy in life, and they should lead a form of life that brings more pleasure than pain, which is what life in the ethics of immediacy promises.

For Woolf, however, this utilitarian boon of the ethics of immediacy, where the presence or absence of utility or satisfaction would be the sole or main criterion for judging the moral value of this ethics, was not its only or main justification. Another reason for the ethics of immediacy to merit our esteem is that it furthers human thriving, the realization of human potential—in Woolf's example, the potential to be an artist creating significant works of literature. Here we remember Woolf's example of a woman of high intelligence and creativity wasting her life doing nothing but housework. Woolf's position would seem to be that such a woman can realize herself and unfold her gifts only by embracing the force of her immediate intersubjective experience vis-à-vis those in her social circle who are demanding that she devote her life to homemaking—only by resisting that social identity through the recalcitrance of her immediate experience and living into her calling as an artist through the futurity of this experience. So even if the utilitarian pursuit of satisfaction is chalked up to a problematic hedonism, the ethics of immediacy is also a path to virtue, an ethics that helps realize a person's purpose to make something noble and beautiful of their life. The ethics of immediacy, Woolf implies, will deliver a world where a greater number of powerful operas and symphonies will be composed, poetic masterpieces written, great scientific discoveries made, and acts of love and justice accomplished.

Living against the grain of immediate intersubjective experience also makes for an unauthentic and untruthful life. An individual lives a life that, in a large sense, is a lie when their action and behavior contradict their interior drive to satisfaction. When life leans into immediacy's energies, however, life becomes more authentic and truthful.

The ethics of immediacy is also a boon to virtue in that an individual who not only embraces this ethics toward themselves but also sees all humans as subjects who can and should follow the lead of their immediate intersubjective experience practices more respect for the other. This respect can be good in itself and can benefit the person bestowing respect themselves. As Lackey notes, Woolf's fiction, by "enabling people to understand and appreciate the inner lives of others ... makes human intimacy possible."[29] Practicing the ethics of immediacy can engender a more humane and peaceable relational world through individuals paying attention to the experiential immediacies of other and self. So, there is a transformation of how the self-other relationship is viewed at the most fundamental level, when immediate experience is made the center of and the context for social coexistence. Social identities—husbands and their wives, employers and their workers, parents and their children—in European life were changing, as the former (more or less willingly) were giving more room to the unfolding of the desire of the latter in a way that was seen as less vitiating and less spoiling of their human potential. In short, life immersed in the ethics of immediacy, a life aware of the importance of the drives of immediate intersubjective experience in human life, can liberate life into new, more empathically attuned, closer forms of human relating.

Social existence will also be more egalitarian. Even if immediate intersubjective experience can involve anger and resentment, as Woolf's example of the cook shows, listening to it does not have to lead to spite or revenge. For the cook, the alternative to having her desire and potential dominated and stifled is not to take revenge or to begin to dominate and stifle the one who dominated and stifled her. In the recalcitrance and futurity of immediate intersubjective experience, there is not necessarily any desire to hurt the oppressor. When these promptings are allowed to unfold—even when they begin in resentment and anger—the end result, Woolf sees, can be a more egalitarian community. The cook becoming more of a sharer of the same space as her employer is an example of the possibility that the ethics of immediacy can help engender a new, freer, more mutually satisfying social existence.

Thus, when immediate intersubjective experience has its rights in human life, life's potential for satisfaction and contentment, thriving and creativity, authenticity and truthfulness, respect and intimacy, and mutuality and community become more possible to realize. The choice to embrace and follow the recalcitrance and futurity of immediate intersubjective experience, as it presses to deconstruct and reconstruct the terms of social existence, can often be profoundly moral. A good argument can be made that—whereas, historically, immediacy had been seen as a cauldron of chaos and vice against which the demands of social identities were seen as bulwarks—now it was these social identities, at least in their current forms, that had to come under judgment, at least at times, for themselves serving as an impediment to the possibility of virtue.

Therapeutic Immediacy: Illusion and Renewal

The therapeutic aspect of Woolf's work is that it dismantles the idea that social identities have objectively given and thus rigid essences. Rather than living in sync with a natural essence, life had been pledging allegiance to a set of tendentious, far from innocent, far from normative, second-order ideals for human social existence. It is an illusion that an eternal, historically unchanging, and invincible set of standards can set the terms for the proper performance of the social identity of wife, a child, or a worker. Any conception of what it means to be of these social identities is a fabrication to the extent that it claims to be necessary, essential, or unchanging. The ethics of immediacy is therapeutic because it can show, by embracing immediate intersubjective experience, that rigid and punitive inherited conceptions of social identities are contingent rather than natural, objective, or necessary. Claims that an inherited form of social identity represents the essence of that identity now will lose legitimacy and authority to the extent that the inherited form inspires recalcitrance and futurity within the realm of intersubjective immediacy.

The shift here is stark. Before, if a conflict arose between the ideals and standards for the performance of social identity, on the one hand, and the phenomena of immediate intersubjective experience, on the other, a person was expected to control the latter so that life, more or less comfortably, could perform the inherited social identity and thus practice the virtues appropriate for someone living in that role. In the ethics of immediacy Woolf's work represents, however, Europeans of her day were reversing this dynamic. Now it was not the insurrectionary momentum of immediacy that was the problem but the restrictive inertia of the inherited forms of social identity. In a reversal of events, the inherited ideals and norms of social existence can sometimes be the social pathology, causing needless suffering, from which individuals need deliverance. Europeans were coming to see that many inherited forms of social identity—of what it means or could mean to be a wife, child, or worker, for example—were, when painful, capable of being diagnosed as merely illusory, arbitrary forms of social identity.

So, being illusory and arbitrary, an inherited form of social identity could be abandoned and replaced by a new form. Social identity could be renewed. Allowing immediate intersubjective experience the freedom to force the renegotiation of the terms and expectations of social identities in feminist, child-centric, and pro-labor directions meant that social identities themselves were open to being changed for the better. Whereas, before, an inherited ideal of the meaning of a social identity imposed unquestionable limits to the range of action and interiority that an individual was allowed, where immediacy's recalcitrant experiential content had to be brought in line with the inherited ideal, now humans could consider the possibility that it was the inherited ideal that was the problem and needed to be rethought in the light of the recalcitrant and future-looking contents of immediacy.

So, although, in this chapter, I have used the word "revolution" to describe the kinds of changes Woolf's work was expressing and evoking, the better word might be "renewal." For Woolf was not striving to jettison categories of social identity, like being-a-wife, being-a-child, or being-an-employee, altogether. Instead, her work showed new possibilities for being a wife, child, and worker and for being a husband, parent, or employer.

A looser, more malleable sense of the nature and authority of inherited forms of social identities was becoming prevalent, a sense that social identities and forms of social existence will always have an element of formlessness. Social identities were coming to be seen as structures that were open to being continually remade in ways that lessen the pain and increase the satisfaction and thriving of those participating in them. This renewal was not a total rupture with the past; instead, it involved both continuity and discontinuity with the shape the social identity had before. The embrace of immediate intersubjective experience as a source for social existence opens up new ways for a woman to be a wife, or for a woman to be a woman, for a spouse to be a spouse, or even for a human being to be a human being in ways that better facilitate chances for individuals to thrive and find satisfaction.[30]

Human life seems to need social identities, social forms, and social ideals, but the ethics of immediacy invites individuals to hold them loosely, to stay open to ways they may need to be reworked in light of the pressures of immediacy. In this more flexible account of the nature of social identity, human life can both inhabit social identities and remain open to how immediacy's recalcitrance and futurity can inspire the remaking of the forms of those identities. It may be the case that no individual, whatever the social identity in which they find themselves, will ever be able to participate seamlessly in that identity. Immediacy's dissonance with whatever happens to be its present social identity may be inescapable. Moments of immediate intersubjective experience in their logic of recalcitrance and futurity will always emerge. So the process of remaking the forms of social identities will be an ongoing one. There are no timeless ideals of social identity. Fashioning social identities is the work of time. It requires remaining open to the ongoing revelations of immediate experience in the time of its becoming, and new, surprising, and improbable meanings of self-other relations will always continue to be discovered and created.

Human life that commits itself to the ongoing renewal of social identities by listening to immediate intersubjective experience is complex and hazardous work. Life has reasons to defend against immediacy by erecting illusions. We can frame the issue by speaking of the pleasures that life must forgo to live in the ethics of immediacy.

First, life lived with the grain of immediate intersubjective experience is difficult and dangerous as it has to renounce pleasures of personal stability and coherence. Life in an unchanging identity can be meaningful and safe in ways that are often pleasurable. These pleasures can create inertia motivating individuals to cling to sedimented shapes of social identity even when such shapes are painful. A wife, child, or worker may suffer, but they know who they are and what is expected of them and others, for better or worse. Here there is a parallel to Freud's insight about the power of sedimented psychological identities, now played out at the level of social identities. Social existence lacking any ongoing stable grammar can be uncertain and anxious. Freedom for identity creation does not always feel like a blessing. The point is even more true when we remember that the process of identity renewal is ongoing and not a one-off event.

Second, the ethics of immediacy is difficult and dangerous because it challenges the pleasures of living with entrenched hierarchies. As the force of immediate intersubjective experience, often pulsing with recalcitrance and futurity, reveals the shape of social identities in some hierarchies as arbitrary and groundless, vincible and vulnerable to change, the process can be painful for those invested in the hierarchies. Difficulty ensues for persons in privileged places in the hierarchy, to be sure, but perhaps also for those who are not. The powerful are required to forgo the pleasures of domination and responsibility, but the less powerful or powerless may have to forgo the pleasures of subordination, innocence, victimhood, and protection, pleasures someone like Freud knew could be powerful. People anywhere in the hierarchy find themselves relinquishing the pleasure of order, as the pressures of immediate experience can threaten chaos and the collapse of social order.

Third, following immediacy's promptings can lead to more intense interpersonal conflict at individual and societal levels. Disunity and instability can saturate personal relationships and communities. As the ethics of immediacy ascends to prominence, it can seem as if relational and social tranquility can disappear.

If the ethics of immediacy threatened the pleasures of personal stability and coherence, of hierarchy and order, and of purported tranquility, then what was its promise? Why did European life seem to have wagered in favor of embracing the ethics of immediacy? First, Europeans sensed that the satisfaction and thriving made possible by listening to immediate intersubjective experience's lead would outweigh the pleasures of an unchanging sense of personal social identity and coherence and alleviate the real pain caused by rigid commitments to the stability and coherence of a social identity. They sensed the promise of a different kind of flourishing that was possible in a social existence that was less coherent and more dynamic. Second, they believed that the satisfaction and thriving of personal relationships and social structures as egalitarian and mutually determined as possible would outweigh the pleasures of hierarchy and order and mitigate the real suffering caused by arbitrary relationships of authority and obedience. They sensed the promise of a different kind of existential fulfillment and joy in relationships that could occur in communities that were more chaotic and creative. Third, they anticipated that the pleasures of truth, intimacy, and authenticity in negotiating the terms and ideals of relationships would outweigh the pleasures of surface tranquility and lessen the toxic pain and resentment often just below that surface. They sensed the promise of a different kind of thriving that could occur when personal and societal conflict over the forms of social identities (however raw and spirited the conflict was) was overt, when the terms and ideals of social existence were negotiated and renegotiated more directly by attending explicitly to the way the self-other relationship was, phenomenologically speaking, being given in the register of immediate experience.

Conclusion: The Danger and Promise of Immediacy

We began this chapter by showing that Virginia Woolf, against the literature of death she saw her contemporaries writing, strove to write a literature of life, a literature that would understand "human nature," discern and reveal "the meaning of existence itself," "the spirit we live by, life itself," a literature that meant not only to describe a certain kind of lived experience but to convey and evoke it. We saw that this meaning—this soul, this spirit of life, embodied in the woman on the train who inspired Woolf's reflections on the nature of fiction, the literary character Mrs. Brown, and human being itself—was the life of immediate experience. Her subject was defined by immediate intersubjective experience, all the thoughts, desires, feelings, and perceptions that arise in the mind in ways that are sudden, unanticipated, unrequested, anomalous, disordered, and spontaneous in the context of the self's relationship with real others in the actual world. This experience, for Woolf, was a register of experience in which acts of surprising and improbable creativity enjoyed a measure of freedom to continually upset and reimagine the traditional authoritative forms of the self-other relation. Within the creative operations of immediate intersubjective experience, the possibilities of the self-other relationship could be given differently: old ways could come to look incoherent, while insurrectionary ways could begin to look reasonable. And these ways in which the self-other relation is now given could conflict with the very social identities that provided the context for the immediate intersubjective experience to happen in the first place.

The particular way Woolf saw the self-other relation being newly and improbably given was through the recalcitrance and futurity that we saw through our analysis of Cam's anger and resentment in *To the Lighthouse*. There we saw the quality of many instances of the experience of being dominated by an oppressor, and resisting that oppressor, in some structure of social existence. This recalcitrance and futurity actually, experientially speaking, was the first step in the subject's relocation of themselves into a new social space where their self-other relation was freer and less painful. Before the force of immediate intersubjective experience was allowed to rewrite the terms and ideals of social identity, many wives in Woolf's time had to waste their lives doing housework when they could have been writing novels or symphonies. Now the subject is recognized as a "flying spirit," an "uncircumscribed spirit" who has the "unlimited capacity" to relocate themselves, in their experiential futurity, "in any place," any social place, as the "fantastic" creative operations of immediate experience determine. Once the work of social relocating that occurs in immediate experience has begun to gain traction, however, developments in social existence become possible, like the transformation in the life of the Victorian cook Woolf describes, who was formerly a depersonalized and invisible servant and is now, through the increased privileges of immediate intersubjective experience to creatively reconceive the shape of her social identity, a personal, visible, more content agent coexisting in a shared time and space with her employer.

In these ways, Woolf's literature was indeed a literature of life, a literature that aimed to inspire a new kind of life in those who read it. It not only represented but expressed and fomented the existential revolution of embracing the improbable and surprising creative powers of immediate intersubjective experience. This experience, in turn, was the first fruits, the future freedom being experienced now, the context making possible the real revolutions in social existence between wives and husbands, children and parents, and workers and employers, real revolutions in which the former demanded and were beginning to receive more space from the latter to live in ways more expressive of their agency and desire. In this existential revolution that Woolf discerned and narrated so brilliantly, it became clear that the immediate experience Freud thought could remain solely psychological was also profoundly and manifestly social. And the consequence was that it was not only psychological existence that would be transformed in liberating ways when human life began to live into the grain of immediacy; social existence, when it lived into this grain in its interpersonal register, would be changed in liberating ways as well.

In Woolf's vision, we also see how the ethics of immediacy was not just a form of hedonism. This ethics was moral, a form of life that could lead to virtue, to human satisfaction, to the realization of human potential and human thriving. We saw how human life could only begin to live according to the ethics of immediacy if certain kinds of therapeutic dismantling of illusions occur in which ideals masquerading as eternal and normative are unmasked as contingent and arbitrary. We saw that social existence lived according to the ethics of immediacy offered the possibility of social renewal at every level of human life through the continual renewing of the forms taken by social identities. And, finally, we saw that, even with all the dangers involved, all the pleasures forgone, the ethics of immediacy, to Woolf's mind, was a risk worth taking—both because of the way it lessened human suffering and because of the way it increased human possibilities for a social existence defined by truth, authenticity, joy, and thriving.

In this chapter, however, we have been examining something larger than just Woolf's work, which is the way that Woolf's genius allowed her to compose criticism and fiction that showed how "human character changed." She helped define and inaugurate a burgeoning existential atmosphere in Europe in the first part of the twentieth century, the Freudian age. Just as Freud's texts showed a vision of human life reclaiming, for the first time, the hazard and promise involved in giving a preeminent place to immediate experience in the shaping of psychological identity and existence, Woolf's sometimes un-Freudian and sometimes even anti-Freudian texts showed a vision of European life reclaiming, for the first time, the hazard and promise involved in giving a preeminent place to immediate experience in shaping social identity and existence. Now social existence would more closely follow the ethics of immediacy, a life lived more with the grain of immediate intersubjective experience, with fewer defenses against the contents and insistences of this specific kind of experience.

Nor was the work ever done. Letting immediate intersubjective experience orient social existence was not only focused on discrete moments of recalcitrant desire and the future that desire posited. Embracing the ethics of immediacy also meant making the choice to live in an ongoing way in the logic of intersubjective immediacy. Individuals' participation in social existence would now develop as they listened attentively to the currents of insistence, recalcitrance, and futurity in their immediate intersubjective experience. Europeans would come to realize that forms of social identities were open to being continually unsettled, interrupted, and deconstructed because of the logic of immediate intersubjective experience. But they could also anticipate more opportunities for social renewal and even healing because of this same logic. Their social existence could become an arena of creativity and development rather than of stasis and reiteration. Woolf's work recommends embracing the ethics of immediacy with its continually renewing adventure of social existence grounded in the lead of immediate intersubjective experience and its logic. For her, life within the framework of this ethics was a difficult and dangerous prospect for European society. Still, it was also an auspicious prospect that offered the possibility for self-other relations that are more virtuous, authentic, satisfying, and free, than the self-other relations that were available without this ethics. We can again remind ourselves of Hölderlin's message: where the danger lies, there is salvation. It was a message Europeans were taking to heart as they embraced the ethics of immediacy in social life, a Freudian ethics that Woolf developed beyond Freud.

Chapter 4

Toward Wondering Life: Mystery, Miracle, and Menace in Merleau-Ponty

Introduction: Was Merleau-Ponty a Freudian?

Maurice Merleau-Ponty felt ambivalent about the truth of Freud's psychoanalysis, and this is evident in the "Preface" he wrote in 1960 for his colleague Angelo Hesnard's *L'Oeuvre de Freud et son importance pour le monde moderne*. In this brief text Merleau-Ponty, from the perspective of phenomenology, suggests that Freud's theory of mind is overdetermined, trapped even, in the language and concepts of science—a broad category for Merleau-Ponty, one that here means natural science. For Freud, "mechanistic and energetic metaphors" define human life, including consciousness and unconsciousness.[1] Merleau-Ponty accused Freud of making a category mistake: "Does not the notion of libido lose all of its meaning if there is a 'cellular libido,' if it is a property of the cells?" (Preface, 82). He thinks it incoherent to say that cells have sexual desire, for desire is a first-person phenomenon. Cells may indeed operate mechanistically: an internal design may cause them to develop in specific ways, and external influence may cause them to exist in particular ways. But cells *qua* cells, considered as objects in nature, do not desire; desire is a different kind of reality, an experiential one. Thus, in Merleau-Ponty's estimation, Freud's attempt to understand desire and mental life in mechanistic instead of experiential terms "leads to misunderstandings between Freud and the hurried reader (perhaps between Freud and himself)" (83).

Merleau-Ponty did not dismiss psychoanalysis; he believed it revealed fundamental truths about the human being, even if it did so in a confused way. He believed Freud understood his achievement only partially: "psychoanalysis is informed with a thought which nevertheless is expressed only very indirectly in certain Freudian concepts" (82). At least in certain respects, Freud's psychoanalysis needs to be saved from itself—by phenomenology: "Here phenomenology brings to psychoanalysis certain categories, certain means of expression that it needs in order to be completely itself. Phenomenology permits psychoanalysis to recognize 'psychic reality' without equivocation" (81). Phenomenology makes visible how human life is saturated with sexual desire as an experiential reality. Freud's scientism threatened to blind him to the actual reality engaged by psychoanalysis: "the treasure of *experience* that is hidden in psychoanalytic communication" (82, my italics). By aiming "to separate psychoanalysis from a scientific or objectivist ideology" (81) and by "reformulating certain Freudian concepts in the framework of a better philosophy" (84), a phenomenological philosopher can offer a more coherent and satisfying understanding of Freud's discoveries.

In Merleau-Ponty's framework, the unconscious is an experiential reality, not a mechanistic one: "the Freudian unconscious as an archaic or primordial consciousness, the repressed as a zone of experience that we have not integrated" (81). Rather than being a machine of impersonal drives, the unconscious is instead a matrix of unintegrated personal experiences.[2] This way of understanding Freud reflects my proposal for understanding him. Even if Freud was never fully aware of it, his psychoanalysis was a theory and a therapy of conscious and unconscious lived experience.

In addition, Merleau-Ponty believed that Freud's psychoanalysis also expanded phenomenology's understanding of what counted as lived experience. Now, phenomenology must acknowledge that lived experiences can be both conscious and unconscious. Exploring the realm of consciousness now entailed exploring the logic of its unconscious dimensions. In this way, phenomenology needed to become "Freudian," just as psychoanalysis needed to become phenomenological.

In this chapter I suggest that Merleau-Ponty's project was also Freudian in its appreciation and development of Freud's revolutionary reclaiming of immediate experience's value in human life. Like Woolf's, Merleau-Ponty's work expressed and inspired the transformation in European life that Freud's work had first named and encouraged. In this chapter we will consider four concise texts from his early period: mainly the "Preface" to *Phenomenology of Perception* (1945), "Cezanne's Doubt" (1945), "The Primacy of Perception and Its Philosophical Consequences" (1947), and *The World of Perception* (1948).[3] Whereas Freud focused on immediacy in psychological life and Woolf focused on immediacy in intersubjective life, Merleau-Ponty concentrated on immediate experience in philosophical life in order to see how philosophy could take a new shape in the Freudian age.

4. Toward Wondering Life

Sunrise and Forest: Perception, Immediacy, and Predication

Merleau-Ponty makes the following claim in the "Preface" to *Phenomenology of Perception*: "we are immediately in touch with the world" (*PhP-CS*, xiii). But what does it mean to be immediately in touch with the world? It means to be in the experience of "perception" (PrP, 30). Perception is the mode of experience the individual has when they watch the sun rise: "I ... perceive the sun on a hazy day as hovering two hundred paces away ... I ... see the sun 'rise'" (*PhP-DL*, 62). Perception is a first-person everyday experience: on an early spring morning, my eyes see a piercingly bright and bulging-forth yellow-orange disc ascend in a pink sky haloed by a black-blue penumbra; my skin feels warmed by heat breaking through the cold air; the space around me expands as the constricted dark that surrounds me gives way to a more capacious atmosphere provided by light. For Merleau-Ponty, such perception is a "truly immediate experience" (*PhP-DL*, 60).[4] Merleau-Ponty calls this perceptual immediacy by many names: "tacit cogito" (*PhP-DL*, 426), "operative intentionality" (*PhP-DL*, lxxxii), "this lived world" and "naïve consciousness" (*PhP-DL*, 59). Here I will focus on his description of immediate experience as "pre-predicative" (*PhP-DL*, lxxix) or as "the unreflective life of consciousness" (*PhP-CS*, xvii)—the world as "what it in fact is for us, prior to every thematization" (*PhP-DL*, lxxix).

Merleau-Ponty shows what he means by "pre-predicative" or "unreflective" experience by contrasting it with another kind of experience that is not immediate: "reflection" (*PhP-DL*, 216). Here, rather than "the perceiving subject," there is "consciousness which 'interprets'" (PrP, 12). Reflection or interpretation is predicative and thus secondary, supplemental, and derivative. To predicate is to make an assertion about something—to reflexively thematize or define something the individual has concretely experienced, to attribute some character to it. Predication presupposes a more basic, spontaneously experienced object of which something additional can be predicated. Two forms of predication are explication and explanation. *Explication* predicates something about the meaning of a phenomenon: the poet might say the sunrise is the world welcoming us back to waking life; the ancient Greek might say that it is the beginning of Helios's daily journey through the heavens. *Explanation* predicates something about the causes behind a phenomenon. The religious person might say that the sun rises because God wills it to rise. And the astronomer might say that the human experience of the sun rising is the effect of the earth's daily rotation on its axis combined with humans' ordinary terrestrial perspective. Both kinds of predication stand at a distance from immediacy, from the unreflective experience of simply seeing the sun rise in the sky. Sunrises can exist even if poems are not composed about them, but poems about sunrises cannot be written unless someone somewhere has seen a sunrise with their own eyes.

In other words, for Merleau-Ponty predication is a form of representation—that is, re-presentation. As pre-predicative, "Perception does not give me truths like geometry but presences" (PrP, 14). In naïve consciousness, Merleau-Ponty takes the rising sun as a presence in human life, one that is directly present. Perception is a realm of direct presence. When I assert that the rising sun has some additional feature or content—it is a symbol, for example, or it is a massive ball of gas and fire, or it is a theophany—I am re-presenting the sun with the addition of an aspect. I see the sun as something, as having some feature. I am now not simply experiencing the presence of the sunrise; I am saying something additional about the sunrise that is present. Hence Merleau-Ponty's comment: "I cannot assimilate perception to syntheses that belong to the order of judgment, acts, or predication" (*PhP-DL*, lxxiv). When I am making judgments about the truth of the sunrise, I am re-presenting the sunrise scientifically, religiously, poetically, and so on. I am operating on a level of explication or explanation in which the immediate presence of the world is lost.

We should note that predication (as interpretation, reflection, explication, or explanation) is not problematic. Merleau-Ponty's phenomenology of perception is itself a second-order, predicative reflection on a first-order, pre-predicative phenomenon. Perception involves immediate experience of something, while predication adds something to that direct experience.

It should be clear that Merleau-Ponty does not consider perception to be merely psychological or mental; perception focuses on something outside the subject that appears to the subject. Perception connects with objects: "Perception opens onto things" (*PhP-DL*, 54); it is "our lived-through relationship to things" (*PhP-CS*, 379). Perceiving a sunrise is not an internally self-enclosed experience; it is not just qualia, in the language of analytical philosophy.[5] Perception is the experience of an object beyond the subject. There is no interiority without exteriority, no subject experiencing without an object experienced: "This phenomenal field is not an 'inner world,' the 'phenomenon' is not a 'state of consciousness,' or a 'mental fact,' and the experience of phenomena is not an act of introspection" (*PhP-CS*, 66). Perception is about both the sun rising and the person watching it. Perception is not more subjective than objective: "Our body and our perception always solicit us to take the landscape they offer as the center of the world" (*PhP-DL*, 299). Perception is not subjectivist. What appears is the center of perception as much as the subject to whom it appears. Subjectivity and objectivity are equally real in the field of perception; this experiential matrix includes self and world as necessary, intertwined poles that exist together or not at all.

The issue concerns not only isolated perceptions of discrete objects. The issue is perceiving the world itself. In other words, "The normal subject does not revel in subjectivity, he flees from it, he is really in the world" (*PhP-DL*, 358). Merleau-Ponty insists upon "the natural and pre-predicative unity of the world and of our life" (*PhP-DL*, lxxxii). In terms of subjectivity, the field of perception is the individual's "naïve contact with the world" (*PhP-DL*, 7); in terms of objectivity, the field is "the world of living experience" (*PhP-CS*, 67), and "the 'lived-through' world" (*PhP-CS*, 69). Hence Merleau-Ponty's critique of Husserl: "Truth does not 'inhabit' only 'the inner man' … there is no inner man, man is in the world" (*PhP-CS*, xii).[6] Subjectivity is ecstatic: it goes beyond itself into the world; it concerns the world's reality as much as the subject's.

This lived-through realm of perception is defined by immediacy. Merleau-Ponty calls it "this *immediately* present world" (*PhP-DL*, 60, my italics). He sees this world as having three aspects: nascency, pastness, and givenness.

First is nascency. Life's first contact with reality is perceptual. Here is the "primordial world" (*CD*, 13), the world of "originary experience" (*PhP-DL*, 259) and "*originary* knowledge" (*PhP-DL*, 45, original italics), the world that contains "originary phenomena" (*PhP-DL*, 25) that initiate humans' sense of reality itself. Unreflective perception provides life's "initial situation" (*PhP-CS*, xvi). Merleau-Ponty's claim is strong: perception is "the layer of living experience through which other people and things are first given to us, the system 'Self—Others—things' in its *nascent* state" (*PhP-DL*, 57, my italics). And also: "The fundamental world is the world of conscious experience … through which from the outset a world forms itself round me and *begins* to exist for me" (*PhP-CS*, ix, my italics). In perceptual experience, the world and its contents first are what they are—at least for human beings. The sun first exists in human life as it rises and sets in perceptual experience. Perception is the experiential matrix in which the meaningful world has its genesis, the nexus in which it first becomes manifest in any way before other kinds of reflective engagement can be undertaken.

Second is pastness. Vis-à-vis reflection, perception always exists in the past. Merleau-Ponty speaks of "the more secret act, *always in the past*, by which we take up a world" (PhP-DL, 293, my italics). We experience "a communication with the world *more ancient* than thought" (PhP-DL, 265, my italics). Just as perceptual experience has logical anteriority (there is no predication without a perception about which something is predicated), perception also has genealogical anteriority. Perception antedates reflection in logical as well as temporal space (to employ inadequate metaphors). An analysis of the cause of a phenomenon is always logically and temporally subsequent to the experience of the phenomenon itself.

Third is givenness. In Merleau-Ponty's mind, the human individual life *finds* itself in the field of perception: "I began to reflect, my reflection is a reflection upon an unreflected ... this involves recognizing, prior to its own operations, the world that is *given* to the subject because the subject is *given* to himself" (PhP-DL, lxxiii, my italics). In predication, I make a claim about something, but this "something" involves receptivity. Predication takes up something given to it: "Perception is not a science of the world, nor even an act or a deliberate taking of a stand; it is the background ... and is thus presupposed" (PhP-DL, lxxiv). Perception and its world exist in human life, and the individual has no choice in the matter. Perception is suffered, painfully or joyfully, apart from any activity of the will.

Here Merleau-Ponty draws on Husserl: "Husserl distinguishes between act intentionality—which is the intentionality of our judgments and of our voluntary decisions ... and operative intentionality (fungierende Intentionalität), the intentionality that establishes the natural and pre-predicative unity of the world and of our life, the intentionality that appears in our desires, our evaluations, and our landscape" (PhP-DL, lxxxii). Perception's field is involuntarily present. It simply appears as a dimension of life without any deliberation or decision on life's part, so Merleau-Ponty speaks of "the unmotivated springing forth of the world" (PhP-D, lxxvii).

So, life is thrown into perception. We find ourselves experiencing certain things in specific ways, and these experiences constitute the given on which human life can reflect. These words encapsulate the point: "We uncovered, beneath act or thetic intentionality—and in fact as its very condition of possibility—an operative intentionality already at work prior to every thesis and every judgment" (PhP-DL, 453). When Merleau-Ponty writes that human life is "*condemned to meaning*" (*PhP-CS*, xxii, original italics), he refers to the way in which human life cannot avoid the givenness of the meaning and meanings of the perceived world. It is as if there is an active perceptual life that preexists us. He claims about life's sensory experience of material objects: "I experience sensation as a modality of a general existence, already destined to a physical world, which flows through me without my being its author" (*PhP-DL*, 224). Immediate perception is unauthored by the reflective, predicative mind; it is mine and at the same time not mine; it comes unbidden; it is always already there. I suffer perception: "Now, at the very moment that I turn toward myself to describe myself, I catch sight of an anonymous flow, an overall project in which 'states of consciousness' do not yet exist" (*PhP-DL*, 458). What pre-predicatively exists as the givenness I have to experience is a realm of pre-predicative meaning-making activity.

For these reasons, Merleau-Ponty affirms that "The world is *always already* constituted" (*PhP-DL*, 480, my italics)—logically, temporally, factically. "The world is there *before* any possible analysis of mine … with … *prior* reality" (*PhP-CS*, xi, my italics); "the field is meaningful *prior* to its being attended to" (*PhP-DL*, 153, my italics). He summarizes his point with an example in these words: "To return to the things themselves is to return to this world prior to knowledge, this world of which knowledge always speaks, and this world with regard to which every scientific determination is abstract, signitive and dependent, just like geography with regard to the landscape where we first learned what a forest, a meadow, or a river is" (*PhP-DL*, lxxii). Any explication or explanation of the rising sun depends—by logic, temporality, or facticity—upon life's perception of it.

We will return to the issue of thetic intentionality—interpretation, predication, explication, explanation, and reflection. But the crucial point to remember is this: "Reflection can never make it the case that I cease to perceive the sun on a hazy day as hovering two hundred paces away, that I cease to see the sun 'rise' and 'set'" (*PhP-DL*, 62). Merleau-Ponty reminded the philosophical community that the reality of the world of pre-thetic perception could not be gainsaid: it exists willy-nilly with its nascent, logically and temporally anterior, given meanings and significances apart from whatever forms of reflection or analysis may come upon the scene to engage it, to explore it, or even to attempt to negate it. Demonstrating and emphasizing the reality of this world was a significant philosophical achievement since Merleau-Ponty believed that modernity had often given little purchase to this reality philosophically or, as we will see, existentially.

Philosophy Begins in Wonder: Interrogation

Merleau-Ponty captures the theme we have been investigating: "Science and philosophy have for centuries been carried along by the originary faith of perception" (*PhP-DL*, 54). We have focused on the latter part of this claim, the character of the perception that is originary in human experience, but now we need to focus on the former part of the claim—on the nature of the science and the philosophy that follow and derive from pre-thematic perception in human experience. For even with everything Merleau-Ponty says about perception's primacy and anteriority, he still knows that science and philosophy must to some degree leave behind the reality of perceptual immediacy: "The center of philosophy is … found in the perpetual beginning of reflection at that point when an individual life begins to reflect upon itself" (*PhP-DL*, 63). Pre-reflective perceptual immediacy is a first-order experience, and reflection is a second-order posture toward it.

Merleau-Ponty follows Plato and Aristotle in believing that philosophy begins in "'wonder' before the world" (*PhP-DL*, lxxvii). Wonder has several aspects. First, to wonder is to question—philosophy is interrogative. The wondering human being asks, in gentle or aggressive, meditative or calculating ways: "What is the meaning of the immediacy and anteriority in which I am immersed?" Second, to wonder is to quest. Philosophy sees the field of pre-thetic perception as an enigma whose truth must be sought after because it is not simply present or apparent. Third, to wonder is to suffer. The one who takes up the posture of philosophical reflection is somehow discontented with the unreflective and naïve life of perception; rather than simply staying within or living out the plane of perceptual life, they feel goaded to reach beyond its brute existence to find a more thematized meaning for what it is and how it works.

In these ways, the rising sun is not just a phenomenon of immediate perceptual experience; it is also a solicitation of contemplation. Yet if the realm of perception is a solicitation to reflection, what is the precise shape of this reflection? If wonder initiates philosophy, what is the aim of the wondering? How does philosophy try to answer the question that perception raises?

Departure and Replacement: Scientific Philosophy

What kinds of reflection and predication are elicited by wonder at the realm of perception? For Merleau-Ponty, there are two main types. The first we can call scientific philosophy, and the second phenomenological philosophy. Let us start with scientific philosophy.

For Merleau-Ponty, the category of scientific philosophy signifies a specific way of approaching questions in both philosophy and the natural and social sciences. What distinguishes this approach is the way the approach distances itself from the plane of perception, the way it departs from immediate experience: "Beginning from our experience of the world, reflective analysis works back ... as if toward a condition of possibility distinct from our experience ... as that without which there would be no world" (*PhP-DL*, lxxiii).[7] Wonder initiates a process of explanation. Wonder inspires the attempt to grasp some reality behind, beneath, or before perceived, pre-predicatively experienced phenomena: "Science neither has, nor ever will have the same ontological sense as the perceived world for the simple reason that science is a determination or an explanation of that world" (*PhP-DL*, lxxii).

Scientific philosophy can take the shape of natural science. Physics provides an example: "The real world is not this world of light and colour; it is not the fleshy spectacle which passes before my eyes. It consists, rather, of the waves and particles which science tells us lie behind" (*WP*, 41). Physics gives a theory of light and color where their ultimate reality is not found in the way they illuminate or hue the world but, rather, in the way they are forms of material energy. Light and color as we unreflectively experience them in everyday life are epiphenomenal—an effect caused by the material interaction between waves and particles on one side and the biological structure and functioning of the eye on the other. The true story about light and color is a story of a reflectively and conceptually known reality that exists behind and before illumination and hue: "the *real* world is the physical world as science conceives it" (PrP, 23, my italics). That world causes phenomena like illumination and sheen to appear.

Scientific philosophy can also take the form of metaphysics. This category would include forms of philosophy like rationalism, empiricism, idealism, positivism, and so on.[8] Here Merleau-Ponty is thinking of the "sense-data" theorized by someone like John Locke or the "substance" theorized by someone like Gottfried Leibniz. In Locke's empiricism, the experience of perception is founded on and caused by the more fundamental reality of sense-data—for example, brute, unreconstructed sensations, such as redness, hardness, and sphericalness. The mind then processes these raw experiences to generate the lived experience of vision—seeing red marbles, for example. Nowhere in everyday, pre-predicative life do human beings directly experience sense-data—Merleau-Ponty says that "we have no experience of sensation" (*PhP-DL*, 7)—yet it is this sense-data and the mind's processing of them that, by causing the experience of perception, constitute the truth of perception for empiricism.

Similarly, in Leibniz's rationalism, the perceptual world is grounded in and generated by the more fundamental world of monads—the discrete, simple, self-contained, perceiving units of force moving in preestablished harmony that Leibniz thought made up the true furniture of reality. Nowhere in ordinary, pre-reflective experience does human life directly encounter monads, yet these monads, causing the phenomena of perception to appear, constitute the final truth of the perceptual world. Both sense-data and monads are abstract postulations of realities that exist behind the scenes of immediate lived experience and cause that experience; they comprise the actual show.

The central issue for Merleau-Ponty is that scientific philosophy, whether natural science or metaphysics, does not keep faith with perception. Through acts of inference, this theorizing postulates a world that departs from and replaces the directly and immediately experienced world. He wrote, "I take flight from my experience and I pass over to the idea .... I no longer pay attention to my body, to time, or to the world such as I live them in pre-predicative knowledge" (*PhP-DL*, 73–4).

For Merleau-Ponty, the consequence of this flight is stark: it signals "the death of consciousness" (*PhP-DL*, 74). The world of immediate experience loses its claim to be real; it becomes a realm of only "*sensory illusions*" (*WP*, 41, my italics). Pre-reflective perception no longer delivers any authentic truth of the world because it is no longer in touch with the genuine reality of the world, which is known and defined by natural or social science and metaphysical philosophy. A new stance toward the world, disengaged conceptual and theoretical reflection, holds all the cards in the game of knowing truth and reality. What is lost when humans put their faith in theory rather than perception is staggering: the loss of "the human world" (*PrP*, 23)—of self, other, and nature in their perceptual nascency, pastness, and givenness. The world of immediate experience, which would seem to be individuals' most primordial world, loses its right to be in touch with reality. A discipline like astronomy can claim that the sun does not rise. A sunrise does not really exist; the sun does not actually move, even though we have the visual illusion that it does. Immediate, direct experience of the world has become spectral; pre-thematic perception's claim to be a realm of truth and reality with its own integrity has been diminished or even eliminated. For Merleau-Ponty, this situation was problematic.

Fidelity and Homecoming: Phenomenology and Reduction

To summarize, Merleau-Ponty believed that scientific philosophy reflects on the realm of pre-reflective perception by departing from it. Wonder at the sphere of nascent perception elicits a search for something that exists before, beneath, and behind it, something that causes it. The problem is that the field of perception in its own right fades away. Merleau-Ponty reminded his readers that "perception owes nothing to what we know in other ways about the world, about stimuli as physics describes them and about the sense organs as described by biology. It does not present itself in the first place as an event in the world to which the category of causality, for example, can be applied" (*PhP-DL*, 240). Hence his comment that the substitution of a nonhuman theoretical realm for the realm of immediate perceptual experience means the death of consciousness as it first presents itself. And this substitution is a problem, for "no analysis of perception can be ignorant of perception as an original phenomenon without thereby being ignorant of itself as analysis" (*PhP-DL*, 40). The very thing scientific philosophy intends to investigate disappears in the investigation. The inquiry becomes absurd.

Yet Merleau-Ponty did not believe that scientific philosophy exhausted philosophy's possibilities. Another approach to philosophy, one advanced by Edmund Husserl and his followers, was phenomenological philosophy. Like scientific philosophy, phenomenological philosophy is a reflection that takes off from the experience of wonder at the world of pre-predicative experience. But phenomenological reflection takes a different shape from scientific philosophy's mode of theorizing.[9]

Merleau-Ponty opens his "Preface" to *Phenomenology of Perception* with the question "What is phenomenology?" (*PhP-DL*, lxx), but we might equally ask another: Where is phenomenology—that is, where is phenomenology's attention? What dimension is its focus? What reality does it engage?

To answer such questions, we need to see how phenomenology's mode of reflection begins with a method: reduction. Merleau-Ponty wrote, "Perhaps the best formulation of the reduction is the one offered by Husserl's assistant Eugen Fink when he spoke of a 'wonder' before the world" (*PhP-DL*, lxxvii). He means that the phenomenologist wonders about the realm of perception itself. The object of inquiry is the perceptual plane itself, the field of pre-thematic immediacy in its own right. This register is where phenomenology operates; it provides the area that reflection, elicited by wonder, seeks to know.

We have explored how Merleau-Ponty named this domain of immediate experience in several ways: the tacit cogito, operative intentionality, the lived world, naïve consciousness, pre-predicative experience, and the unreflective life of consciousness. He also calls this domain "existence itself" (*PhP-DL*, 426) or "facticity" (*PhP-DL*, lxx) or simply "life" (*PrP*, 30). We need to remember that this life is not merely subjective: it is "being in the world" (*PhP-DL*, 81). Facticity includes subject and objective poles of experience: self, other, nature, world, and so on. Defined in all these ways, the field of immediate perceptual experience is where phenomenology focuses its investigation. In this way, phenomenology is "remaining faithful to the phenomena" (*CD*, 14). There is a kind of intentional, explicit fidelity and loyalty to existence, perception, and life, to nascent and given immediate experience, to perceptual experience within its own terms. Now we can understand better these famous words of Merleau-Ponty that we have already reflected upon once: "Phenomenology is the study of essences … the essence of perception, or the essence of consciousness, for example. But phenomenology is also a philosophy which puts essences back into existence, and does not expect to arrive at an understanding of man and the world from any starting point other than that of their 'facticity'" (*PhP-CS*, vii). There is a refusal to depart from, abandon, or replace the human world—to stay with that world, to remain with the world in which the sun rises. If we want to know the logic of perception, we cannot transition into a realm before, behind, or underneath perception. No, the essence of perception has to be found within the experience of perception itself.

Merleau-Ponty believed that fidelity to the realm of immediate perceptual experience almost inevitably involves returning to it. The inaugural gesture of phenomenology is "the return to the world of perception" (*WP*, 105), the "return to lived experience" (*PhP-DL*, 57). The phenomenological reduction is a homecoming to the immediate phenomenal plane after being away.

In other words, this homecoming first requires a departure; every turning-toward is also a turning-away-from. Philosophy, when it is scientific philosophy, is far from home. To come home, to focus on the plane of perception itself, philosophy must turn away from scientific philosophy. Hence phenomenology begins with this declaration: "The world is not what I think, but what I live through" (*PhP-CS*, xviii). The world that I think is the world of theories both scientific and metaphysical. Phenomenology is interested in a realm that I do not think in these ways: "'lived' space, 'lived' time, and the 'lived' world … our experience such as it is, and without any consideration of its psychological genesis or of the causal explanations that the scientist, historian, or sociologist might offer of that experience" (*PhP-DL*, lxx). Turning toward the plane of pre-predicative perception means leaving behind the scientific philosophy that leaves perception behind. The quest for scientific or metaphysical substrates of perception is renounced in the phenomenological attitude.

An example brings out the point. Consider psychological depression. Biological psychiatry will be interested in how brain biochemistry causes depression. A philosophical approach like that of Arthur Schopenhauer will say that depression has its source, metaphysically speaking, in the reality of a cosmic will underlying all things, a will that vacillates between boredom and discontent. But the phenomenology of depression will take neither of these paths. Instead, it will ask what it is like to be depressed, how self and world pre-thematically appear in depression as a first-person experience, and how the depressed person finds themselves and their world before they are explicitly aware of doing so. To arrive at a place where it can ask about what depression is like, phenomenology must leave behind biological psychiatry and speculative metaphysics—at least while the phenomenologist is doing phenomenology.

Thus, the phenomenological reduction involves investment and divestment: it can put naïve, unreconstructed perceptual experience before the philosopher's eyes only by putting something else out of mind (at least, while the philosopher is doing phenomenology), making a deliberate decision not to pass from the phenomena of perception to an inferred or speculated theoretical realm behind it. The reduction says to philosophy, concerning first-order immediate experience: do not separate from it, do not replace it, do not derive anything from it. We can know self, other, nature, and world as they are given in perceptual life only by turning away from them as they are given in second-order theoretical life. For this second-order abstract theoretical life is an avoidance of concrete existence.

The phenomenological reduction is an act of unforgetting, an intentional remembering of immediacy: "The fundamental philosophical act would thus be ... to thwart the ruse by which perception allowed itself to be forgotten as a fact" (*PhP-DL*, 57). When human life is captivated by theory, it will need to unforget a pre-reflective world that it has always lived but that it has little acknowledged: "Consciousness must be faced with its own unreflective life in things and awakened to its own history which it was forgetting" (*PhP-CS*, 36). Consciousness will need to become aware of itself and its first world in which it has been dwelling unaware.

Merleau-Ponty describes this process in several ways, all with the prefix "re-," which in Latin means "back." The phenomenological reduction is an act of *restoration*: "we will have to restore the perceptual experience of the thing" (*PhP-DL*, 191). The phenomenological reduction restores us to, and restores to us, the original givenness of perceptual life. It is an act of *reawakening*: "we must begin by reawakening the basic experience of the world" (*PhP-CS*, ix)—that is, we must seek "a reawakening of the world of perception ... the same world which we had turned away from" (*WP*, 69). Human awareness has been asleep to its fundamental way of encountering itself and reality; phenomenology brings the truth of this encountering to awareness. In this way, the reduction is therapeutic. Therapeutic here does not mean "making happy"; it means reconnecting life with itself and its world, eliminating our blindness to the rich and previously passed over reality of self, other, nature, and world that is most immanent and imminent to life. The reduction facilitates *rediscovery*: "Our task will be ... to rediscover phenomena, the layer of living experience through which other people and things are first given to us" (*PhP-CS*, 66) and "to rediscover the world as we apprehend it in lived experience" (*WP*, 52). Merleau-Ponty compares this process to the process pursued by a painter such as Cezanne: "The artist is the one who arrests the spectacle in which most men take part without really seeing it and who makes it visible" (CD, 18). Similarly, in the process of return, reawakening, restoration, rediscovery, and reconnection, the phenomenological reduction renders seen what scientific philosophy has often left unseen—the immediate perceptual realm of life.

Before moving on, one more point needs to be made. Merleau-Ponty has been trying to show that the world of perceptual immediacy has its own rich truth and reality: "The sun 'rises' for the scientist just as much as it does for the uneducated person. ... The rising of the sun, and the perceived in general, is 'real'" (*PhP-DL*, 359). Yet Merleau-Ponty thought that human reflection, via the reduction, needs to embrace the field of immediate perceptual experience in its own right—to return to it, remain with it, reconnect with it, reclaim it, immerse itself in it, focus on it, explore it—not just because the hitherto unseen world of perception is an actual reality that merits philosophical attention (against, for example, astronomical approaches that claim that the rising sun is unreal, that it is just a perceptual illusion). Merleau-Ponty did want to reclaim the right of the perceptual world to exist and have meaning in its own right, but he also thought that human reflection needed to attend reflectively to the world of pre-thetic perception because this field is the first, most fundamental locus of reality itself.

To reflect phenomenologically in response to wonder at the perceptual world is not to reflect only on the truth and meaning of the perceptual world in its own right as one register of reality among others—as if the sun's rising were one dimension of its existence equal to others. Merleau-Ponty claimed that phenomenology, by returning to the plane of original phenomenal experience, reflects on the grounding, central truth and meaning of reality as such, the world that is fundamental and foundational for all other worlds of reflection. The world of perception is the "primordial world" (CD, 13); it is "the real" (*PhP-DL*, lxxiii).

The reduction was required to allow humans to remember that perception—the subject's immediate experience of the lived world—and not science or metaphysics is their truest contact with reality, the mode of experience in which reality and its truth are most authentically given and presented. To know reality at all, we have first to know the reality of perceptual life. To quote Merleau-Ponty again, "phenomenology is … a philosophy which puts essences back into existence, and does not expect to arrive at an understanding of man and the world from any starting point other than that of 'facticity'" (*PhP-CS*, vii). Immediate perceptual experience is the locus in which we first and best encounter all reality and should seek to know its truth.

Without the reduction, then, we might think from the perspective of natural science that there is no sunrise, that the sunrise is not real because the sun is stationary (at least as far as the solar system is concerned). Because the earth spins on its axis as it orbits the sun, the human eye has an illusion that the sun rises. But with the reduction, we can recognize that, when the untutored human eye sees the sun rising, we know the sun's first and fundamental reality and meaning in human life. The sunrise is first and foremost the sunrise as it has meaning in the naïve experience of sailors, soldiers, workers, or sleepers awakening. The sunrise as it exists in the music of Richard Strauss, the poetry of John Keats and Joy Harjo, and the painting of Claude Monet is the truest reality and meaning of the rising sun. The reduction suggests that we should question the authority of scientific astronomy to teach us to disbelieve the original, primordial evidence of our own eyes and the evidence expressed in art, in waking, and in working that the sun does rise. For the poet, the sailor, and the laborer, the sunrise of immediate perceptual experience is the most real and meaningful sunrise there is. The reduction opens the mind to see the world of perception because, for Merleau-Ponty, perception is life's initial and most authentic contact with the world. The world of pre-reflective perception is human life's first and most real realm, a world that is more genuine than any theoretical world or reality speculated about by any form of scientific philosophy, a concrete, first-order world in relation to which any scientific or metaphysical account of what is beneath the universe of perception will be a second-order abstraction that is derivative from perception's prior and concrete reality. If life wants to know the deepest and broadest meaning and truth of reality, reflective life needs to immerse itself in the world of pre-predicative perception.

Home Away from Home: Phenomenology as Reflection

Merleau-Ponty has been asking the question "What is phenomenology?" (*PhP-DL*, lxx), and the first part of his answer was negative: it is not natural science or philosophical metaphysics, for these approaches depart from and annul immediate perceptual experience. The phenomenological reduction annuls the annulment, so to speak; it turns our attention away from explanations for perceptual immediacy toward that immediacy itself. This acknowledgment of the reality and integrity of the phenomenal plane was itself a philosophical achievement. Yet, once this reorientation toward phenomena *qua* phenomena has been made, once attention is focused on the right place, what happens next?

To be sure, Merleau-Ponty does not simply want his reader to stand silently dumbstruck before the register of perception. Once attention focuses on the plane of immediate perceptual experience itself, the interesting work is just beginning. The next stage in answering the question "What is phenomenology?" is to ask another question: "Is it the decision to ask experience itself for its own sense?" (*PhP-DL*, 305). In other words, phenomenology asks about the "lived logic" (*PhP-DL*, 50) of pre-thematic perceptual life.

Phenomenologists are not content simply to know that this experience exists. They believe that this register of reality exists in a certain way, that there is a way it goes. So phenomenological philosophers do not only turn to pre-predicative experience; they ask how this experience goes the way it does; they want to explore this experience's nature, sense, and logic as experience. Phenomenological reflection begins in wonder, like scientific philosophy in natural science or metaphysics. Yet, instead of wondering why pre-reflective experience is the way it is, phenomenologists wonder how this lived experience is the way it is, the way this experience goes in itself, its intrinsic logic.

One way to indicate this next stage in phenomenological work is to take the latter part of the word "phenomenology": "logos." The reduction first calls attention to the existence of phenomena. But there is also the dimension of the logos, which is about knowledge of the phenomena. Hence Merleau-Ponty writes, "our actual commitment in the world is precisely what must *be understood* and *raised to the concept*" (*PhP-DL*, lxxviii, my italics). Phenomenology is logos because it seeks to articulate in concepts the logic of lived through pre-conceptual perceptual experience—that is, phenomenology's turn to perception is a turn to *philosophical* awareness of perception: "all its efforts are concentrated upon re-achieving a direct and primitive contact with the world, *and endowing that contact with a philosophical status*" (*PhP-CS*, vii, my italics). The purpose of the reduction is to allow philosophical life to seek the essences of the perceptual plane.

Philosophy needs to pursue the logos of immediate perceptual experience because humans usually dwell within that experience without being aware of it. We live an existence we do not know. In fact, in some sense, we have to dwell in pre-thematic perception without thematizing it—otherwise, perception would not be the experience that it is. Thus, Merleau-Ponty says this about phenomenology's task: "it is the attempt to match reflection to the unreflective life of consciousness" (*PhP-DL*, lxxx). Phenomenology conceptually unfolds the implicit and pre-conceptual logic of perceptual life—the plane of existence we embody tacitly without the explicit awareness that we do so, a plane that Merleau-Ponty sometimes says is anonymous. In this way, phenomenology is itself a science—in the sense of the German term *Wissenschaft*—although not a natural one. Phenomenology is the science of seeking the truth of pre-reflective life, the science of immediate perceptual experience: it investigates and elucidates the nature of this field of reality. Phenomenology's return to pre-predicative phenomena is a philosophical return. As a philosophy, phenomenology remains abstract—it tries to generalize from the concrete to a knowledge of the universal—but its generalizing stays with perceptual immediacy by describing and understanding this on its own terms rather than by speculating or inferring from it to something else behind or beneath it. The goal is to know pre-conceptual life conceptually, to thematize unthematized immediacy.

Here we can also see why Merleau-Ponty needed to ward off a misunderstanding of the phenomenological reduction. Phenomenology is a philosophical restoration of immediacy, not a restoration of brute, unreconstructed immediacy as such. He writes: "Assuredly a life is not a philosophy. I thought I had indicated in passing that description is not the return to immediate experience; one never returns to immediate experience. It is only a question of whether we are to try to understand it" (PrP, 30). We remember from above that immediate perceptual experience is a first-order realm of presence: the actual sun rising before me in itself, in the flesh, seen directly by me. But phenomenology is reflection—a turning back toward or upon something preexisting it. Phenomenology is thus a second-order practice of representation—it retrieves perceptual immediacy in the process of re-presenting its presence in the derivative form of knowledge of it. Awestruck by wonder at the world of perception, human life has a philosophical reawakening to and immersion in perception. The goal is "to return *to the pure description* of phenomena" (PhP-CS, 300, my italics), not to return to naïve participation in the phenomena themselves. Understanding the logic of the experience of seeing the sun rising is phenomenology's focus, not the experience itself, even as returning to focus on the experience itself is the condition of such understanding. Not presence but the logic of presence is the issue, not naïve experience of the world but reflection on naïve experience, not unselfconscious existence but self-aware philosophical existence, not phenomena directly encountered but phenomenological knowledge of phenomena.

So, Merleau-Ponty is not recommending intellectual suicide, where we trade in reflection for some pure immersion in perception and its world. The point is not re-immersion in perceptual life itself. In phenomenology, life's direct participation in immediacy is put at a distance: "Because we are through and through related to the world, the only way for us to catch sight of ourselves is by suspending this movement, by refusing to be complicit with it … to put it out of play" (PhP-DL, lxxvii). Although Merleau-Ponty does not often use the term, this suspension he is recommending is what Husserl and many of his followers refer to as the epoché: "breaking with the originary faith of perception, I adopt a critical attitude toward perception and wonder 'what I actually see'" (PhP-DL, 251). Human life steps back from its investment in immediate perceptual experience in order to understand it. As Merleau-Ponty said in prefacing a set of his lectures, life must step back from immediacy in order to appreciate its presence and logic:

> The world of perception, or in other words the world which is revealed to us by our senses and in everyday life, seems at first sight to be the one we know best of all. For we need neither to measure nor to calculate in order to gain access to this world and it would seem that we can fathom it simply by opening our eyes and getting on with our lives. Yet this is a delusion. In these lectures, I hope to show that the world of perception is, to a great extent, unknown territory as long as we remain in the practical or utilitarian attitude.
> (*WP*, 39)

When we are immersed in perceptual immediacy, we do not and cannot know it. While nothing is closer to us than this pre-predicative experience, we remain ignorant of it while we are living through it.

Paradoxically, Merleau-Ponty wanted phenomenology to remain as close to perceptual immediacy as possible while also remaining outside it. Phenomenology is never beyond immediacy, and it is always beyond immediacy. He could write: "Reflection is only truly reflection if it does not carry itself outside of itself, if it knows itself as reflection-upon-an-unreflected" (*PhP-DL*, 63). Reflection must be distant from perception and thoroughly immersed in it. The situation is one of "both/and" and "either/or," and thus he wrote, "the naïve view of the world is included and transcended in the reflective view" (*PhP-DL*, 221). Phenomenology is a new form of philosophical life that is inextricably intertwined with perceptual existence. In phenomenology, philosophical life both leaves and does not leave immediate perceptual experience; it stays with perception and does not stay; it reclaims and dwells within perceptual life, but it does so reflectively, in awareness not only of perceptual immediacy but equally of this immediacy's logic. Phenomenology and its reduction bring life back home to immediacy, but it is always a home away from home.

Space, Time, Aesthetics, Interpretation: Presence and Absence

Merleau-Ponty's work has been advancing two claims. First, phenomenology is a quest to reconnect with perceptual immediacy: "one of the great achievements of modern art and philosophy (that is, the art and philosophy of the last fifty to seventy years) has been to allow us to rediscover the world in which we live, yet which we are always prone to forget" (*WP*, 39). But, second, phenomenology seeks not to re-immerse life in raw immediacy but to become aware of the logic of immediacy—hence his insistence that "Phenomenology is the study of essences ... which puts essences back into existence" (*PhP-CS*, vii). But what are the logics—the essences—of perception that phenomenology wants life to comprehend? How does this practice of unforgetting pre-reflective perception and articulating its logics take shape? Merleau-Ponty gives answers to these questions at both more general and more specific levels.

At the broadest level, what are the essences of perception? An essence is something's "mode of appearance" (*PhP-DL*, 322). The phenomenology of perception asks after the mode of givenness of the perceived object—whatever it may be—in perceptual experience. So, the questions phenomenology seeks to answer are not precisely "What is perception?" or "What is the perceived object?" The questions are "How is perception?" and "How is the perceived perceived?" What is sought is the logic of appearance—not just what is appearing, but how what appears does appear. If it inquires into the nature of an immediately perceived material object, phenomenology will explore how something we take to be a material thing is given in and to lived experience. The truth about what something is always is connected to the truth about the manner in which it appears; if we do not consider how something appears, we cannot give an adequate account of it. Merleau-Ponty's insight was that we do not know the world we dwell within or its objects because we try to understand what they are without knowing how they are given. If we want to understand the world and all that is in it, we must understand how what appears is given to experience.

One example of a phenomenology of perception concerns the issue of sensation. Earlier, we heard Merleau-Ponty say that "we have no experience of sensation." What do we experience? He wrote, "We observe at once that it is impossible, as has often been said, to decompose a perception, to make it into a collection of sensations, because in it the whole is prior to the parts" (*PrP*, 15). A red marble is given to perception as a whole—not as a collection of discrete separate sensations of "materialness" and "redness" and "shininess" and "sphericalness" and "smoothness" and "hardness." Perceiving a marble in a pre-reflective experience is to have an object given as a whole object. It is the object as a whole that is given to experience. The thing is not the constellation of sense-data that get put together by the mind to make up a red marble. Instead, from the beginning, the marble itself is given in perception as a material, red, shiny, spherical, smooth, and hard object, as an object with these qualities. The point Merleau-Ponty is making is that it is the experience of the red marble as a red marble that comprises perception. Philosophy or science may certainly abstract from the original perception of an object with its qualities to ask about the qualities themselves—redness, smoothness, and so on—but then inquiry has moved somewhere else, for these qualities are never perceived immediately. Perception is the nascent experience in which what is given is first given as a whole with qualities and not as a conglomeration of qualities that somehow later gets synthesized into a whole.

We can say more about the nature of perception and its objects when we see the way in which the perceived is given in the horizon of space. When we speak of the perceived thing's givenness in the horizon of space, we encounter the dimension of Merleau-Ponty's philosophy for which he is best known: the embodied character of perception. He wrote, "To perceive is to render oneself present to something through the body" (PrP, 42). Embodied experience is not just the experience of the body; it is the experience of the world as it immediately appears to the body-subject.[10]

How is a perceived object in space given to the body-subject? While perception can engage material and nonmaterial objects, we can consider another example of perception vis-à-vis a material object. Let us say I am hiking in Colorado's Pike National Forest, and I find my eyes alighting on a columbine on the side of the trail. My immediate perception is of the flower as a whole. Before I even know what I am doing, I see and delight in the flower with its blue and white spurred petals that resemble the claw of an eagle, with its golden stamens bursting forth like a sun exploding.[11] Here I have a first-order immediate perceptual experience.

But then I can step back to reflect in a second-order way on how the flower appears to me as an object of pre-reflective experience, on how it is originally given to me as an embodied perceiver—in fact, the way it has to be given to me as an embodied perceiver. Merleau-Ponty would want us to notice some features of the flower as it is first perceived in embodied experience: it has a front and back; it is a more or less clear center surrounded by a vaguer halo; it has a top and a bottom and left and right sides; it has both surface and depth, exteriority and interiority, volume and texture. To see a flower is necessarily to see it in these ways; a flower is what it is for the hiker who delights in it because it is given in these ways, and the flower can show itself to the hiker in these ways only because the hiker is an embodied experiencer.

What is interesting to notice is that, while the perceived is always given as a whole, the whole of the perceived is never given. The perceived object appears in what phenomenologists call profiles or adumbrations. The seer sees a specific side of the columbine from a particular perspective. Hence Merleau-Ponty's observation: "what we do see is always, in some respect, not seen: there must be hidden sides of things ... if there is to be a 'front' of things" (PhP-DL, 289). If there is a front of a perceived object that I see in my visual field, then there must be a back I do not see and cannot see. Otherwise, the notion of "front" would be incoherent. And we have to be careful here, for the point is not that we only perceive part of the object. We perceive the whole object, but only through seeing it in one or another profile, from one or another perspective: "present vision is not limited to what my visual field actually presents to me, and ... the interior or the back of this object is not evoked or represented" (PhP-DL, 344–5). The observer perceives the whole flower, but not all its ways of showing itself. The interior or back of the flower is not imagined or thought; the flower is experienced as a whole, but it is present in some profiles and not in others. Or, to put it paradoxically, the back of the flower is present as absent. There are always more profiles according to which the spatially perceived can be apprehended and more perspectives in space to see it or touch it. Again, the whole object of perception is experienced, but never in its totality. There is always more to see of every actual or possible perceivable thing than is currently seen. From my actual perspective, I experience the whole object in its presence and absence, in its given and ungiven profiles. The pre-predicatively perceived object is experienced as a whole object, the flower itself, but the experience is always also shot through with absence—and necessarily so, otherwise we would not be dealing with a pre-predicatively perceived material object.[12]

The body-subject is also a temporal perceiver, and there is a similar logic of presence and absence in perception with respect to time. Just as there are always more spatial profiles of an object than the one currently seen, there are always more temporal profiles of a thing than the one presently seen. Merleau-Ponty writes: "Naturally there is a development of perception; naturally it is not achieved all at once" (PrP, 42). Perception takes place in time. As I walk around the flower, I see it in different temporal profiles. My perspective on the columbine changes not only in space but in time. Again, I perceive the whole object, but I do not perceive the whole of it because it has temporal profiles or adumbrations that are not present in my perception. It is not just that perception is not achieved all at once; it is never fully achieved. I experience the perceived object through a spatial profile and a temporal profile. Merleau-Ponty would agree with Husserl's conviction that a temporal profile is a distended present in which the now-moment includes horizons of the just-has-been and the about-to-be—but there are always going to be absent temporal profiles (past and future) that are not given in the present moment even as retentions or protentions.

At the same time, we do not want to think that Merleau-Ponty took the objects of immediate perceptual experience to be only natural objects. Literary, artistic, and musical works also comprise objects of immediate perception: "The world of perception consists not just of all natural objects but also of paintings, pieces of music, books and all that the Germans call the 'world of culture'" (*WP*, 101). While the pre-reflective aesthetic and interpretive experience of a cultural artifact such as a poem, a painting, or a symphony is different from the experience of a natural object, both kinds of experience are perceptual and thus share, at least at one level, a similar logic (e.g., cf. *PhP-DL*, 338).

The work of art—especially the modern work of art, a category which for Merleau-Ponty would start with impressionist art and lead up to his own time—is itself an object that shows itself while never showing all of itself. A modern artwork embodies "a kind of ... art that is characterised by difficulty and reserve" (*WP*, 105). Experiencing the beauty and meaning of an artwork is also an activity saturated with presence and absence. As Merleau-Ponty wrote, "'mental' or cultural life borrows its structures from natural life and ... the thinking subject must be grounded upon the embodied subject," so there are always new and different spatial and temporal perspectives from which we can engage the artwork—and also new and different interpretive and aesthetic perspectives from which we can do so as well (*PhP-DL*, 199). Time, space, interpretation, and aesthetic response all open into infinity. Again, modern art—whether visual, literary, or musical—explicitly opens to infinity: "Cezanne ... was, in any case, oriented toward the idea or the project of an infinite Logos" (*CD*, 19). Merleau-Ponty means that Cezanne sought in his paintings both to represent a natural world whose truth lends itself to a non-appropriating appropriation that is in principle and essence unending and also for them to be a form of representation whose truth and aesthetic as representational could be grasped and interpreted only as ultimately, in principle and essence, ungraspable and uninterpretable.

Merleau-Ponty believes that, as perceptual immediacy engages reality spatially, temporally, aesthetically, and interpretively, the perceived object retains a transcendence in relation to the perceiver. The pre-reflectively perceived object is not perceived without the perceiver's act of perceiving, but nor is it reducible to the perceiver's act of perceiving: "What is given is not the thing on its own, but the experience of the thing, or something transcendent standing in the wake of one's subjectivity" (*PhP-CS*, 379). There is always more of the object to perceive. Indeed, a perceived object is a perceived object precisely because there is always more of it to perceive:

> Thus there is a paradox of immanence and transcendence in perception. Immanence, because the perceived object cannot be foreign to him who perceives; transcendence, because it always contains something more than what is actually given. And these two elements of perception are not, properly speaking, contradictory. For if we reflect on this notion of perspective, if we reproduce the perceptual experience in our thought, we see that the kind of evidence proper to the perceived, the appearance of "something," requires both this presence and this absence.
>
> (PrP, 16)

To be in the realm of immediate perceptual experience is not to drain the world of its otherness or its in-itself-ness. It is not to collapse reality into the subject. The world of pre-thetic perception is a world for the subject, but it is not the world of that subject, not a world invented by or circumscribed by that subject. The perceiving subject's grasp of the perceived object is always incomplete. Immediate perceptual consciousness makes authentic contact with the perceived in the manner of encounter, not comprehension: "consciousness itself as a project of the world, meant for a world which it neither embraces nor possesses, but toward which it is perpetually directed" (*PhP-CS*, xx). In a moment, we will see just how radical Merleau-Ponty's belief that the logic of appearing is a logic of encounter without embrace or possession is.

The Universal Style of Being: Phenomenological Ontology

In describing the logic of immediate perceptual experience, Merleau-Ponty first focuses on how concrete perceptual phenomena, like a flower or a sunrise or a painting, appear in spatiotemporal experience.

4. Toward Wondering Life

But he also asked a further philosophical question, which has to do with ontology, the science of the meaning and truth of being as being. The phenomenology of perception, as Merleau-Ponty understands it, seeks after the logic of "ontological structure" (*PhP-DL*, lxxxiii) and "ontological sense" (*PhP-DL*, lxxii). Phenomenologists investigate not only natural objects but reality as such: "phenomenology … is a study of the advent of being to consciousness" (*PhP-CS*, 71). This issue is not just the advent of a flower or a sunrise, or even the advent of the whole material world, but the advent of being itself.

A reader might wonder whether phenomenology and ontology are compatible bedfellows. Does phenomenology not bracket ontological questions about reality itself to focus on reality as given to human subjectivity? Yes, and this is the reason Merleau-Ponty distinguished his phenomenological ontology from metaphysical ontology.

What is a metaphysical ontology? In Merleau-Ponty's words, in this ontology, "the attempt is made to reach being without passing through the phenomenon … [this] conception is Spinoza's" (*PhP-DL*, 418). Spinoza conceived ultimate reality as a monistic substance by inferring from and speculating about which reality grounds the field of perception while remaining different from it. Such an ontology is experience-distant. No one encounters monistic substance directly, concretely, or immediately—it is a second-order, abstract, mediated creation of cognition. So, in the framework of metaphysical ontology, perceptual immediacy does not offer access to being. To make contact with being, reason has to transition from perception toward some other reality that exists beneath and before perceptual life and that founds this life. Metaphysical ontology thereby replaces the realm of perception, substituting something else in its place. Merleau-Ponty called this approach (and Spinoza was not the only philosopher to take it) *pensée de survol*, which Donald Landes translates as "thinking from above" or "high-altitude thinking" or even "thinking from a God's-eye view."[13] The metaphysical philosopher is not in touch with the being of the immediately perceived world; he or she is involved with something else.

Merleau-Ponty's brilliant insight was to ask whether there could be a different kind of ontology from metaphysical ontology, a different way of approaching *ontos* and its *logos* in which the realm of pre-predicative perception is not abandoned. And he thought there was a different kind of ontology—phenomenological ontology. But his position was subtle. He agreed with the promoters of metaphysical ontology that being is not encountered in the same way as trees, people, or paintings are. Ontology is a conceptual, reflective discipline that is disengaged from perception itself. But he thought that philosophy could reflect on ontological questions so that its results did not so much replace the data of perception but, rather, articulated that data at a deeper level. Ontology would remain abstract and general, but it would not substitute anything that had to compete with the phenomena of perception. How did such reflection—which would be both experience-near and experience-distant—work?

Phenomenological ontology stayed with the realm of immediate perceptual experience by asking about that realm's own logic at the broadest and most profound level. Phenomenological ontology delineates in the most conceptually unrestricted way the manner in which perceived immediacy appears: "the world itself ... is the totality of perceptible things and the thing of all things ... the universal style of all possible perceptions" (PrP, 16). Here, being is the implicit yet general and universal structure of the immediate perceptual experience of self, other, nature, artwork, and world. Phenomenological ontology renders this structure explicit; it thematizes the logic of the pre-thematic variegated world of perception to the broadest degree conceptually possible. Being is what human life knows philosophically when it abstracts from how the particular things of the world appear in perception to elucidate conceptually the ultimate truth and reality of how anything and everything does and can appear in immediate perceptual consciousness.

In this picture, being is not exactly an object in its own right; it is not a super-entity. Instead, being is the most universal and general form or mode in which anything and everything that appears does so. As the logic of givenness of everything—of trees, flowers, poems, sonatas, and sculptures—being is more a "how" reality than a "what" reality. What reality is becomes known through understanding how reality is given. Phenomenological ontology teases out the logic that defines immediate perceptual experience tout court—the logic of it and within it, not behind or underneath it. Phenomenological ontology seeks to know the most primordial reality of perceptual immediacy, the fundamental sense of this reality. The way phenomenologists aim to understand the most comprehensive, most inescapable meaning of the plane of perception is by becoming as clear as possible about how objects (from a flower to the perceptual world as a whole) appear—how things in the broadest sense are immediately given in the broadest sense.[14] The aim of phenomenology is to seek the logos of ontos by seeking the logos of phenomena; it seeks the universal meaning of being by tracing the givenness of things, which saturates and characterizes the world of pre-thetic perception.

Being is a philosophical concept, but it is not one opposed to the register of perception. This concept, instead, articulates the logic of the world's pre-conceptual appearing. Whereas metaphysics gives an ontology of what exists behind and before perception, phenomenology provides an ontology of perception itself, a way of considering the shape of the register of immediacy itself, the logic within it, and the style that determines how it goes the way it does.

Consider an example: a chair. We can predicate of a chair that it is wooden or metal, blue or orange, low or high off the ground, modern or antique. These are descriptive predicates that define the subject. They tell what kind of chair it is; they specify its type. But a thing has being, in a phenomenological sense, differently than how a subject has a predicate. In phenomenology, when we speak of the being of the chair, we are not playing the subject-predicate game anymore. The being of the chair consists not in what is predicated of it as a type, but instead in how it is given, its logic of appearance in lived experience. When we say that the chair is a gift, a burden, a marvel, a comfort, or an eyesore, we are engaging its being, thinking about its ontology, in a phenomenological way. Phenomenological ontology clarifies the grammar of givenness that defines everything that is exclusively in terms of how it is given in lived experience at a level of philosophical universality and generality. In words that Merleau-Ponty would affirm, Husserl wrote, "In opposition to all previously designed objective sciences ... this would be a science of the universal *how* of the pregivenness of the world."[15]

So, to be clear, Merleau-Ponty was not just seeking a regional ontology of the perceptual world that would be merely one among others. He believed that, at some level, "all consciousness is perceptual" (PrP, 13). The ontology of the world of perception is pervasive and fundamental because it inquires into the logic of anything and everything that does or could appear in human experience. Perception gives humans "our primordial knowledge of the 'real'" (*PhP-CS*, xviii). The being of immediate perceptual experience is without qualification, and the questions phenomenological ontology asks relate to the meaning, essence, truth, logic, and sense of being *qua* being, which we remember is being *qua* appearing. In Merleau-Ponty's words, "perception ... [is] the paradoxical phenomenon which renders being accessible to us" (PrP, 17). Understanding the logic of perceptual immediacy, the way perception goes, is the way to understanding being—the way to conceiving the truth of reality at the most fundamental level.

So, it is a misunderstanding of phenomenology, at least Merleau-Ponty's, that phenomenology cannot be ontological. Although the phenomenologist is not after a metaphysical ontology, they are after an ontology that posits what is the ultimately real. But the ultimately real, being as such, is pursued through attending to the logic of the world of perceptual immediacy rather than through making an inference from the perceptual world to a different ontological domain: "There is thus no destruction of the absolute ... here, only of the absolute ... separated from experience" (PrP, 27). Because perceptual ontology is the first ontology, the philosopher does not need to leave perception behind to understand the nature of being. They know being through perception because being is the logic of perception.

Here Merleau-Ponty is significantly revising and inverting the conviction running from Plato to Leibniz that ontology must abandon and surpass perception, that being can only be known through deduction or speculation. On the contrary, for phenomenology, "The perceived world is the always presupposed foundation of all rationality, all value and all existence. This thesis does not destroy either rationality or the absolute. It only tries to bring them down to earth" (PrP, 13). To bring ontology down to earth—to ground it in pre-reflective immediacy—is the goal of phenomenology.

At its most fundamental and pervasive level, being is the way the world is given in pre-predicative experience. And phenomenology is the form of reflection that seeks to give voice to this being's logic. In phenomenological ontology, philosophy articulates the sense of perceptual immediacy, thereby going beyond it—without departing from it. This logic of perceptual immediacy is the being that is investigated by phenomenology. For Merleau-Ponty, phenomenological ontology parallels a practice like painting, in which "Art is not imitation, nor is it something manufactured. ... It is a process of expressing" (CD, 17). Phenomenological ontology does not reiterate perception, nor does it abandon perception; rather, it expresses perception in the idiom of ontology by outlining perception's style and logic. But what are these, its style and logic?

Mystery and Miracle: The Logic of Being

Merleau-Ponty wanted to explore how immediate perceptual experience—the touched, seen, heard, smelled, tasted, desired, emotionally felt world and its objects—is given. For him, the world's being is the way this world is given. In perceptual ontology, the focus is on how the world is given, and it focuses on what the world is only in the horizon of how the world is given. The world's being is not an object but a manner of givenness. We can understand what the world is only when we see how the world is given to immediate perceptual and embodied consciousness. The logic of being is the logic of the world's appearing.

Here some specific questions arise. What is this perceptual ontology? What is the logic of the immediately perceived world's givenness? What is the truth and meaning of the being of the pre-thetic world that phenomenology implores human reflection to unforget? We can attempt to understand Merleau-Ponty's answers to these questions by considering his thoughts on the givenness of "the thing," "the world," and "the real."

First is the givenness of the thing—the being of the thing, in the phenomenological approach. A thing like a columbine is spatiotemporal, for example, in the way it is given to our immediate perception. The flower's being, its logic of appearing, is an appearing in space and time, and the thing given in space and time has a crucial feature: "It is thus of the essence of the thing and of the world to present themselves as 'open,' to send us beyond their determinate manifestations, to promise us always 'something else to see'" (*PhP-CS*, 388). In pre-reflective perceptual experience, the spatiotemporal thing gives itself in spatial and temporal profiles. Perception encounters the thing only in one spatiotemporal profile that has the horizon of other, different profiles. Perception never grasps all the profiles; perception cannot do so. Perception is a journey: "each aspect of the thing which falls to our perception is still only an invitation to perceive beyond it, still only a momentary halt in the perceptual process" (*PhP-CS*, 271). The pre-reflectively perceived thing's being is always beyond itself. Whatever spatial or temporal aspect perception is experiencing entails many others that it is not presently experiencing. In terms of spatiality, the realized experience of seeing a flower from one perspective in space always points to other possible but unrealized experiences of seeing other sides of the flower from other perspectives. In terms of temporality, any present perception points to past perceptions and possible future perceptions. However the thing may be perceived, it always has a horizon of other aspects that are not yet perceived.

In these ways, the thing's being—the way a thing is originally, nascently, given in time and space—has a special quality. That quality is "depth—that is, the dimension in which the thing is presented not as spread out before us but as an inexhaustible reality full of reserves" (*CD*, 15). This depth is a necessary feature of the openness of the thing's identity. A thing perceived is never perceived in all its aspects; there is always more to perceive. The thing never gives itself fully in perception; by definition, it always promises that there is more than currently meets the eye, an excess that will come to light only through other spatial and temporal perspectives. Because it never shows all its cards, the perceived thing's nature and identity remain somewhat indeterminate. To say as much is to say that the being of the thing has a depth that cannot be eliminated.

This indeterminacy and depth mean, furthermore, that the immediately perceived thing will always be, by definition, something of an enigma. Merleau-Ponty wrote, "This is what is sometimes expressed by saying that the thing and the world are mysterious. They are indeed, when we do not limit ourselves to their objective aspect, but put them back into the setting of subjectivity. They are even an absolute mystery, not amenable to elucidation" (PhP-CS, 388). In perceptual ontology, in which the being of the thing is the logic of the thing's pre-thetic appearing in perception, being is a mystery. This mystery is ongoing by necessity. The pre-reflective truth of the thing is always excessive and, to some degree, unavailable. If the thing itself is entirely available in pre-reflective experience, then it is not a thing at all. Of the thing-in-itself Merleau-Ponty explains:

> The ipseity is, of course, never reached. ... If the thing itself were reached, it would be from that moment arrayed before us and stripped of its mystery. It would cease to exist as a thing at the very moment when we thought to possess it. What makes the "reality" of the thing is therefore precisely what snatches it from our grasp. The aseity of the thing, its unchallengeable presence and the perpetual absence into which it withdraws, are two inseparable aspects of transcendence.
>
> (PhP-CS, 271)

The truth of the thing in immediate perceptual experience, in other words, is always future, never entirely given in the present but pointing to different profiles and perspectives to come—and there are always profiles and perspectives to come. The thing-in-itself is unreachable in principle in perceptual immediacy. The meaning of the thing is never static, never fully achieved, never final; it is promissory and unending, comprehensible only as also incomprehensible, known only as also unknown, visible and standing forth only as also invisible and withdrawn, present only as absent, describable only as also indescribable.

In sum, the truth of the perceived thing—the thing as it is given to uncalculated, pre-reflective, primordial experience—always remains other, forever transcendent, perpetually excessive. There is no total possession of a thing in pre-reflective experience; possession always entails dispossession. When we reflect in this way, this is phenomenological ontology. We are speaking about the being of the thing—the way the thing is given in immediate perceptual experience. And since this perceived thing's identity and truth are always somehow excessive, transcendent, hidden, absent, excessive, and future, Merleau-Ponty characterizes the being of the perceived thing as a mystery.

Next is the givenness of the pre-conceptual world. The logic of the world's givenness, as Merleau-Ponty indicates, is also temporal. The world, as it appears to perception, is "a world in which being is not given but rather emerges over time" (*WP*, 54). The truth and meaning of the immediate present world are never simply present; this truth and meaning are always being disclosed anew and are never definitively or conclusively revealed. Merleau-Ponty makes his point in stunning language by speaking of "perception ... as a re-creation or re-constitution of the world at every moment" (*PhP-CS*, 240). Reflecting phenomenologically, we realize that the world—the field of immediate perceptual experience of self, other, nature, and culture—is constantly appearing in changing ways; perceptual immediacy's truth is dynamic, not static. Merleau-Ponty did not mean that the truth of the immediately perceived world is revealed in a progressive, accumulating, or teleological way. He meant that the meaning of the world as it appears in unpremeditated and pre-thetic perception is always appearing differently from how it appeared before; the meanings of the world are excessive, never just reiterative, vis-à-vis the boundaries of the immediately perceived world's previous meanings. The being of the world is always, to some degree, unorthodox.

Other features of the givenness of the pre-predicative world are its impenetrability, ambiguity, and paradoxicality. Merleau-Ponty wrote that "Obscurity spreads to the perceived world in its entirety" (*PhP-DL*, 205); the immediately perceived world is shot through with "opacity" (*PhP-CS*, xiii). This opaque, puzzling world is challenging to know. Thus, Merleau-Ponty's positive estimation of Proust's project is that "the world he describes for us is neither complete nor univocal" (*WP*, 107). The world of perception is intrinsically ambiguous; its truth is "equivocal" (*PhP-DL*, 309). The truth of the nascently given universe of perception is not perspicuous or seamless; it lends itself to multiple interpretations. These interpretations are often mutually incompatible: "we arrive at contradictions when we describe the perceived world" (PrP, 18). Every immediate perspective on the world's truth enables vision even as it entails blindness. We confront in perceptual immediacy "an enigmatic world of which we catch a glimpse ... but only ever from points of view that hide as much as they reveal" (WP, 70). Revelation and concealment go together.

For all these reasons, Merleau-Ponty concludes, "reflection ... reveals the world as strange and paradoxical" (PhP-DL, lxxvii). The immediately given world's meaning is never transparent or straightforward. Being is inherently extraordinary and unusual if we see it correctly. Being is always a foreign country, and as contradictory, strange, and paradoxical, being is never at home with itself—that is, the foreignness of being is internal to being itself and is not something to overcome (as if it ever could be).

Last is the real. The being of the real is the logic of givenness of anything and everything—self, other, nature, or world—that exists taken just as existing. Here two passages are key. First: "The real lends itself to an infinite exploration, it is inexhaustible" (PhP-DL, 338). Second: "The real ... does not await our judgment before incorporating the most surprising phenomena, or before rejecting the most plausible figments of our imagination" (xi). In these passages, Merleau-Ponty makes ontological and epistemological points about the real—about pre-predicative reality. He claims that this real is endless and limitless; it is excessive; it is astonishing—unpredictable, unimaginable, and implausible. He claims that knowledge of the real is by definition ongoing, inconclusive, and revisionary. If we look closely, we can see that pre-reflective perception is constantly being taken aback by the real's manifestations, for the real feels no obligation to manifest in reasonable or probable ways. The pre-thetic real is continually clashing with our most quotidian or most fantastic, most commonsense or theoretical conceptions of it: the being of the real is unceasingly new, astounding, and confounding.

In all these ways, Merleau-Ponty in his phenomenological ontology shows that the realm of immediate perceptual experience—as the thing, as the world, as the real—is an ongoing "miracle" (PhP-CS, xxiii). Being is not taken to be something existing behind the deliverances of immediate perceptual experience; it is not metaphysical, and it is not a super-object. Instead, being is the logic of the pre-predicative realm's appearing. That appearing, that givenness of things, world, and real is the absolute and ultimate context in which human life exists. Here being is not covered by the shroud of pre-reflective perception;

being is the logic of that perception, a logic that is always shrouded in itself; being is intrinsically shrouded. In this picture, "the thing and the world are mysterious. ... They are even an absolute mystery, not amenable to elucidation" (*PhP-CS*, 388). Merleau-Ponty's project of phenomenological philosophy was to elucidate the truth of being as miracle and mystery—the marvelous and wonderful ways in which thing, world, and the real are given in pre-reflective experience—to help make us reflectively aware of the logic of the immediate perceptual experience that is our first home but about which we often are not aware because of its imprisonment in commonsense, natural science, or philosophical metaphysics. How we can or should respond to the miracle and mystery of being, how we should engage the actual logic, meaning, and truth of the thing's, the world's, and the real's givenness—a givenness whose logic comprises the most fundamental meaning and truth of being and reality there can be—is a question that we now have to take up.

The Hostility of Being: Menace and Danger

For Merleau-Ponty, the mysterious and miraculous nature of being does not have anything to do with the supernatural. Nor is the benevolence, malevolence, or indifference of being at issue. Rather, being—that is, how thing, world, and real are given in immediate perceptual experience—is mysterious and miraculous because, as Romand Coles writes, "the world as it is given to us in our primitive experiential contact with being" is permeated with "depth."[16]

Sometimes, Merleau-Ponty seems to see perception's continual engagement with reality as an ever-deeper journey in one direction toward an ever-deeper truth of the thing, the world, and the real. In this deeper experience of reality, the truth of the perceived is constantly being revealed in new ways consistent with the inherited ways of knowing it. Ever-deepening engagement with being would bring out more extensive or precise meaning and truth in the perceived, but this elucidation would move in a cumulative trajectory. In saying that "The perceptual 'synthesis' must be incomplete" (*PhP-DL*, 396), Merleau-Ponty would have been emphasizing that perceiving is always not perceiving, that every perceptual presence is permeated with absence, that perceiving never exhausts the perceived, that the givenness of thing, world, and real is always excessive. But this excess is experienced in consistent ways. Thus, he could write

> The tacit thesis of perception is that at every instant experience can be co-ordinated with that of the previous instant and that of the following, and my perspective with that of other consciousnesses—that all contradictions can be removed, that monadic and intersubjective experience is one unbroken text—that what is now indeterminate for me could become determinate for a more complete knowledge.
>
> (PhP-CS, 62)

In this framework, perception, its depth, and its truth develop in an ever-deeper yet consistent direction.

Yet we also need to see that Merleau-Ponty sometimes conceived of perception, its depth, and its meaning differently. Sometimes he accented the inconsistency of perception and the perceived. He did so in two ways.

First, he thought that perception, its depth, and its truth can be saturated with inconsistency because of the temporality of pre-predicative experience. He wrote, "on the level of perception, our certainty about perceiving a given thing does not guarantee that our experience will not be contradicted" (PrP, 20). Sometimes it is in the nature of being to interrupt and undermine previous perceptual grasps of thing, world, and real. The truth and meaning of the perceived can always be different—often is always becoming different. The nature of the perceived can always be unsettled and transformed in the process of its givenness; in the register of perceptual immediacy, present truth can contradict inherited truth.

Hence Merleau-Ponty's conviction that incompleteness entails equivocity—what he calls "the ambiguity in which we live" (WP, 111). In immediate perceptual experience, because reality is unfinished, reality can always arrive at a new meaning, even one that contradicts the meanings that have come before. The truth of the perceptual plane is therefore always underdetermined and unstable—it can always go in different ways. Every inherited meaning is open to judgment—we do not know how meaning will unfold. Because the perceived meaning is temporal, that meaning can never be perspicuous, transparent, or secure. The truth of thing, world, and real is enigmatic and polysemic; this truth can develop in unpredictable, even contradictory ways that make meaningful perception an intrinsically uncertain and imperiled endeavor: "perception can only present a 'real' to me by exposing itself to the risk of error" (PhP-DL, 396). The meaning of thing, world, and real is always contingent, provisional, and unguaranteed. Every pre-thematic embodied experience is precarious and risky. This insecurity and hazardousness comprise what Merleau-Ponty called "the danger of time" (*PhP-DL*, 359). Being as mystery and miracle is temporal, and being as temporal is dangerous.

All of which is to say that unreflective, nascent experience, its depth, and its meanings are always vincible and vulnerable. Merleau-Ponty wrote, "There is meaning. But rationality is neither a total nor an immediate guarantee. It is somehow open, which is to say that it is menaced" (PrP, 23). The truth of every intelligible perception is endangered because pre-predicative consciousness never sits still. The present meaning of thing, world, and real is always threatening to be dissolved. This menace is real whether the meaning of the perceived changes is desirable or undesirable, teleological or random, developmental or fragmenting. What makes perception risky and menacing is the temporality of being—the instability of the pre-thetic givenness of thing, world, and real. Pre-theoretical meaning is constantly deconstructing and transcending itself in time.

In addition to being dangerous because of its temporality, being is dangerous for another reason: its irreducible otherness. To say that there is no thing, world, or real that is unperceived—no object without a subject—does not mean that the object's meaning collapses into the subject's. Merleau-Ponty wrote:

> One cannot, as we said, conceive of a perceived thing without someone who perceives it. But moreover, the thing is presented as a thing in itself even to the person who perceives it, and thereby poses the problem of a genuine in-itself for-us. We do not ordinarily catch sight of this because our perception, in the context of our everyday dealings, bears upon the things just enough to find in them their familiar presence, and not enough to rediscover what of the non-human is hidden within them. But the thing is unaware of us, it remains in itself …. The thing is then hostile and foreign, it is no longer our interlocutor, but rather a resolutely silent Other [Autre], a Self that escapes us.
>
> (*PhP-DL*, 336)

So, although Merleau-Ponty affirmed the traditional conception of phenomenology that asserts that thing, world, and real have meaning only insofar as they appear in lived experience, he also affirmed that thing, world, and real have meaning that is not given in lived experience.

Pre-reflective perception also experiences thing, world, and real as unexperienceable. The perceptual object is *for* the subject, even as it is *not for* the subject. Being does not lodge itself in subjectivity; in Emmanuel Alloa's words, being is always "being-at-a-distance." There is a "resistance" to perceived reality (*WP*, 53).[17] Being as mystery and miracle is alien and strange. Perceived reality does not oblige our inherited conceptions; it can undo any attempt to grasp, assimilate, or domesticate it. Merleau-Ponty wrote that "all living things, ourselves included, endeavour to give shape to a world," but it is "a world that has not been preordained to accommodate our attempts to think it and act upon it" (*WP*, 73–4). To say that the thing, world, and real are foreign and hostile is to say that their givenness can be radically other, uncontainable, and uncontrollable. Their being has a depth that can never be fully accessed, a depth that can be antagonistic to attempts to access it.[18] And, it bears saying again, being is hostile not only when it deconstructs the trajectory of inherited meanings in painful ways but simply whenever it deconstructs the trajectory of consistency. Being, whether gift or curse, can be menacing. Whether for good or ill, inherited meanings of thing, world, and real in immediate perceptual experience are continually subject to the possibility of being reenvisioned for a subjectivity that never entirely possesses them and never has.

Phenomenology is sometimes conceived of as a discipline that recuperates and tries to understand the ordinary workaday world (as contrasted with the world of explanatory science or metaphysical ontology). The aim of phenomenology is to rehabilitate the value of the familiarly and naïvely lived world—that world gets its rights to "reality" back from the dogmatists of natural science or metaphysics who claim that they and only they deliver the real world and its truth. But, the phenomenology of perception also helps us see that being can be strange. Philosophical attention to the logic of perceptual immediacy can help us understand our experiential world as a world of irrepressible unfamiliarity. Phenomenology shows that immediate perceptual experience is not always a realm of commonsense experience, for the former often can bristle against the grain of the latter. Phenomenology shows that perception can be and often is unsettling. Phenomenology shows how the pre-thetic meaning of the perceived can be ambiguous as much as perspicuous, contradictory as much as consistent. Perception aims to constitute an intelligible, coherent world, but perception often finds a world with depths that upend much of its inherited intelligibility and coherence. We might say that, for common sense, reality is given without givenness, and beings are considered without being; phenomenology shows that givenness always overflows the given, and being is always more than beings. Hence meaning is intrinsically vincible and contingent.

Here we see a fundamental reason why Merleau-Ponty did phenomenology. He did his work because the logic of common sense—like that of natural science or metaphysics—is not the logic of perceptual experience. Common sense is clear enough and available enough already—it does not need to be revealed by philosophy. Phenomenology is essential because the sense of perceptual appearing is one we often do not recognize. We dwell within being as mystery and miracle without realizing that we do. We find ourselves in being that is incomplete, contradictory, strange, menacing, and other. This being's meaning is present, yet not perspicuously so. Thus Merleau-Ponty's phenomenology aimed to aid human life in explicitly acknowledging the nature of being as revealed in perceptual immediacy—but not only to acknowledge it.

The Stance of Wonder: The Phenomenology of Phenomenology

For Merleau-Ponty, phenomenological ontology does not replace the reality of pre-thetic perception; it enriches that reality. To see why, we must understand phenomenology as a form of experience in its own right—in Merleau-Ponty's terms, the "phenomenology of phenomenology" (*PhP-DL*, 382). What is the experience that is phenomenology? What is phenomenology's lived stance toward reality, and how is reality given within that stance?

Phenomenology is a re-seeing or re-experiencing of something already perceptually seen or experienced, as Merleau-Ponty makes clear when he says, "Whether it is a question of things or of historical situations, philosophy has no other function than to teach us to see them anew" (*PhP-DL*, 483); and, more extensively, "True philosophy entails learning to see the world anew" (*PhP-DL*, lxxxv). Reexperiencing thing, world, and real is to see them in a new way under the aspect of their givenness, to see them in their being as miracle, mystery, and menace. But what is the concrete subjective intentionality of this reexperiencing?

We have seen that Merleau-Ponty believed that the phenomenological stance is epistemic—knowledge of the style of being. But he also noted another dimension to phenomenological subjectivity. Phenomenology is a perspective of "attentiveness and wonder" before being (*PhP-CS*, xxiv). Doing phenomenology means "*standing in wonder* before the world" (*PhP-DL*, lxxvii, original italics). As phenomenology reveals being to be miracle, mystery, and menace, the phenomenological subject enters a posture of awe and amazement. When we look at the word "miracle" etymologically, as in the Latin *miraculum*, it simply means "object of wonder" or even "a wonder." Both subjectivity and objectivity are transformed: "We must not merely practice philosophy, but also become aware of the transformation that it brings with it in the spectacle of the world and in our existence" (*PhP-DL*, 63). In perception, thing, world, and real appear in a certain way with a certain logic—a logic that phenomenology makes explicit and calls being. As the phenomenologist realizes that the character of being is astonishing and awesome, they themselves appear in a new way as the subject of a new and richer life of wonder. Doing phenomenology makes possible a way of being present to the world that is more than epistemic: the way of wonder before being.

For Merleau-Ponty, this existential stance of wonder is not a paroxysm of silent astonishment. This wonder at being is a form of reflection; it is a philosophical posture. He writes, "Reflection ... alone is conscious of the world because it reveals the world as strange and paradoxical" (*PhP-DL*, lxxvii).[19] The wondrous character of being becomes evident when philosophy articulates the logic of how reality presents itself in pre-thematic, pre-theoretical embodied experience. Philosophy re-presents in concepts the logic of givenness of the originally presented preconceptual world: "Philosophy is not the reflection of a pre-existing truth, but, like art, the act of bringing truth into being" (*PhP-CS*, xxiii). Phenomenology manifests the truth of being as astounding, astonishing, and hostile—and it ushers human subjectivity into wonder at being that is understood in this way. The philosophical stance surpasses perception without abandoning it: phenomenology is "a philosophy ... whose entire effort is to rediscover this naïve contact with the world in order to finally raise it to a philosophical status" (*PhP-DL*, lxx). Merleau-Ponty was articulating an experience not unlike what Virginia Woolf described in *To the Lighthouse*: "One wanted, she thought, dipping her brush deliberately, to be on a level with ordinary experience, to feel simply that's a chair, that's a table, and yet at the same time, It's a miracle, it's an ecstasy."[20] The embodied subject spontaneously perceives thing, world, and real in the infinity, unknowability, inexhaustibility, and paradox of their givenness.

The pre-thematized and thematized coalesce in Merleau-Ponty's vision of phenomenology. Second-order thinking deepens first-order perception and even transfigures it. Rather than producing a metaphysical ontology that replaces the immediate perceptual plane with being that is abstract, thinned out, and spectral, phenomenology does ontology by expressing and elucidating the logic of that plane. In phenomenology, ontology does not compete with perceptual reality. Pre-predicative perception becomes more of what it is in predication because its logic of givenness is made explicit.[21] In other words, phenomenology brings us not only back to an immediacy we once had but have since lost; it brings us forward to an immediacy the depths of which we never have fully encountered before because we have not yet known it ontologically.

Merleau-Ponty's phenomenology was charting a mode of reflection and representation where reality is encountered in its determinate specificities as well as in its broad ontology; where life is explicitly attuned to how thing, world, and real are given in unceasing and uncircumscribable ways, to the truth and logic of the appearing of reality; where concrete perceptual life expresses itself philosophically without finding itself lost, negated, or replaced. The goal is not to return to immediate phenomenality but to enrich and dwell in this phenomenality philosophically—to taste it, see it, hear it, feel it, smell it, love it, hate it in embodied perception, and at the same time (or as close to the same time as possible) to experience it on another plane as miracle, mystery, and menace, to bring the experience of the phenomenal into the closest possible contact with awareness of phenomenality's logos—even as a gap or distance between phenomenal awareness, on the one hand, and phenomenological awareness, on the other, may always remain.

We have never fully understood how to live perception philosophically, and this is the lesson Merleau-Ponty was trying to teach: to be reflectively alive in the pre-reflective realm. As George Marshall notes, Merleau-Ponty was offering "a new conception of philosophy"—a radically new conception in which philosophy is reflective but not theoretical; it exists beyond nascent perception but also remains faithful to it; it does not try to go before, behind, or underneath the nascently perceived.[22]

Merleau-Ponty believed that if human life does not meet reality with wonder, it does not meet it authentically. Human life is constantly being taken aback by reality. The answer to Merleau-Ponty's fundamental question "What is phenomenology?" (*PhP-DL*, lxx) is that it is a reflective practice of unending wonder at being—wonder at the givenness of immediate perceptual experience. In this philosophy, because the meanings of reality are always ambiguous and opaque, implausible and surprising, unanticipatible and inexhaustible, dynamic and strange, wonder is where philosophy should begin, and wonder is where philosophy should remain.[23]

Knowledge and Reason: Thinking and Time

The world of perception, met philosophically with wonder, shows that being can be uncontrolled and uncontrollable, unknown and unknowable. More than anything, being is not owned and unable to be owned. Phenomenologically understood, immediate perceptual experience makes contact with being but never comprehends it: "The world is not an object such that I have in my possession the law of its making. ... I am open to the world. ... I am in communication with it, but I do not possess it" (*PhP-DL*, xi–xii, xix). Being is encountered but unmastered and unmasterable.

Correlated to Merleau-Ponty's new understanding of the nature of being was a new conception of the nature of reason and knowledge. There are a few different dimensions of this process to note, the first of which is that the scope and limits of knowledge have to parallel those of perception. David Michael Kleinberg-Levin writes, in contrast to Husserl's phenomenology, "The subsequent phenomenologies of Sartre and Merleau-Ponty are ... more radical enterprises, inasmuch as knowledge is shown to be grounded 'outside' itself, in the (philosophically prior) *lived* (simply experienced) acts of intentional meaning, whence our knowledge is constituted."[24] For Merleau-Ponty's epistemology, knowledge is not fundamental or self-grounding; perception is fundamental, and knowledge is based upon perception. Knowledge can have contents and logics that exceed the contents and logics of perception and differ from them—but it cannot have contents or logics that contradict those of perception. What is interesting is that Merleau-Ponty's way of grounding knowledge outside of itself in immediate perceptual experience leaves knowledge profoundly ungrounded. What Donn Welton says of Husserl's epistemology characterizes Merleau-Ponty's (and perhaps even more so): "all knowledge based on perception is presumptive, provisional, fallible, undergoing constant change."[25] For Merleau-Ponty, immediate perceptual experience is characterized by uncertainty, opacity, dynamism, and mutability, so the knowledge that builds on it and expresses it will also have to be uncertain, opaque, mutable, and dynamic.

In fact, we might say that Merleau-Ponty offers a phenomenology of phenomenological reason that charts the logic of the experience of reflecting philosophically on the field of pre-predicative immediacy. He shows the temporality of phenomenological reason—that is, the way that phenomenological reason discovered the truth of the being of the world in a temporal manner. The temporality of perception

4. Toward Wondering Life

and its field implies the temporality of philosophical reflection on that field as wonder. He wrote: "perception *and* thought ... appear to themselves as temporal" (PrP, 21, my italics). Philosophical reason, in phenomenology, is itself characterized by becoming, not being: "our reflections are carried out in the temporal flux on the which [*sic*] we are trying to seize" (*PhP-CS*, xv).

This temporality of phenomenological reason becomes manifest when the issue of knowledge's justification is raised. In knowledge, Merleau-Ponty wrote, "Evidence is never apodictic, nor is thought timeless" (PrP, 13). It is because evidence is never certain that thought is never timeless. The consequences of admitting the temporality of thought are powerful:

> Can I seriously say that I will always hold the ideas I do at present—and mean it? Do I not know that in six months, in a year, even if I use more or less the same formulas to express my thoughts, they will have changed their meaning slightly? Do I not know that there is a life of ideas, as there is a meaning of everything I experience, and that every one of my most convincing thoughts will need additions and then will be, not destroyed, but at least integrated into a new unity? This is the only conception of knowledge that is scientific and not mythological.
>
> (PrP, 20)

Because the subjective and objective reality of pre-reflective experience is dynamic, and because this world's phenomenological truth (its ontology) is dynamic, the philosophical reasoning of phenomenology must be dynamic.

Reason and its perceptual evidence, as temporal, will always remain incomplete, contingent, and provisional because the being of thing, world, and real always resists being possessed. Being has an "infinite logos," and thus, phenomenological philosophy must understand itself as a project with its own infinite logos (CD, 19). This philosophy's process is endless. To articulate being, its ways, and its instantiations, phenomenological reason must always be *in via*: "Expressing what *exists* is an endless task" (CD, 15, original italics). Wondering reasoning is unceasing.

Phenomenological reason does not always go unceasingly deeper into the truth of reality in one direction; it is a process but not a unilinear one. The givenness of reality is not always continuous; it can deviate from its past trajectories. Merleau-Ponty wrote:

> [P]hilosophy ... will be, as Husserl says, an infinite dialogue or meditation, and, to the very extent that it remains loyal to its intention, it will never know just where it is going. The unfinished nature of phenomenology and the inchoate style in which it proceeds are not the sign of failure; they were inevitable because phenomenology's task was to reveal the mystery of the world and the mystery of reason.
>
> (*PhP-DL*, lxxxv)[26]

The only definitive thing we can phenomenologically say about phenomenological reason is that this reason's deliverances will never be conclusive; the only absolute trajectory of phenomenological reason we can discern is this reason's departure from any final trajectory. Wondering reason will be unstable; it will not possess the truth; it will be constantly dispossessed of the truth. Only such reason can genuinely make contact with being. When reality is taken in terms of how it is given, every idea about reality is by definition incomplete, contestable, developable, and mutable because the world of pre-thematized experience is incomplete, contestable, and mutable.

Most radically, a phenomenology of phenomenological reason shows the way that this reason can and must accept the contradictory character of both thought and world. Merleau-Ponty wrote: "if there were such a thing as a non-contradictory thought, it would exclude the world of perception. ... But the question is precisely to know whether there is such a thing as logically coherent thought or thought in the pure state" (*PrP*, 18). Only a form of thinking open to contradictions can mirror a reality permeated with contradictions and ambiguities. In contrast, thought that seeks to resolve all contradictions would entertain only coherent and consistent ideas about a coherent and consistent world. Merleau-Ponty's point is that, because the realm of perceptual immediacy is inevitably contradictory and ambiguous, phenomenological reason itself has to be willing to entertain ambiguities and contradictions. Only a contradictory thought can represent a contradictory reality—a reality that is one of the causes that sustains ongoing wonder against any attempt at epistemic closure.

All the same, Merleau-Ponty does not consider phenomenological reason irrational. It is because "world and reason ... we might call them mysterious, this mystery is essential to them" that a non-possessing, self-dispossessing, contradictory form of reason will provide the only rational way to know the truth about being (*PhP-DL*, lxxxv). It is only when we embrace the fact that we reason wonderingly in time that our human being is reasonable. He wrote:

> Finally, the contingency of the world should be understood neither as a lesser being, a gap in the tissue of necessary being, a threat to rationality, nor as a problem to be resolved as soon as possible through the discovery of some deeper necessity. This is an ontic contingency, or contingency within the world. Ontological contingency or the contingency of the world itself, being radical, is on the contrary what establishes once and for all our idea of truth.
>
> (*PhP-DL*, 419)

Phenomenological thinking is truthful because it refuses to try to be a form of thinking that would possess being. Being cannot be truthfully known unless it is known in its temporality with the depths, deviations, contradictions, and ambiguities this temporality entails. The reason that truthfully encounters being will have the same characteristics that characterize being.

Merleau-Ponty realized that we would find reality and reason pictured in this way hard to handle: "It is an unfamiliar world in which one is uncomfortable" (CD, 16). The world of fissures, contradictions, reserves, and ambiguities generates anxiety and resistance in the human mind. The uncontrollable, and frequently unknown, nature of being can seem so hazardous for us to acknowledge that we take drastic measures to deny that being is what Merleau-Ponty has shown.

The concrete form this resistance takes is scientific and metaphysical reason, the kind of reason that delivers empirical or metaphysical ontology. This knowledge flees perceptual immediacy and distances itself from phenomenological ontology. It is a reason marked by its quest for a definitive understanding of a definable reality. This form of thought forecloses on the possibility of reason as a practice of ongoing wonder because it refuses to acknowledge the temporality of reason and its evidences, the way that philosophy should be an unending process of beginning again. In this philosophy, "domination of time ... is the work of thought" (PrP, 20). Metaphysical or scientific reason seeks some form of definitive knowledge that would define what reality is without wrestling with how reality is given in time. The ontologies generated by these forms of reason try to determine what being is and what beings are, rather than describing how being and beings are given to naïve experience in the actual logic of their appearing. What being and beings are is privileged over how being and beings are given because of the anxiety provoked by givenness.

For this reason, Merleau-Ponty believed, it is "the ambitions of classical science, art and philosophy ... to know nature through and through and to purge its knowledge of man of all mystery" (*WP*, 105)—and not only knowledge of "man" (i.e., humanity) but knowledge of anything and everything that can be known at all. In other words, this reason demands that the identity of thing, world, or real be definable without reserve, alterity, or difficulty: "It is striking to see that classical transcendental philosophies never question the possibility of carrying out the complete making-explicit that they always assume is completed somewhere" (*PhP-DL*, 62). With this form of thinking we seek to possess and master being through definitive, timelessly valid concepts; we believe that such possession and mastery are possible and desirable.

For Merleau-Ponty, however, this account of reason is inadequate to capture the fundamental nature of being. Thinking that tries to master being "is always somewhat deceiving" (*PrP*, 20). Not just deceiving, in fact, but blasphemous: scientific and metaphysical reason pursue an "idol of absolute knowledge" (*PrP*, 21). Merleau-Ponty implies that this deceptive and idolatrous form of so-called timeless reason is defensive. This kind of reason is a self-protective strategy against acknowledging the marvelous, disorderly, uneasy reality of being with its evolving ambiguities, uncertainties, and contradictions. Readers familiar with the story of the golden calf in the Hebrew Bible/Old Testament will remember that humans make idols in the attempt to achieve a measure of security, however illusory that security might be. The ancient Israelites fashioned the golden calf because their God seemed distant, uncontrollable, and unpredictable; to assuage their anxiety, they made a god who would be totally present, available, and manageable. Metaphysical or scientific reason follows a similar path.

All these non-phenomenological philosophies are problematic because their ideal of absolute timeless knowledge is illusory and destructive. Instead of being an ideal that could inspire philosophical life to move closer to a genuine understanding of being, if we hold this ideal we take life farther away from such knowledge by imagining that being can be entirely transparent for present knowledge. Our ideal of absolute knowledge is a misguided standard for knowledge that engineers and perpetuates an ultimately futile attempt to shield embodied life from perceptual immediacy and philosophical life from phenomenological ontology; the purpose is to protect human beings from perceiving the world's actual dynamic and wonderful appearing and the process of reflecting on the logic of this appearing. Our anxiety in the face of perception and its logic of givenness generates an ideal of timeless, objectivist, definitional thought, which then causes anxiety about perception and its logic of givenness.

The phenomenology of perception is therapeutic in the way that it turns us philosophically away from a dishonest and impious form of timeless and totalitarian reason and toward a truthful and reverent reason that faces up to the complex, dangerous, unpredictable, and inconsistent temporal givenness of thing, world, and real. Hence Merleau-Ponty states, "This is why, of all philosophies, only phenomenology speaks of a transcendental field. This word signifies that reflection never has the entire world and the plurality of monads spread out and objectified before its gaze, that it only ever has a partial view and a limited power" (PhP-DL, 62). In this philosophy of wonder, the philosopher is a perpetual wonderer: "the philosopher is a perpetual beginner ... philosophy itself must not take itself as established in the truths it has managed to utter ... philosophy is an ever-renewed experiment of its own beginning" (PhP-DL, lxxviii). The kind of philosophical life Merleau-Ponty invites his readers into dismantles the defensive strategy of metaphysical or scientific philosophical life that deceptively and idolatrously aims at the control or manipulation of being, philosophical life that fails to do justice to "the aseity of things" (PhP-CS, xvii), the way things, world, and real proceed in time of their own accord, not as human will demands them to be. In his philosophy he was therapeutically trying to restore life to a form of temporally structured philosophical reason, a dynamic form of philosophical life that will do justice to the temporal essence of the field of perceptual immediacy and its logic, which comprise the most fundamental reality of human life in its "opacity and its transcendence" (PhP-DL, lxxv).

Phenomenology thus is therapeutic in how it challenges and dismantles the ideal of absolute, timeless knowledge in philosophical life along with the metaphysical productions inspired by this ideal and which we confuse with reality. Phenomenology relieves human life of the illusion that timeless knowledge can be the ideal of reason; it shows that total clarity, completeness, certainty, and comprehensibility in present knowledge are misguided ideals, which take knowledge away from the truth, not near it. Such ideals are illusions; they serve as defenses against confronting being in its difficult temporal givenness, being that is as much future as it is present. Such ideals are defenses against wonder.

Interestingly, in much of the history of philosophy, the ideal of absolute knowledge has inspired philosophical projects meant to deliver truth-seeking life from the vicissitudes of perception and its uncertain logics—projects that Merleau-Ponty characterizes as *pensée du survol*. But now Merleau-Ponty's phenomenology is claiming that this ideal of timeless valid knowledge is itself the pathology from which philosophical life needs deliverance. Now it is not temporality that is the problem but the illusory forms of thinking that try to escape temporality.

Because the philosophical possession of being is always a myth (we never possess being in the present with any epistemic closure), part of phenomenology's work is to pull us away from philosophies that pretend to such present possession and epistemic closure. Thus, Merleau-Ponty was opposed to rationalism, empiricism, naturalism, and idealism or intellectualism because of his conviction that none of these forms of philosophical thinking were forms of ongoing wonder at how the world dynamically appears. Philosophical life in the grip of timeless, absolute definitions of what reality is seems safer than philosophical life immersed in the world of time, but the former's demand for closure leads to inaccurate representations of reality. Reality is not seen as wonderful, which is the ultimate truth of reality.

Phenomenology is thus an invitation into a new epistemic life, a less defensive form of always provisional and unfinished reason in time. By giving up the idol of absolute knowledge, this form of philosophy goes with, rather than against, the grain of perception and its logic. Phenomenological philosophy—by remaining committed to attending to how being is ongoingly given, as continually strange upsurge, flux, and difference, rather than to pinning being and beings down as static entities, amenable to being captured in definitional concepts—is thus a therapy for helping us engage the reality of self, other, thing, nature, and world more authentically and truthfully. Phenomenology's therapy fosters the practice of phenomenological thinking—temporal thinking, in all that this temporality entails—as an endeavor of philosophical wonder in which all thinking proves difficult and dangerous.

It should be clear that Merleau-Ponty offered the phenomenology of perception as a difficult philosophical therapy, and he did not deny the anxiety and discomfort of truth-seeking life immersed in pre-theoretical perception and phenomenological reflection. His phenomenology is not an easy therapy, but he did think it a truthful one. Merleau-Ponty's phenomenology might even be a form of moral or political therapy, as we will now see.

Without Restriction: The Reach of Phenomenological Ontology and Reason

The interpretation of Merleau-Ponty offered here draws on and extends the insights of other readers of his work. Romand Coles has explored the way in which pre-reflective experience and its ontology always involve "depth," which makes our reasoning about the world "a continual questioning engagement."[27] For Emmanuel Alloa, Merleau-Ponty's work is "an obstacle to the grasping of being with no remainder," since the pre-predicatively experienced reality exists not only on what Alloa calls "the side of presence." For Alloa's Merleau-Ponty, epistemically encountering this world of experience entails our perpetual "unlearning what we believed we knew."[28] For the reasons highlighted by Coles and Alloa, Jessica Wiskus believes that Merleau-Ponty's "philosophy ... is ... an expression that could never be finished .... This work of philosophy must ever be taken up again." For Wiskus, Merleau-Ponty's phenomenological "work promises an opening—an initiation to a philosophical discourse that by its very nature could be nothing other than ongoing and incomplete."[29]

But here, we can ask two questions about what Merleau-Ponty took to be the scope of his phenomenology. What does the being engaged by phenomenological ontology include? What realms of understanding is phenomenological reason involved with and relevant to?

Merleau-Ponty's answer to the first question is: everything. The being whose logic phenomenology can investigate and articulate is being without qualification or limit. Ontology can seek to know any reality insofar as it is given to pre-reflective experience—and Merleau-Ponty believes that every reality, in some way, is so given. As he said about politics, for example:

> Leaving the sphere of knowledge for that of life and action, we find modern man coming to grips with ambiguities which are perhaps more striking still. There is no longer a single word in our political vocabulary that has not been used to refer to the most different, even opposed, real situations: consider freedom, socialism, democracy, reconstruction, renaissance, union rights. The most widely divergent of today's largest political parties have all at some time claimed each of these for their own. And this is not a ruse on the part of their leaders: the ruse lies in the things themselves.
>
> (*WP*, 108–9)

Reality as such, in the logic of its appearing, is contradictory, ambiguous, and unfinished. In pre-predicative experience, being (natural, aesthetic, political, social, economic, or religious) is defined—non-definitively—by mystery, miracle, and menace.

The critical point is that the aim of Merleau-Ponty's phenomenology of perception is not to seek to understand the truth of only an esoteric or rarefied field that is of interest only to philosophers—being as some kind of grand abstraction. Instead, he believed that "all consciousness is perceptual," and he sought to describe the fundamental logic of all of human life's pre-thetic lived worlds, whether these worlds be natural, political, religious, or so on. Through phenomenology we see that the ontological truth of all these worlds is enigmatic, excessive, unexpected, opaque, paradoxical, implausible, and inexhaustible, and that all the things, worlds, and realities in these registers need to be met with wonder.

And what about the domain of reason, even scientific and metaphysical reason? Merleau-Ponty wrote,

> I do not detract anything from the more complex forms of knowledge; I only show how they refer to this fundamental experience as the basic experience which they must render more determinate and explicit. Thus, it has never entered my mind to do away with science, as you say. It is rather a question of understanding the scope and the meaning of science.
>
> (PrP, 34)

When all reasoning is first and fundamentally phenomenological, reason has to avoid being idolatrous, whatever it aims to understand; it must resist the temptations of closure and definition; it must accept its being in time. Reason will not try to stabilize reality by pinning it down in concepts but will try to articulate the ways in which reality is continually being de-familiarized in our immediate perceptual experience in such a way that all concepts and definitions of reality are by definition vincible, interruptible, and provisional—whether the concepts and definitions belong to common sense or to high-level science and theory. We never know quite what democracy or freedom or society is. In the philosophy of wonder, knowledge is always being upended because what is known is strange, opaque, and hostile in itself. The situation could not be otherwise when, as Merleau-Ponty said, "The entire universe of science is constructed upon the lived world" (PhP-CS, lxxii). George Marshall has noted that, in Merleau-Ponty's philosophy, "Both scientific explanation and the analytic reflection of the philosophers offer accounts or reconstructions of the world."[30] But now, we have a form of reasoning conceived not as a reconstruction but as an articulation of pre-thetic perception and its miraculous, mysterious, enacting logic of givenness.

The upshot is that any attempt to understand anything of thing, world, or real without phenomenology and its perpetual wonder before being is an inauthentic and untruthful attempt. Any theory's genealogy leads back to the soil of perceptual immediacy and its phenomenological ontology. So theorizing of any kind—such as science or metaphysics—that through inference or deduction seeks to leave the realm of immediate perceptual experience and its truth behind will produce a problematic theory. Whereas constructive theory—for example, of social or political notions like freedom or psychological concepts like mind and sensation—will stay close to perception and its phenomenology.

In sum, philosophy not only brings us light; it reminds us that we are always also in the cognitive dark. In the face of the pre-reflective world's awesome and uncomfortable unfamiliarity, Merleau-Ponty's phenomenology of perception reminds us that we will never quite have our footing in our attempts to know any reality. Every familiar and habitual pattern of knowing in any dimension of reality is essentially vulnerable when we do epistemic justice to thing, world, and real by seeing thing, world, and real in their logic of givenness. For something to be is for it to be given. And seeing what something is while attending to how it is given will always unsettle our understanding of what we know it to be. Understanding the world without understanding—the way the phenomenology of perception lays out—is the only genuine and authentic way to understand the world.

Conclusion: Responsible Life

This discussion of Merleau-Ponty has not covered everything in his phenomenology of perception. I have tried to show that human life's first encounter with reality is found in immediate perceptual experience. This immediate experience can take place in any realm: religious life, political life, aesthetic life, epistemic life, and so on. In every domain, the logic of this experience is mystery, miracle, and menace. It is a logic that holds before we actively think or reflect or judge—it is the experience in which we always find ourselves before the fact, the experience we think about and reflect on. Immediate perceptual experience is primary in human life—whether the experiencer is politically conservative or progressive, religious or atheist, romantic or rationalist—and its world with that world's logic is the world that is originarily given to us in human life, the world that is the source for all later attempts to know reality.[31]

I have tried to show how Merleau-Ponty's phenomenology, understood in this way, can be read as a moment of the existential revolution of the Freudian age. Merleau-Ponty advanced an ethics of immediacy: his work called people in the first half of the twentieth century in Europe to embrace a philosophical life in which reflection remained deeply connected to perceptual immediacy and its ontology. Here his goal of centering philosophical life on immediate perceptual experience and its logic of appearing developed Freud's goal of grounding psychological life within immediate psychological experience and its logic, and it paralleled Virginia Woolf's goal of orienting social life around immediate intersubjective experience and its logic. In Merleau-Ponty's phenomenological reflection, philosophy becomes attuned to the truth of being by exploring the logic of how thing, world, and real are given within first-order, nascent, originary, pre-thematic experience, the kind of embodied and interpretive experience in which we always already find ourselves.

Now up to this point, we have read Merleau-Ponty's project to be an epistemological one. In this framework, his philosophy would consist of an attempt to help readers, first, to leave behind a set of tempting but inadequate and defensive ways of seeking to know being found in scientific philosophy and metaphysical ontology and, second, to embrace a more fitting and less defensive mode of knowing being, which is found in phenomenology. Merleau-Ponty's goal, when we conceive his thought in this way, was to invite philosophical experience to contemplate being by unknowingly knowing it as mystery, miracle, and menace and then to contemplate the truth of everything else within this ontological context, whether the phenomenon under consideration was one of nature, art, politics, religion, or anything else.

Even so, Merleau-Ponty may not have conceived of his project as only epistemic or reflective. In his mind, phenomenology may have aimed at a goal beyond just acquiring more authentic and truthful knowledge. He left hints that phenomenological reflection can lead to phenomenology as a way of life. Phenomenology strives to *intellectually* reflect more truthfully and authentically so as to inspire us to *practically* engage with reality more truthfully and authentically.

Here phenomenology is a practice of articulating and clarifying the essences of perception and also a practice of fostering an existential transformation that allows humans to embody a new way of life, which can be called phenomenological life. This way of life is one we humans are always, to some degree, tacitly already living out but often in an inauthentic and unaware fashion.

What hints does Merleau-Ponty leave that his phenomenology of perception might have included the reflective aim but also gone beyond it? It is uncontroversial that Merleau-Ponty's philosophy sought to understand pre-predicative embodied existence—what he called, in words that should make sense in light of these inquiries, "the lack of completion and the ambiguity *in which we live*" (*WP*, 111, my italics). The claim is descriptive: we not only know in ways shaped by incompleteness and ambiguity; we live with incompleteness and ambiguity in every domain of life. And the first goal of phenomenology is for the phenomenologist to become aware of the logic of their pre-reflective experience, to have conceptual contact with the pre-conceptual.

But Merleau-Ponty also says something that moves beyond the descriptive. We, as human beings, are called not only to know the nature of being, not only to become aware of perception and its logic. We are called to shape our lives in a way that is consonant with the actual logic of being, in a way that is aware of perception and its structures. This call is "taking our own history upon ourselves" (*PhP-CS*, xxii). Phenomenology's ultimate aim is for us to know the true nature of being, to be aware of perception and perception's grammar, so that we can live within the true nature of being and navigate the circumstances of love, sex, politics, art, religion, society, and more within the ontology of mystery, miracle, and menace. A more authentic and truthful knowledge leads to a more authentic and truthful awareness, and this awareness leads to a more authentic and truthful life.

In phenomenology, Merleau-Ponty wrote, "We take our fate in our hands, we become responsible for our history through reflection, but equally by a decision on which we stake our life" (*PhP-CS*, xxiii). Through phenomenology, we become aware of the content of perceptual immediacy but, even more so, of its logic—its logic of givenness that is its ontology. This awareness of being is the condition for our ability to take responsibility for practically engaging reality in terms of what it is and how it is given. In phenomenology as a way of life, we will intentionally subjectify our pre-reflective, naïve experience and its logic of givenness to allow every dimension of action and practice to be attuned to the inescapably temporal, dynamic, incomplete, and endlessly surprising essence of being. Learning to know the ontology of religious, aesthetic, or political phenomena is the first step toward learning to negotiate these phenomena practically. The goal is to acknowledge and respect the nature of being in whatever we think or do.

Ontology may seem a long way from everyday life. But Merleau-Ponty's point is that human life always stands in an ontological horizon that provides a background for all of life's concrete practices and engagements, an overall sense of reality, a pervasive sense of the logic of how thing, world, and real exist and appear. We love, strive, gain, build, lose, hope, fear, fight, accept, destroy, and repair within a horizon of being.[32] Merleau-Ponty developed a more truthful ontology that could be a new horizon for more truthful concrete acts of knowing and doing. He wanted us to lessen our defenses against perception and its logic—in which we always already stand. He wanted us to dwell within perception and its being as revealed by phenomenology: as paradoxical, other, ambiguous, incomplete, strange, surprising, and inexhaustible. Lawrence Hass offers a keen insight here: "certain modes of thinking get in the way of seeing important features of our living experience ... get in the way of *realizing* our living experiences—'realizing' them in the sense of understanding them, but also in the sense of living in consonance with them."[33] Merleau-Ponty offered an art of living, a possibility for a transformed life, in which human life renounces the idol of the absolute in every area of knowing and acting.

All meanings—political, moral, aesthetic, and so on—are recognized as inherently vulnerable and vincible, never static, settled, complete, or controllable. The ideal of a life that would have a full and unchanging handle on things, in any way, is left behind as a defensive illusion that phenomenology has dismantled. In this way, phenomenology was a therapeutic endeavor for Merleau-Ponty, a project meant to foster a profound existential transformation in the lives of those who practice it.[34]

This way of conceiving phenomenology as existentially therapeutic does not negate how phenomenology has been historically understood as a reflective, second-order practice of understanding the logic of first-order experience.[35] But it does mean seeing how phenomenological understanding can be a means of becoming more aware of and attuned to being as we live life. Saying that phenomenology is a practical philosophy can supplement an understanding of phenomenology as a reflective philosophy by acknowledging that knowledge affects life. This way of conceiving phenomenology as an existential therapy also does not mean that phenomenology is an attempt to relieve suffering or engender an easy life of psychological peace or contentment. The therapy that is offered by reading Merleau-Ponty's philosophy is the entrance into a certain kind of awareness—a wondering life—that is not always easy, peaceful, or content. Wondering life is difficult; it means learning to live with being's ability to constantly upset our conceptions of thing, world, and real. Life lived with the grain of being as mystery, miracle, and menace is uncomfortable by definition because the phenomena of the world will always appear in unfamiliar ways. Because the meanings of reality will never be completely constituted or possessed, phenomenology as a way of life will be perpetually unsettled and unstable. Living in the posture of wonder means being open to the violence of being undone on an ongoing basis by the foreignness of being, the strange momentums, deliverances, and logics of perception. Thus, reading Merleau-Ponty's phenomenology as a form of existential therapy does not necessarily increase psychological joy or relieve psychological suffering; rather, it ushers us into the life of wonder before reality.[36] For a text like "Cézanne's Doubt" ultimately centers its reflection on the experience of Cézanne the painter, and, mutatis mutandis, the experiential possibilities for human life as such. Recall Merleau-Ponty's conviction that Cézanne's existence was "a single adventure of his life and work" (CD, 20). This single adventure was primarily emotional: "Only one emotion is possible for this painter—the feeling of strangeness—and only one lyricism— that of the continual rebirth of existence" (CD, 18). This feeling of the strangeness of the ceaselessly dynamic nature of reality—as mystery, miracle, and menace—was not just a discrete emotion of Cézanne as a specific individual; this sense of the strangeness of being—the strangeness of being found in our immediate perceptual experience of being—embodied "a general possibility of human existence" that humans would and should feel when they authentically and honestly encountered reality (CD, 20).

If immediate perceptual experience and its logic are dangerous, if this experience's world always feels strange, if life with the grain of wonder is difficult, why should humans embrace wondering life? Merleau-Ponty would answer that only wondering life can honestly engage with reality. The promise of phenomenology is that it leads to a way of life that is more consonant with actual reality. Phenomenology leads to a way of life that engages reality directly instead of trying to engage it within the illusions of science or metaphysics. This more truthful encounter with self, other, nature, world, and the divine would seem to be a necessary— though not sufficient—condition for living more virtuously. True generosity and justice in any domain of life are impossible if one lives within the terms of a false ontology.

And a false ontology is an ontology of completeness, an idol of the absolute. Political, sexual, social, and moral life can flourish only when the truth of thing, world, and real is incomplete, to some degree absent, unfinished, and future. The meanings of political, moral, social, artistic, sexual, and religious being—because these meanings are defined by the mystery, miracle, and menace of being—are irreducibly dynamic. These phenomena always chafe against any established comprehension of their meanings; their inherited and sedimented meanings are constantly being upset in more or less significant ways. Yet it is a life lived in this framework of phenomenological ontology that has a chance to be truthful and authentic. Here is the condition for the actual practice of virtue, even if it cannot guarantee it.

Moreover, we have to admit that embracing the themes and forms of perceptual immediacy—perception and its ontology—in the experience of philosophical wonder entails risk. The dynamism and futurity of being can be destructive or constructive. To say that being is mystery, miracle, and menace is to say something about ontology's excessiveness and openness; it is not to offer a philosophy of history, and certainly not a progressivist philosophy of history in which the surprises of being are always for the best. Moral and political judgment will still be required, but now this judgment will at least judge reality as it is in its becoming, not as a reductive science or an illusory metaphysical ontology might wish it to be. Phenomenological ontology promises a more genuine encounter with being than any scientific theory or metaphysical ontology ever could, even though it is a less stable and certain encounter, a more hazardous one.

In conclusion, this discussion of Merleau-Ponty's brilliant work has attempted to show that his phenomenology of perception is a philosophy that explicates the logic of experience in a new way for its readers at the same time that it is a philosophy that invites these readers into a new form of conscious experience. We can hear how Merleau-Ponty's remark about Cezanne may have captured his own aims in doing philosophy: "It is not enough for a painter like Cezanne, an artist, or a philosopher, to create and express an idea; they must also awaken the experiences which will make their idea take root in the consciousness of others" (CD, 19). Merleau-Ponty offered his phenomenology of perception as an appeal, as a spiritual exercise to help his readers to have an experience of knowing the content and logic of perception anew and of living life anew within that new knowledge and awareness of its content and logic.[37] Reading his text is a therapeutic experience because it returns the reader to the pre-reflective world and its logic epistemically, a return that creates the condition for turning to the pre-reflective world and its logic practically and existentially.

Immediate perceptual experience and its logic are dangerous, and wondering life does not come naturally. But reading Merleau-Ponty can be a way into wondering life, even as the entrance into this life can feel like a violence to readers being sprung from their entrapment in the perspectives of natural science or metaphysical ontology. Merleau-Ponty's remarkable "Preface"—and the other texts we have encountered—was and is self-implicating for its readers. To read Merleau-Ponty's work as therapeutic is to see how it aims to enlarge its reader's knowledge and change its reader's life. Not only to describe perception, its world and its logic, but to draw us into a life and world characterized by the ambiguity, surprise, mystery, implausibility, inexhaustibility, strangeness, opacity, and paradox that only become evident when we are aware of perception and its ontology. This work presented an ethics of immediacy, a vision of human life that takes responsibility for immediate perceptual experience and its logic in its concrete existence, one that lives in awareness of perception's ontology of mystery, miracle, and menace. As such an ethics of immediacy, Merleau-Ponty's work stood in the wake of the horizon inaugurated by Freud, but it also surpassed that horizon. Merleau-Ponty's work was indeed Freudian; it was Freudian beyond Freud.

Conclusion
The Freudian Age: A Contemporary Horizon

Introduction: Ethics and History

The ultimate aim of this book has been to consider an ethics—the ethics of immediacy—by means of sketching an intellectual history that suggests the possibility that there was an era we can justifiably call "the Freudian age" from around 1895 to around 1945. Regarding this age, I have tried to make two different historical claims in the book. One claim (perhaps harder to prove) concerns direct historical influence. The claim here is that (1) we know Woolf read Freud seriously, (2) we know that the kind of immediate intersubjective experience described and championed in her literary criticism parallels very closely the kind of immediate psychological experience described and championed in Freud's psychoanalysis, and (3) we can thus conclude that Woolf was actively and explicitly taking up the logic of Freud's project in her own work. Mutatis mutandis, the same line of argument applies in tracing the specific historical connections between Merleau-Ponty's work and Freud's. The other historical claim (perhaps easier to prove) is that Freud and Woolf and Merleau-Ponty, very different figures from very different cultural registers, were all, in their distinct ways yet at around the same time, creating work that articulated, embodied, and fostered a significantly new existential or experiential mood in European culture, a mood explicitly evoked in Freud's work before Woolf's and Merleau-Ponty's.

In charting this history, in either version, I have not meant to claim, of course, that Freud, Woolf, and Merleau-Ponty's projects were identical. Their endeavors of Austrian *fin de siècle* clinical psychoanalysis, English modernist literary criticism, and French existential phenomenology, respectively, differed from each other in both theme and scope. Without denying their differences, I have nevertheless tried to argue that their three very different projects resemble each other in the way they all, uniquely and distinctly, foreground the reality of—and promote the value of—a hitherto under-noticed and under-appreciated region of lived experience, namely, immediate experience in its dangerous dimensions. Their work *does* coalesce around the endorsement of different versions of an ethics of immediacy—which is not to say that in other ways, in content and form, their work does not significantly diverge! I have certainly accented the common threads in these writers' works, but I would never deny that differences remain in their very different projects found in very different domains of culture.

In sum, there are good reasons for seeing that Woolf's and Merleau-Ponty's works build on the work of Freud and for seeing that Freud, Woolf, and Merleau-Ponty are three diverse representatives of a shared existential zeitgeist, even as I admit that other historical and theoretical narratives could and would frame what these three figures' works have in common—and what they do not—in different ways. Even so, I hope that the historical and theoretical narrative I have offered in this project is justifiable, evocative, and illuminating in trying to show how these three roughly contemporaneous figures were partisans calling in various ways for a new kind of human life that would follow the lead of the ethics of immediacy, were writers advocating from very different cultural and intellectual backgrounds for human beings to embrace our immediate experience.

Immediate Experience: Defamiliarizing and Dangerous

What is the set of historical and theoretical convergences and affinities between Freud's psychoanalysis, Woolf's modernism, and Merleau-Ponty's phenomenology? In different but overlapping ways, these writers investigated a specific phenomenon in human life. Merleau-Ponty's work was explicitly phenomenological, but Freud's and Woolf's works were also often implicitly phenomenological—each offered, at the least, something like a phenomenology, a phenomenology of the kind of experience we can call *immediate experience*. Together, all three conceived that immediate experience has specific contents and structures that distinguish it from other kinds of experience. For them, immediate experience includes the thoughts, perceptions, feelings, and desires vis-à-vis self, other, thing, world, and real that appear in human life in one or more of the following ways: interruptive, involuntary, uninvited, interfering, unexpected, anomalous, aberrant, implausible, unsettling, pre-reflective, seemingly insane and immoral, recalcitrant, insurrectional, revolutionary, creative, foreign, wonderful, mysterious, miraculous, and menacing—and more.

Because immediate experience is defined in these ways, this field's contents and logics are defamiliarizing. Self, other, thing, nature, world, and real appear in strange new ways in this domain. Moreover, immediacy is dangerous. Immediacy can threaten and problematize tightly held forms of psychological, social, and philosophical existence. I have tried in the chapters to show how immediate experience threatens stable and often dear forms of human life because the momentums and deliverances of immediate experience defy and undermine the power of several central and defensive illusory projects to which human existence often commits itself. Immediate emotional and desiderative experience challenges any project to attain an always settled, consistent, and coherent form of psychological life; immediate intersubjective experience troubles any attempt to possess an always permanently entrenched, familiar, and rewarded form of social life; and immediate perceptual experience critiques any effort to have an always clear, indubitable, and foundationalist form of philosophical life. Deeply cherished assumptions about the interior psyche's virtue and coherence, the social self's identity and essence, and the epistemic mind's certainty and reach find themselves upended. An existential revolution in human life in the direction of embracing immediate experience is indeed dangerous—as has become clear, I hope, as the arguments and interpretations of this book have unfolded—and embracing immediate experience can seem like a painful prospect. But, we have also seen how Freud, Woolf, and Merleau-Ponty all believed that immediate experience might actually be most painful, even most dangerous, when it remains unembraced.

Beyond Reflection and Description: The Ethics of Immediacy

Whether they used standard phenomenological terminology or not, Freud's, Woolf's, and Merleau-Ponty's work was phenomenological. They reflected upon the unique region of human existence that is immediate experience as dangerous and attempted to delineate this region's contents and logics.[1] At this level alone, their work is fascinating.

The phenomenological work of these writers can also be interpreted as a sign of a historically and sociologically significant shift in human life. In this framework, their work expressed an existential revolution in

European society. We remember that, in an existential revolution, one conception of human flourishing gives way to a different conception.[2] In this shift, the value of different forms of lived experience changes. Across society, once privileged kinds of experience diminish in value, then denigrated types of experience increase in value. So, in this way of reading them, Freud's, Woolf's, and Merleau-Ponty's work signaled an historical sea change in how people in Europe understood themselves between roughly 1895 and 1945. The region of immediate experience, which had always existed in human life in some inchoate way, increased in value and purchase. The sea change was revolutionary because, historically speaking, the realm of immediacy had often been seen in a negative light. This experience, in contents and forms, was thought to endanger moral virtue, social stability, and certain knowledge. So, figures such as Plato and Kant believed that human flourishing required immediate experience to be dismissed, repressed, and at best, disciplined and reconstructed in light of another more valuable kind of experience such as religious or rational experience. But Freud, Merleau-Ponty, and Woolf demonstrated that a new way of life was being developed that reversed the traditional denigration of immediate experience and elevated its value to surpass the value of other forms of experience as the primary tool for negotiating psychological, social, and epistemic life.

In other words, their work showed that many Europeans were reimagining—more or less consciously—their idea of human nature and its proper ideals. For Europeans, and the wider western world, the register of immediate experience was coming to stand at the heart of what it means to be human. Historically influential ideals for psychological, social, and philosophical life—which had previously claimed authority to judge and reshape immediate experience—were losing prestige. These ideals included having a perfectly moral, sane, and coherent psychological life; being bound to an unchanging essence of what it means to be a man, woman, worker, or child; and needing to pursue truth in a way that achieves total transparency, objectivity, and certainty. In the Freudian age, however, these ideals were gradually seen as illusions, defending life from the truth and power of immediate experience. Now human life would find its ideals within immediate experience.

We can also interpret the work of Freud, Woolf, and Merleau-Ponty as having an agenda that included but also reached beyond both phenomenological reflection and sociological description. Each of them invited us to turn to immediate experience in a new way—to affirm it rather than to oppose it. We were called to embrace immediate experience in a particular domain—psychological, social, philosophical—more explicitly and with more commitment. The point was for us to lean into the current of immediate thoughts, feelings, desires, and perceptions, to live a life that went with the grain of immediate experience and its logic.

For this reason, it makes sense to interpret Freud, Woolf, and Merleau-Ponty as significant contributors to the formation of an ethics of immediacy. Their work was not only phenomenological or sociological reflection; it was an encouragement to make the momentums, deliverances, and logics of immediate experience normative in psychological health, political and moral action, and knowledge-seeking—in human life at almost every level. Their work advocated the authority of immediacy in psychological, social, and philosophical life. This authority could, if necessary, subordinate the content, pressures, and forms of other kinds of experience in these areas of life.

Freud, Woolf, and Merleau-Ponty made the energies and aspirations of immediate experience into the polestar for human identity and human action. Human life should intentionally and deliberately place immediate experience and its logic at the center of everything it is and everything it does—acknowledging it, welcoming it, learning from it, emphasizing it, and following it. Their work was therapeutic—explicitly in Freud and implicitly in Woolf and Merleau-Ponty.[3]

One other point needs to be briefly made. The ethics of immediacy does not call for a return to naïve or unreconstructed immediate experience itself as it is first given. It is not an attempt to reenter the original brute contents of immediate experience. Instead, the ethics of immediacy invites us to consciously embrace the contents and logics of immediate experience and live into its contents and logics in a self-aware way. Freud, Woolf, and Merleau-Ponty are interested in immediate experience *as it is engaged and claimed* in psychological insight, intersubjective awareness, and reflective knowledge. Immediacy is mediated immediacy.

And this ethics of immediacy was not a way of life for just the cultural elite. This ethics was for everyone. This ethics signaled that Europeans were valuing and embracing—as our authors thought they should—immediate experience in ways both large and small, whether they were psychiatric patients in Vienna, women fighting for the franchise in London, or philosophers contemplating ontology in Paris.

Satisfaction, Virtue, Ideals: The Promise of Immediacy

The work of Freud, Woolf, and Merleau-Ponty also acknowledged the difficulties and dangers of human life that leans into the grain of immediate experience and its logics. They knew that this new form of life can entail neurotic insanity, social instability, and philosophical perplexity and uncertainty. Even so, they summoned us to comport ourselves positively toward immediate experience with all the risks that doing so involves. When immediate experience and its logics are disregarded, diminished, or crushed, human life is stunted and diminished: neurotic pain, social oppression, and philosophical falsehood ensue. When we welcome immediate experience and its logics, psychological, social, and philosophical existence can be reconstructed and renewed in more truthful, authentic, and sometimes more satisfying directions. More psychological health, social vitality, and philosophical truth can ensue. It is not difficult to see that the decision to put immediate experience at the heart of human life is closely connected, for example, with the revolutionary movements for gains in freedom and satisfaction in the lives of the mentally ill, women, workers, people of color, sexual minorities, and the colonialized in Europe and beyond during the rise and reign of the ethics of immediacy—movements whose work continues today. Today the ethics of immediacy is even more influential in moral and political life in the North Atlantic world—and beyond—than it was in the first half of the last century in Vienna, Bloomsbury, and Paris. Indeed, the way that humans in contemporary Western culture negotiate contested questions of identity, morality, and politics may be incomprehensible outside the horizon of the Freudian age, and outside the ethics of immediacy it identified and advanced. In many areas, the Freudian age is far from over.

In these ways, we can see how the turn to the ethics of immediacy was also, at least in some ways, a turn to virtue. Immediate experience was historically considered a realm of vice, irrational and immoral instinct, and epistemic illusion. To be morally good, life had to resist this realm. Yet Freud, Woolf, and Merleau-Ponty unveil the realm of immediacy as the source, when we embrace it, of more rational and virtuous action and more truthful knowing. For Freud, living into psychological immediacy and its logic frees up energy and space to live a moral life; for Woolf, living into intersubjective immediacy and its logic promotes a social world with more justice, equality, freedom, and dignity; for Merleau-Ponty, living into philosophical immediacy and its logic allows the philosopher to know the truth of the world more genuinely.[4] The turn to the ethics of immediacy can usher in a more—not less—moral life.

Another way to describe the radical shift found in Freud, Woolf, and Merleau-Ponty is to focus on the language of ideals. For a long time, immediate experience had suffered the judgment of ideals outside itself—ideals of the psyche like sanity and coherence, ideals of sociality like the teleological essences of genders, and ideals of knowledge like transparency and certainty. These ideals demanded that immediate experience and its logics be ignored, suppressed, negated, or reconstructed if human thriving was to be possible. The irony was that these ideals and their judgment did not protect psychological, social, or philosophical thriving; they attacked and undermined the possibility of thriving in these areas. Thus Freud, Woolf, and Merleau-Ponty worked to therapeutically dethrone and dismantle the various misguided ideals that were having unsalutary effects in psychological, social, and philosophical life, ideals such as the defensive illusions that psyches must be moral, social identities must be immutable, and knowledges must be metaphysical, certain, and total. These writers elevated immediate experience and its logics to be the new ideal governing the way we should engage self, other, nature, and world emotionally, intersubjectively, and reflectively. The truth and value of immediate experience were seen as truer and more valuable than the truth or value of any ideal external to immediate experience that would seek to deny or vitiate immediate experience. Instead of immediate experience being judged by ideals external to it, ideals for human life—what human beings are, how society is supposed to work, how knowledge functions—now have to align with the register of immediate experience, its logics, and its teleologies.

In sum, Freud, Woolf, and Merleau-Ponty shared a faith that a life committed to immediate experience without defenses (or at least with fewer of them) and without ideals external to immediate experience (or at least fewer of them) is not only possible but desirable for human thriving. In promoting moral goodness and desiderative satisfaction, life that leans into immediate experience and its logics is richer than life that does not. And, even where leaning into immediate experience and its logics does not directly lead to more obvious forms of human thriving, these writers believed that embracing immediate experience and its logics would always therapeutically expand and deepen the possibilities and realities of human existence. Embracing immediate experience fosters a fuller human life that contains more suffering and more joy—a life that is more alive, a life that has more life.[5] For these reasons, immediate experience and its logic (which has always been inchoately with us) should provide the deepest, most authentic, most enriching center from which humans could live; it should constitute the main compass orienting human identity, meaning, and action. For Freud, Woolf, and Merleau-Ponty, the ethics of immediacy is an ethics human life should welcome and pursue.

Freud and Beyond: Intellectual and Existential Revolutions

After Freud died in 1939, W. H. Auden famously wrote that he was "no more a person / now but a whole climate of opinion."[6] This climate of opinion—which in this project we call "the Freudian age"—was focused on the ethics of immediacy, with all its threat and promise, and it had begun even before Freud died. The climate of opinion was revolutionary, and the revolution took two forms. One was intellectual; one was existential.

Intellectually speaking, Freud's psychoanalysis created a theoretical atmosphere. Freud's focus on immediate experience and its logic opened a theoretical horizon in which others could also reckon with the same omnipresent, yet historically unacknowledged and denigrated, phenomenon. Virginia Woolf and Maurice Merleau-Ponty were two such figures who worked, more or less consciously, within the horizon Freud created. To fully understand the significance of their engagement with lived experience, their work needs to be contextualized in the horizon of immediacy Freud opened. Even so, it is far from the case that Woolf or Merleau-Ponty merely reiterated Freudian ideas about immediate experience. Rather, they creatively unfolded and extended the spirit of Freud's focus on immediate experience, its logic, and its place in psychological life by focusing on how immediate experience is also at play in social and philosophical life. In this way, Freud's early psychoanalysis embodied and set a pattern for an exciting period in intellectual history to take place, a period in which figures from diverse disciplines (psychology, literature, philosophy) and approaches (psychoanalysis, modernism, phenomenology) all converged on a project to encourage us to intentionally value the dangerous experience that is immediate experience, to embrace the hazards and promises this experience offers. In this project, Woolf and Merleau-Ponty followed Freud, but they did so in ways beyond what Freud himself had imagined or anticipated. Their work showed that Freud may have had one of the first words about the phenomenon of immediate experience, but certainly not the only word or the last.[7]

Freud's work expressed a climate of opinion that referred to an existential atmosphere gaining ground in European life in the first half of the twentieth century. Yet Freud did not singlehandedly express or define this atmosphere. Instead, his work inaugurated an existential mood or atmosphere whose reality and purchase Woolf and Merleau-Ponty, in their unique ways, further advanced in realms beyond psychological life. The texts of Freud, Woolf, and Merleau-Ponty were signs of a sea change in the existential atmosphere of European life in the first half of the twentieth century.

Their works neither initiated nor concluded the existential revolution of the Freudian age; they stood in the middle of it. Inheriting the inchoate momentums of the new existential revolution and developing its latent possibilities, their work expressed what had already begun in European life, articulated new dimensions of the structure of this reorientation, and deepened European life's awareness of and participation in its newfound existential modus vivendi of living into immediacy and its logic. The work of Freud, Woolf, and Merleau-Ponty were signs of a transformation in European life concerning what it means to be a human being in the world. As manifested in their writings, human life was coming to take on a new qualitative tone and feel as immediate experience was coming to be given in a new way as the most valuable kind of experience in human life.

Hermeneutics: Interpreting Life, Interpreting Texts

Is there a register of immediate experience in human life whose insistences and logics are simply waiting to be embraced or refused in psychological, social, or philosophical life? Concerning this issue, someone like Derrida has encouraged the practice of suspicion with regard to stories of immediacy or presence: to his mind, nothing is simply or directly present; nothing is unmediated in some way.[8] If we attend to it carefully enough, we will see that every immediacy is somehow mediated. There is no pure immediate experience with which human life can come into complete contact.

Derrida could criticize Husserl for believing that phenomenological reflection and representation could capture lived experience in its entire presence and immediacy, but he would have a harder time criticizing Merleau-Ponty for the same reason.[9] For Merleau-Ponty, lived experience, including immediate experience, is never simply reflectively represented: "Philosophy is not the reflection of a preexisting truth, but, like art, the act of bringing truth into being" (*PhP-CS*, xxiii). Philosophy's task is "to express immediate experience."[10] Immediate perceptual experience and its logic, for Merleau-Ponty, cannot be simply reported or reiterated by the mind. Instead, for him, the work of reflection on and representation of experience is expressive. To say that phenomenology is the work of expression is to say that it is neither mirror nor fiction.

Merleau-Ponty loved the French impressionists and post-impressionists for just this reason: their paintings do not try to mirror the world in a photographic way like the works of someone like Canaletto, but neither do they try to invent images that are bizarrely disconnected from ordinary experience like the works of someone like Salvador Dalí.[11] Monet and Cézanne painted cathedrals, haystacks, mountains, fruit, and tables: their paintings were mimetic without being copies, were imaginative without being inventive. Their paintings gave a kind of interpretation of their perceptual experience, a perceptual experience that is only accessible through the mediation of their painterly expression. Similarly, phenomenological philosophy for Merleau-Ponty expressed the truth of immediate perceptual experience: its representation of immediate experience was not simply a reflection of something preexisting the representation, nor was its representation an entirely constructed picture of this experience with no connection to anything that preexisted it.

Merleau-Ponty's work shows that Freud, Woolf, and Merleau-Ponty did not discover the realm of immediate experience, but neither did they invent this realm: they expressed it and imagined it in the form of interpretations of human life and lived experience. The very idea that there is a realm of immediacy to which human life must comport itself in one way or another—affirming it or trying to negate it—is itself the result of an act of theoretical imagination. The variety of experiences—ratiocinative, emotional, religious, immediate—are not just readymade and waiting to be valued or not. The very terms in which these different kinds of experience are perceived and classed depend upon their being understood and engaged in specific ways. We only have immediate experience within the ways we comport ourselves to it.

Yet, at the same time, whatever experience is identified, it is a case of imagination and interpretation responding to something that preexists them. Do immediacy and its vicissitudes precede their reflective articulation? Yes. Does the full experience of immediacy follow only upon our comportment to immediacy? Yes. A specific theoretical hermeneutic makes it possible to see that there is the phenomenon of immediate experience in the first place, yet without some intuitive sense that there is something identifiable as the phenomenon of immediate experience that exists before it is theoretically taken up we would have a difficult time accounting for any turn of attention in its direction. It is a kind of hermeneutical circle.

The idea that the human being is caught in the dilemmas of having immediate experience and having to negotiate it is not the only hermeneutic that can be used to read the human condition and the complicated phenomena of its lived experience. But this hermeneutic is one way of reading the human condition and its lived experience; it is a way that can be generative; it is a way that can disclose something fundamental about human existence, its challenges, and its possibilities. Merleau-Ponty wrote: "Human life confronts itself from one side of the globe to the other and speaks to itself in its entirety through books and culture."[12] Any way in which human life speaks to itself about itself and its experience will not be the only way. But through the books of Freud, Woolf, and Merleau-Ponty, many readers would say that human life was undoubtedly speaking to itself in a way that is both fascinating and generative.

And the story in this book about the meaning of the texts of Freud, Woolf, and Merleau-Ponty and about the existential atmosphere and revolution these texts reveal is not the only story that could be told about the connections between them or the transformations in human existence and experience their works defined and encouraged. Instead, this book is one possible story of the meaning and significance of the authors explored in these pages—an expression of expressions, if you will. And the author hopes that this expression itself, this possible reading, has proved interesting and generative.[13]

Dangerous Experience: Past, Present, Future

Freud's early focus on immediate experience and the ways human life defends against it inaugurated a process of encouraging Europeans to reckon with the omnipresent yet historically unacknowledged and denigrated phenomena of immediate experience and its logic. Freud's achievement was to show how human life has traditionally seen this realm of experience as profoundly threatening and has defensively taken up various purportedly self-protective strategies that keep us at a distance from it. Yet Freud also showed how holding to these defensive strategies constrains and diminishes human reality and its possibilities. He believed that by renouncing our defensive strategies, ideals, and illusions, we could more deeply live out the whole gamut of our humanity.

Thus, Freud's writings, and the writings of Woolf and Merleau-Ponty in his wake, signaled a fundamental transformation in how self and world were experienced in European culture in the first half of the twentieth century. In this way, their works were therapeutic—and they remain therapeutic. They show the advent of a new way of understanding and living out human existence, and they summon their readers to embrace this new transformed sense of what it means to be human. Freud, Woolf, and Merleau-Ponty pushed their readers to participate in the register of immediate experience intentionally, to move it and its sometimes difficult logics self-consciously to the forefront of psychological, social, and philosophical life, to deliberately give the sometimes disturbing deliverances and momentums of this register of experience a privileged place in their understanding of interior, intersubjective, and ontological reality. Their ethics encouraged readers to situate immediate experience at the center of what it means to be human. Although they knew that such a center could be dangerously unsettling for human life in various ways, they wagered that it was ultimately a profoundly enriching center from which humans can and should live. Freud, Woolf, and Merleau-Ponty articulated and encouraged what we have called an ethics of immediacy, and their texts are something like spiritual exercises helping readers begin to practice this ethics.

This ethics consists of a way of life—psychological, social, and philosophical—that is committed to embracing the contents and currents of immediate experience and its logics rather than to refusing and suppressing them. This way of life is devoted to valuing immediate experience and its logics positively rather than to denigrating it and its logics as evil or base. It is inclined to seeing immediate experience and its logics as a fundamental and preeminent source for fashioning identity and existence psychologically, socially, and philosophically, rather than to seeing it and its logics as a peripheral, destructive, or insignificant dimension of the human adventure.

Yet in this book my interest in the existential revolution of the ethics of immediacy has never been only historical. My interest is also in the contemporary relevance of this ethics. What this project has called the Freudian age was not just a moment of the past that is over now.

In the wake of their work, the ethics that Freud, Woolf, and Merleau-Ponty articulated and recommended gained purchase that became almost undeniable and momentum that became virtually unstoppable. In Europe and almost everywhere, the commitment to the ethics of immediacy is stronger today than it was when they wrote. In essence, the Freudian age and its ethics of immediacy remain with us today. It is the existential atmosphere that provides much of the air we breathe as we fashion identities, the horizon that gives the light in which we see how to make moral decisions, the framework within whose terms we live with our own minds, with others, and with reality at the deepest and broadest levels. Whereas once it was held to be dangerous to accept immediate experience, now it is seen as hazardous not to do so; suppressing immediate experience is now perceived as often destructive of human thriving and authenticity. The ethics of immediacy is not just an historical artifact; it is a constructive proposal to orient many aspects of human life around immediate experience. Hence my attempt to offer, through an investigation of the history explored in this book, a constructive reflection on the significance and power of immediate experience and the possibility of the kind of human life that takes this experience seriously.

Yet we should not forget that immediate experience, even when we comport ourselves to it positively rather than negatively, remains a dangerous kind of experience—the promise it offers to human life does not cancel out the hazards it poses. Leaning into immediate experience and its logics fosters unsettled, conscious, creative, wondering life but is, by definition, difficult and disturbing. Life will probably always struggle to embrace this register. After all, if immediacy and its logics were easy to affirm, Freud, Woolf, and Merleau-Ponty would not have needed to develop an ethics that recommends embracing this kind of experience and its logics.

Nor is it clear that immediate experience and its logics should provide human life with its sole resource and compass for orienting psychological, social, and philosophical existence. It may remain the case that the data, drives, and logics of immediate experience can be destructive as well as constructive, can be the nemeses of authenticity, virtue, and truthfulness as well as their support. Even with its manifest benefits, an unconditional affirmation of immediate experience might pose problems.

One of the remaining issues to ponder about the ethics of immediacy is whether there are limits to the respect we should give immediate experience to found and guide human existence. Are there ways in which immediacy and its logics need to remain open to judgment if human life is to thrive, find satisfaction, practice virtue, and embody authenticity and truthfulness? Case-by-case judgment about when, where, and how to listen to the lead of immediate experience may remain necessary.

Yet even if some ambivalence remains about the value of the ethics of immediacy, there are powerful reasons to celebrate the ascendance of the ethics in Europe and beyond. We must be mindful of the psychological and social suffering and the philosophical untruth that came from the ways in the past that immediate experience and its logics were put under judgment. For these reasons, the ethics of immediacy should have a fundamental role in human self-understanding, identity-fashioning, decision-making, and knowing.

Perhaps the crucial point to remember from this discussion is that human life will truthfully and authentically engage self, other, thing, world, and real only when immediate experience in its many forms receives its due, when human life recognizes, attends to, and respects this experience and its logics as a central dimension of its existence and a valuable source of motivation and even wisdom. The fundamental lesson of the Freudian age's ethics of immediacy is its claim that human life must be aware of, live with, and learn from immediate experience. In this ethics, human life is called to welcome the register of spontaneous, unexpected, unplanned experience in which human life always already finds itself. Human life is invited to embrace this experience that can be anomalous, insane, amoral, incoherent, recalcitrant, mysterious, miraculous, menacing, and defamiliarizing. Immediate experience can be dangerous. Yet this register of experience, this ethics claims, is a dimension of human life that is as real and valuable as any other dimension—perhaps one of the most real and valuable, maybe the most real and valuable. In Freud, Woolf, and Merleau-Ponty, immediate experience with its insistences and logics found its place as a dimension that is now seen as being an essential and constructive dimension of what it means to be human. As such, studying the ethics of immediacy in the Freudian age will never be a topic of just historical interest, theoretical interest, or even contemporary sociological interest. Reflecting on the ethics of immediacy, and considering whether to live a way of life that is somehow committed to this ethics, will always be a personal task as well.

NOTES

Introduction

1   I take the language of an "almost tactile sense" from Michael Rosenthal's remark that Virginia Woolf's *To the Lighthouse* does much "to produce for the reader an almost tactile sense of felt experience." See Michael Rosenthal, *Virginia Woolf* (New York: Columbia, 1979), 104–5.
2   See Charles Taylor and Hubert Dreyfus, *Retrieving Realism* (Cambridge, MA: Harvard University Press, 2015), chapter 5.
3   The concept, phenomenon, and problem of immediacy, in different forms, has been present for centuries, and probably millennia, in Western philosophy. Some interesting diverse examples are Rousseau's promotion of spontaneity in *Émile*, Fichte's meditation on the feeling of necessity in the "Introduction to the *Wissenschaftslehre*," Hegel's discussion of sense-certainty in *Phenomenology of Spirit*, and Kierkegaard's account of the aesthetic in *Either-Or*. It would be an interesting project to finely trace the relationship of the different accounts of immediacy in these texts to Freud's account, but that is not the project of this book. In the phenomenological tradition itself, the language of immediacy is already found in Husserl. See, for example, Edmund Husserl, *Ideas Pertaining to A Pure Phenomenology and to a Phenomenological Philosophy*, First Book: *General Introduction to a Pure Phenomenology*, trans. F. Kersten (The Hague: Martinus Nijhoff Publishers, 1983), 51. The phenomenological concept and language of "immediate experience" is found in Merleau-Ponty's *Phenomenology of Perception*. See Maurice Merleau-Ponty, *Phenomenology of Perception*, trans. Donald A. Landes (New York: Routledge, 2012), 60. The third chapter of this book will be dedicated to parsing out Merleau-Ponty's conception of immediate experience. In the literature composed after the work of the founders of phenomenology, my project is not the first or only philosophical book to investigate the phenomenon of immediate experience and the issue of human life coming to terms with it. One study that I discovered after finalizing my manuscript is Hermann Schmitz, *New Phenomenology: A Brief Introduction*, trans. Rudolf Owen Müllan with support from Martin Bastert (Milan: Mimesis International Press, 2019). Schmitz's book focuses on the reality of spontaneous, involuntary, sudden, and immediate affective experience and on the nature of freedom vis-à-vis this experience. His final concern in his book seems to be an argument for a vision of the nature of freedom as the personal embrace of the immediate individual or social affective states—he calls them "atmospheres"—in which one finds oneself living. The larger teloi of his

focus on freedom seems to be a defense of the fact that human action truly makes a difference to reality and that therefore human life is desirable and worth living as well as an insistence that this conception of freedom can undergird a conception of moral responsibility that also justifies retribution against wrongdoers. Another study that I did not discover before finalizing my manuscript that also explores immediate experience is Charles E. Scott, *Boundaries in Mind: A Study of Immediate Awareness Based on Psychotherapy* (New York: Crossroad, 1982). From a brief perusal of Scott's book, his book and mine may have significant ideas in common.

4 See Eric Hayot, *The Elements of Academic Style: Writing for the Humanities* (New York: Columbia University Press, 2014), chapter 11, for an argument about why introductions do not, and perhaps should not, outline the rest of the book in detail.

5 The Freud, Woolf, and Merleau-Ponty examined in this book are only one set of possible Freuds, Woolfs, and Merleau-Pontys. The meaning of a text is generated at the nexus of the life and mind of the author, the meanings of the words at the time the author put them down, the ways the author chafed at and developed those meanings, the life and mind of the text's reader, the meanings the words in the texts have come to have in a later historical moment, and more. So I will try to avoid clunkily saying "Freud, as I read him ..." or "Woolf as I take her to say" or "Merleau-Ponty's philosophy, as interpreted here" and simply say "Freud wrote" or "Woolf thought" or "Merleau-Ponty believed," and so on. I simply want to state that I am not naïve about such a way of putting matters.

6 I follow Bernard Williams in making a distinction between ethics and morality. The ethical life is something everyone lives; it is a choice of and a living out of a vision of the meaning and purpose of life; the moral life is one way in which the meaning and purpose of human existence can be conceived. A way of life can be devoted to virtue, duty, holiness, and so on, but an ethical life does not have to be, as we can witness in writers like the Marquis de Sade, Nietzsche, or Foucault, all of whom sought to live and think ethically but not necessarily morally. See Bernard Williams, *Ethics and the Limits of Philosophy* (Cambridge, MA: Harvard University Press, 1985).

7 Pierre Hadot also shows that this conception of ethics is more ancient than a program of ethics that deals only with principles or judgments about good and evil, virtue and vice, duty and transgression, and so on. See Pierre Hadot, *Philosophy as a Way of Life*, trans. Michael Chase and ed. Arnold I. Davidson (Oxford: Blackwell, 1995).

Chapter 1

1 Defined in this way, a phenomenological investigation does not necessarily have to closely follow a rigorous Husserlian method, which includes procedures like the epoché, transcendental reduction, eidetic reduction, and so on.

2. Josef Breuer and Sigmund Freud, *Studies on Hysteria*, trans. and ed. James Strachey (New York: Basic Books, 2000), 4. I will give further citations parenthetically in the text. This volume is an American version of James Strachey, *The Standard Edition of the Complete Psychological Works of Sigmund Freud, Volume II (1893–1895): Studies on Hysteria* (London: Hogarth Press and the Institute of Psychoanalysis, 1955).

3. Anticipation, a phenomenologist like Edmund Husserl holds, is a necessary structure of experience. One version of anticipation is what Husserl calls "protention." See Edmund Husserl, *The Phenomenology of Internal Time-Consciousness*, trans. James S. Churchill (Bloomington, IN: Indiana University Press, 1964). I suggest that, just as anticipation is a constitutive element of human experience, so is the thwarting of what is anticipated by advents of the anomalous.

4. Jacques Derrida has called into question the very idea that a strict distinction can be made between the original and the derivative (in his terms between speech and writing) since the derivative always haunts the original from within. I do not mean to challenge Derrida's point, only to say that, somewhat phenomenologically, Freud is describing an experiential process in which it does make sense to speak of a first experience and then a second experience, which is dependent upon, subsequent to, and derivative from the first as a defense against it. So when I speak of immediate experience, I am not claiming that it is an absolute ur-region separate from language, history, culture, and so on. I claim only that, in many experiential situations, certain experiences (or certain modes of experience) precede others, temporally, that the former are more passively undergone than the latter, that the former are unexpected and unsummoned. Immediate experience is also experience that becomes mediated; non-immediate experience is experience that mediates. For a famous example of Derrida's approach to this topic, see his famous discussion "Plato's Pharmacy" in his *Dissemination*, trans. Barbara Johnson (Chicago, IL: University of Chicago Press, 1981), 61–171.

5. Adam Phillips, *Becoming Freud: The Making of a Psychoanalyst* (New Haven, CT: Yale University Press, 2014), 9, 7.

6. Wiktionary contributors, "good," *Wiktionary, The Free Dictionary*, https://en.wiktionary.org/w/index.php?title=good&oldid=60469678 (accessed October 9, 2020); Wiktionary contributors, "evil," *Wiktionary, The Free Dictionary*, https://en.wiktionary.org/w/index.php?title=evil&oldid=60469514 (accessed October 9, 2020).

7. Donnel Stern, *Relational Freedom: Emergent Properties of the Interpersonal Field* (New York: Routledge, 2015), 108. Stern speaks of "unbidden experience" specifically in the context of the analyst's self-monitoring of their own countertransference. Stern believes that the analyst needs to welcome just these seemingly chance moments of their own psychological life because these moments give unique information, unavailable elsewhere, which can help the analyst understand and help their patients. Even so, I would hope that Stern would agree that "unbiddenness" is a structural essence of lived experience in psychological life as such.

8   See Jonathan Lear, *Happiness, Death, and the Remainder of Life* (Cambridge, MA: Harvard University Press, 2002). Lear is speaking about analysands who find themselves perceiving themselves, their analyst, and their world in ways that are extremely surprising to themselves because they seem irregular. Yet, Lear believes, the openness to learning from just these ateleological moments is where there is potential healing from neurotic pain. In fact, for Lear, an ateleological moment of psychological experience, when embraced, can become the cornerstone for a radical and ameliorating restructuring of an individual's psychological existence, a transformation for the better of their lived experience of self and world. Lear writes about an analytic patient of his who lived in what he calls "a disappointing world." He discusses this particular patient—her entrapment in neurosis and her journey out of it through noticing and appropriating moments of her psychological experience that failed to line up with her ordinary disappointing experiential world—in several of his books, including in the second chapter of his *Happiness, Death, and the Remainder of Life*.

Chapter 2

1   See Jonathan Lear, *Freud*, 2nd ed. (New York: Routledge, 2015), especially the introduction. My discussion of Freud in this chapter is significantly indebted to Lear's work.
2   Laplanche writes: "in the period before 1897 and for a long time afterward, the unconscious will be considered as essentially the result of repression." Jean Laplanche, "The Unfinished Copernican Revolution," in Luke Thurston, trans., Jean Laplanche, *Essays on Otherness* (London: Routledge, 1999), 63.
3   Immediacy is not a foreign concept in psychoanalysis—it has been worked on a great deal, both implicitly and explicitly. One area where the concept has had purchase is in Heinz Kohut's recommendation of "experience-near" interpretations that are more therapeutically useful for the analysand. See Heinz Kohut, *The Restoration of the Self* (New York: International Universities Press, 1971). Immediacy has also been the focus of thought in the Lacanian tradition with its focus on the barriers to, and problems with, making contact with immediacy as it found in, for example, "the Thing" and "the Real." The mediations of "the Imaginary" and "the Symbolic" (in fact, "Symbolic Castration") take the human subject outside of any realm of pure immediacy and allow us to become a subject. Too much uninterrupted proximity to the "Thing" (for example, "the mother" is too immediately present in the psyche or the fragmented, chaotic "Real" is experienced too immediately) means that the distanciating processes of Imaginary and Symbolic mediation have

never taken place—which can entail profound anxiety and psychosis. That is, it is being in touch with immediacy, or desiring to be, and insisting on being in touch with it, that is the problem. See, for example, the many discussions of mediation throughout Jacques Lacan, *Écrits*, ed. and trans. Bruce Fink, in collaboration with Héloïse Fink and Russell Grigg (New York: Norton, 2006) and the discussion of "the Thing" in Jacques Lacan, *Anxiety: The Seminar of Jacques Lacan—Book X*, ed. Jacques-Alain Miller and trans. A. R. Price (Malden, MA: Polity, 2014). In addition, the post-Lacanian Julia Kristeva has written that the depressive is the person who refuses to enter a symbolic realm that would, through its mediations, distance the mourner from the immediacy of the internal lost and mourned-for object. See Julia Kristeva, *Black Sun*, trans. Leon S. Roudiez (New York: Columbia University Press, 1989).

4 Another caveat. Some might think it odd that this book is based on my decision to phenomenologically conceive Freud's work to be focused on immediate experience. There are many Freuds, of course, and every reading of Freud focuses on specific ideas and specific texts from his oeuvre. My reading of Freud results from how I emphasize specific texts, a specific period, and specific dimensions of Freud's work. Another reader of Freud might develop a conception of his work based on the later Freud (e.g., the Freud of the structural theory of the 1920s in which almost the entire mental apparatus is unconscious), while I focus in my project on the earlier and more experience-near Freud (e.g., the Freud of the investigations into hysteria of the 1890s). The latter Freud is interested in mental life's conscious immediate experience in all its vicissitudes—one of which is the possibility that this conscious content is repressed, becomes unconscious, and wreaks symptomatic havoc in human life. I have evoked this early Freud because he gives one of the first full articulations of human life's revolutionary turn to immediate experience. I certainly do not intend this chapter to suggest that my way of reading Freud is the only way to read him. Nor do I claim that the dimensions of his thought, the texts, and the time period I explore in the book are the only ones that are of interest in our study of Freud. The later Freud of the structural theory is just as Freudian as the early Freud of immediate experience. Moreover, this later Freud is equally interesting, albeit for different reasons.

5 Both texts are found in Breuer and Freud, *Studies on Hysteria*, 4. I will give further citations parenthetically in the text. This volume is an American version of Strachey, *The Standard Edition of the Complete Psychological Works of Sigmund Freud, Volume II (1893–1895)*. My focus is on the theory and clinical material from *Studies on Hysteria*, but much of the same ground is covered also in three other famous early papers: "The Neuro-Psychoses of Defense," "Further Remarks on the Neuro-Psychoses of Defense," and "Sexuality in the Aetiology of the Neuroses." These papers are in James Strachey, *The Standard Edition of the Complete*

Psychological Works of Sigmund Freud, Volume III (1893–1899): Early Psycho-Analytic Publications (London: Hogarth Press and the Institute of Psychoanalysis, 1962).

6   To be clear, physical abuse, sexual assault, or war violence trauma are profoundly real, painful, and damaging traumas, but Freud's focus in these texts is on the subjective experiences that can go along with them or that can also happen without them.

7   The rage could never happen unless the young man also felt humiliated, exposed, and shamed in the real intersubjective world. Anger does not come out of nowhere. But in this situation, Freud is interested specifically in the rage as a phenomenon in its own right and not so much its intersubjective genealogy.

8   In this discussion, I am indebted to and drawing upon Charles Taylor's notion of "moral space" in his presentation of a phenomenology of morality in part 1 of his *Sources of the Self: The Making of Modern Identity* (Cambridge, MA: Harvard University Press, 1989), 3–107.

9   I take the language of "neurotic life" from Jonathan Lear.

10 I sympathize with criticisms of notions of mental privacy and interiority that writers such as Wittgenstein have offered. A person's thoughts and feelings are bodily and transparent in many ways; it is difficult to hide the fact that one is deeply sad or extremely happy: "The body is the best picture of the soul." Wittgenstein, *Philosophical Investigations*, 3rd ed., trans. G. E. M. Anscombe (Oxford: Blackwell, 1958), Part II, 178. At the same time, many human thoughts and feelings, perhaps especially in the realm of fantasy and reverie, are not always transparently available to public view.

11 I am giving "spontaneity" a sense different from that which Immanuel Kant famously gave it in his discussion of the mind's formation of concepts. Broadly speaking, for Kant the mind's spontaneity is its freedom vis-à-vis what has been more or less passively received by the mind. The kind of spontaneity I am intending, in contrast, is on the passive and receptive side of the psychological mind and includes internally generated yet unpremeditated content that has arisen suddenly in the mind and has not yet in any way been taken up and mediated by the mind's operations. See Immanuel Kant, *The Critique of Pure Reason*, ed. and trans. Paul Guyer and Allen W. Wood (Cambridge: Cambridge University Press, 1998), 205.

12 Stephen Mitchell and Margaret Black, *Freud and Beyond: A History of Modern Psychoanalytic Thought* (New York: Basic Books, 1995), 118.

13 The following account is also relevant to Freud's understanding of obsessional neurosis and phobia, even as he understood them to be significantly different from hysteria in that they did not concern the lived body in the same way.

14 I do not mean that an emotion like anger is not felt in the body. It is. But there is still a useful distinction to be made between experiencing something like anger, on the one hand, and experiencing something like stomach nausea, on the other. When I speak of "bodily" suffering, I mean the latter.
15 This discussion highlights only one of the ways Freud thought symptoms functioned. Symptoms can also have to do with partial wish fulfillments, self-punishments, and retaliations, and with avoiding consequences. My thanks to Janet Mooney for reminding me of the overdetermination of the symptom.
16 Jonathan Lear discusses how utterance in psychoanalytic treatment is never only objective or dispassionate. See Jonathan Lear, *Therapeutic Action: An Earnest Plea for Irony* (New York: Other Press, 2003), and Jonathan Lear, *A Case for Irony* (Cambridge, MA: Harvard University Press, 2014).
17 The sentence continues: "*and it subjects it to associative correction by introducing it into normal consciousness.*" I am not going to address the issue of associative rectification, which, while important, is not crucial for my overall argument.
18 There are connections here with Jonathan Lear's understanding of how unconscious wishes are not fully formed intelligible wishes—as if the unconscious were a second, fully developed mind underneath the conscious one. See Lear, *Freud*, 2nd ed., ch. 1.
19 As an aside, we might ask two questions. First, is language the only way experience can be expressed and embodied? Or can the play of art and sport, perhaps, be equally effective ways of experiencing our experience? Second, do words have a kind of protective feature? In this framework, words would be a kind of safe way of experiencing experience. By putting my experience into words—by speaking or thinking words as a way of experiencing—I would experience my experience but in a still mediated way. Speech itself would be a sublimation that made it possible for me to experience dangerous experience. Speech lets us experience our experience to a greater degree without defenses, though perhaps still within the medium of what we might call the "defense" of speech that distances us from what can be a psychologically shattering traumatic rawness of what Lacan would call the Real of affective life.
20 Elisabeth has died to some degree too through becoming immobile and corpse-like.
21 A feminist critique could accuse Freud of reading too much into this study. Must Elisabeth be sick because of her singleness? Is this thinking patriarchal? Freud might respond in two ways. First, his understanding depended upon Elisabeth's own self-reporting, which would seem to confirm his interpretation, although questions about whether Elisabeth's suggestibility prompted her to confirm Freud's biases would still remain.

Second, even if Freud misunderstood the details of Elisabeth's illness, his conviction that she is ill because she has repressed some immediate psychological experience would still hold.

22. Freud mentions a wide variety of the forms sex and aggression can take. See Sigmund Freud, *The Psychopathology of Everyday Life*, ed. James Strachey, trans. Alan Tyson (New York: Norton, 1990) for mention of jealousy and ambition (248), guilt (42), hostility (50), shame (112), death wishes toward others (137), exhibitionism (141), sadness (151), self-criticism (217), suicidal death wishes toward oneself (231), homosexuality (253), racism (287), perversion (326), masochism (326), sadism and cruelty (332), pleasure (344), and egotism (352). This volume is an American edition of James Strachey, *The Standard Edition of the Complete Psychological Works of Sigmund Freud, Volume VI (1901): The Psychopathology of Everyday Life* (London: Hogarth Press and the Institute of Psychoanalysis, 1960). Freud gives a few more examples in Sigmund Freud, *The Interpretation of Dreams* (New York: Basic Books, 1955): criminality (94), bisexuality (346), and in his famous Oedipus complex, incestuous wishes (408–10). This volume is an American edition from James Strachey, *The Standard Edition of the Complete Psychological Works of Sigmund Freud, Volume IV (1900): The Interpretation of Dreams (First Part)* (London: Hogarth Press and the Institute of Psychoanalysis, London, 1953) and James Strachey, *The Standard Edition of the Complete Psychological Works of Sigmund Freud, Volume V (1900–1901): The Interpretation of Dreams (Second Part) and On Dreams* (London: Hogarth Press and the Institute of Psychoanalysis, 1953). Freud's thinking here, however, may be culturally determined. In a different culture, it may be kind, pro-social feelings that are anomalous and therefore difficult to handle and repressed. An aggressive person—a person who enjoys being tough, who likes seeing himself as dominant—may resist, even repress, feelings of tenderness, weakness, or sympathy. For neurotics the issue is how their immediate psychological experience conflicts with their hopes for the kind of mind they believe they have and want to have. If the *Iliad's* Achilles is neurotic, his cure will not involve getting more in touch with his aggression—quite the opposite. Erich Fromm's work made this point. See Erich Fromm, *Beyond the Chains of Illusion: My Encounter with Marx and Freud* (New York: Simon and Schuster, 1962). Also see the discussion of this issue in Daniel Burston, *The Legacy of Erich Fromm* (Cambridge, MA: Harvard University Press, 1991), 144–84.

23. Psychotic insanity is the subject of Freud's discussion of the famous case of Judge Schreber. See Sigmund Freud, *The Case of Schreber*, in James Strachey, *The Standard Edition of the Complete Psychological Works of Sigmund Freud, Volume XII (1911–1913): The Case of Schreber, Papers on*

Technique and Other Works (London: Hogarth Press and the Institute of Psychoanalysis, 1958).

24 If the neurotic is, in a way, psychotic, then the psychotic is, in a way, neurotic. The psychotic's wishes, for example, are present not in their original form but in the form of delusions and hallucinations that do not explicitly reveal the story, for delusions and hallucinations distort and reconstruct the story. This reconstruction is itself a kind of symptom.

25 Wiktionary contributors, "Sanus," *Wiktionary, The Free Dictionary*, https://en.wiktionary.org/w/index.php?title=sanus&oldid=58841297 (accessed October 28, 2020),

26 Wiktionary contributors, "Zoen," *Wiktionary, The Free Dictionary*, https://en.wiktionary.org/w/index.php?title=zoen&oldid=60065176 (accessed October 28, 2020).

27 Freud sometimes speaks of the process of conversion involving "the genesis of hysterical symptoms through the conversion of psychical excitations into something physical." Freud and Breuer, *Studies in Hysteria*, 157. This quantitative theory of energy transfer has been judged, even by Freud himself, as a weak part of his early theory.

28 Here we might recall Freud's later notion of the body ego: physical and psychological experiences are in a profound sense convertible.

29 Phillips, *Becoming Freud*, 7, 9. Citations will be given parenthetically in the text.

30 Here Phillips seems to be echoing, in part, the notion of Lacan's imaginary and the need to move beyond it.

31 Again, this pattern holds true for certain kinds of morally determined experiences. For other kinds of experiences, such as trauma, the picture will be more complicated.

32 In biography, but perhaps especially in autobiography, there is the pressure to describe someone's conversion—for example, political or religious—as being in some way an intelligible, even if surprising, development out of what came before in the person's life.

33 Here I have drawn on Google Dictionary but also expanded upon its definitions.

34 There may be similarities here with Hume's discussion of selfhood. See "Of Personal Identity," in book 1, part 4, section 6 of David Hume, *A Treatise of Human Nature*, vol. 1, ed. David Fate Norton (Oxford: Oxford University Press, 2007), 164–71.

35 Incidentally, here we can question Jean Laplanche's claim that Freud wanted to eliminate otherness from psychological life. For Laplanche, Freud's "dominant tendency is always to relativize the discovery and to re-assimilate and reintegrate the alien." See Jean Laplanche, *Essays on Otherness* (New York: Routledge, 1999), 65. On the contrary, we have been seeing just how Freud wants the neurotic to accept that their immediate thinking, feeling, and wishing, in content and form, are always being and

becoming alien—and should be freely allowed the time and space to do so. Freud emphasized how strangeness, difference, and alterity define, in themes and shape, the human mind in its most fundamental, immediate reality. He suggested that the only possible psychological homecoming is to a kind of psychological homelessness, and that the only kind of sense to be made is a kind of nonsense. Here we might also wonder if Lear is quite correct when he says of the psychoanalytic process that "This developing 'self-knowledge' is in and of itself the active, self-conscious unifying of the psyche." See Lear, *Freud*, 2nd ed., 18. It seems rather that the spontaneity of the psyche, its unpredictable spontaneity, seems to be in tension with an uncomplicated sense of its unity and the horizon of memory and anticipation that such unity entails.

36 A marked lack of coherence in parenting behavior, for example, can do profound emotional damage to children.

37 It bears saying that, structurally, Elisabeth is neurotic, not psychotic. Freud often, but not always, upheld a clear distinction between neurosis and psychosis—someone could have one psychic structure or the other but not both. The difference concerns the presence or absence of repression. Neurosis and psychosis both concern the way the individual negotiates the dangerous, insane wishes of immediate psychological experience. The neurotic represses them, and they become unconscious— or differently conscious—and do damage in the form of the symptom, be it hysterical, obsessive, or phobic. The psychotic, however, does not repress these insane desires in a neurotic way; instead, they allow these desires to remain conscious and wreak havoc in a way that can only appear to those around them as delusions and hallucinations. The conclusion is thus that, since analytic treatment aims to abreact repressed psychological content, and repressed content exists only in neurotics, abreaction is not a relevant or effective treatment for psychotics. So the goal is not for Elisabeth to become psychotic as such. To do so is impossible, since she already has a psyche that operates by means of repression, a psychic structure that is by definition neurotic. See Freud, *The Case of Schreber*. While some approaches to psychoanalysis, like the Kleinian and the British Object Relations, have softened the theoretical and therapeutic dividing line between neurosis and psychosis, other schools, like the Lacanian, have vigorously sustained the distinction. For Lacan, once an individual has entered language, the Symbolic, they are neurotically structured forever; repression will always be their tool for managing hazardous desires. See Bruce Fink's discussion of neurosis in chapter 8 of *A Clinical Introduction to Lacanian Psychoanalysis: Theory and Technique* (Cambridge, MA: Harvard University Press, 1997).

38 Freud also speaks of the symptom as symbolic. Elisabeth "had done nothing more or less than look for a *symbolic* expression of her painful

thoughts" and "somatic symptoms of hysteria can be brought about by symbolization of this kind." In other words, "the patient had created ... her functional disorder by means of symbolization." Freud and Breuer, *Studies in Hysteria*, 153, 176.

39 I take the language of "subjectification" from Bruce Fink, *The Lacanian Subject: Between Language and Jouissance* (Princeton, NJ: Princeton University Press, 1995), 63–6, although I do not claim to mean by it the same that he does.

40 Nancy McWilliams, *Psychoanalytic Diagnosis: Understanding Personality Structure in the Clinical Process*, 2nd ed. (New York: Guilford, 2011), 307; Norman O. Brown, *Life against Death: The Psychoanalytic Meaning of History* (Middletown, CT: Wesleyan University Press, 1959).

41 In his later more developed metapsychology Freud will speak of therapeutically lessening the power of the too-strict superego.

42 Janet Mooney has suggested to me that it might be better to say that the symptom is "more tolerable" or "more acceptable" rather than "easier."

43 Elisabeth is going through a process that Jonathan Lear nicely captures in the phrase "Educating oneself to the truth of oneself." This process, he writes, "is not merely a matter of learning new facts about oneself, but is rather the activity of self-consciously appropriating those wishes, efficaciously taking responsibility for them as one's own. It is a matter of actively integrating unfamiliar ways of thinking into self-conscious thinking." By "thinking," Lear does not mean abstract reflection but, rather, all of Elisabeth's strange psychological experiences: thinking and feeling and desiring. See Lear, *Freud*, 2nd ed., 18.

44 Lear, *Therapeutic Action*, 204.

45 In ideal circumstances, Freud might say, a neurotic's joys will be enough of a counterweight to their sufferings to enable them to have, in psychoanalyst David Moore's phrase, "a good-enough life."

46 Freud uses the language of the "fundamental rule" preeminently in the 1913 paper "On Beginning the Treatment," in Strachey, *The Standard Edition of the Complete Psychological Works of Sigmund Freud, Volume XII*, 121–44. The concept is present from the beginning of Freud's work.

47 Freud deserves part of the blame for this understanding, as he sometimes described his work in terms of "detection" and the methods of analytic interpretation as "detective devices." See, for example, the 1906 paper "Psycho-Analysis and the Establishment of the Facts in Legal Proceedings," in James Strachey, *The Standard Edition of the Complete Psychological Works of Sigmund Freud, Volume IX (1906–1908): Jensen's "Gradiva" and Other Works* (London: Hogarth Press and the Institute of Psychoanalysis, 1959), 97–114. The literary critic Peter Brooks has used the hermeneutic of the detective story to interpret Freud's case study of "the Wolf Man," in Peter Brooks, *Reading for the Plot: Design and Intention*

in Narrative (New York: Vintage, 1984), 264–85. Recall also Anton Kris's comment: "I do not picture the analyst as 'curing' the patient or even as 'analysing' the patient. I ascribe such functions to the method of free association." See Anton Kris, *Free Association: Method and Process*, rev. ed. (Hillsdale, NJ: Analytic Press, 1996), 30.

48 Quoted in Kris, *Free Association*, xv.
49 See Mark Edmundson, *Towards Reading Freud: Self-Creation in Milton, Wordsworth, Emerson, and Sigmund Freud* (Chicago, IL: University of Chicago Press, 1990).
50 Quoted in Adam Phillips, *On Flirtation* (Cambridge, MA: Harvard University Press, 1994), 67.
51 Another cultural myth is that Freud's neurotic is cured by having a single "Aha!" moment of remembering a single memory. This picture of Freud's therapeutic action is largely mythical and depends upon a superficial reading of isolated passages of his writings, taken out of context.
52 Again, one possibility—sometimes Freud's own—is to conceive of Freud as a storyteller, whose writings fall into the genre of the detective narrative, the line of interpretation of Freud's case studies pursued by Brooks.
53 Hadot's path-breaking work argues that ancient philosophical writers such as Plotinus, Marcus Aurelius, Sextus Empiricus, and Saint Augustine did not write philosophy in the same way that many modern philosophers do. For many modern writers, philosophy aims at disinterested truths that are knowable at a cognitive or discursive level—be they truths about the nature of knowledge, morality, aesthetics, or metaphysics. The philosopher's job is *knowing*, which is taken to be something of value in its own right. Hadot thinks that when we assume the ancients were also interested in disinterested knowledge for its own sake, we do them an injustice. The Hellenistic philosophers were not first of all engaged in the disinterested work of discovering truths to be only cognitively apprehended. Rather, they were offering visions of what they took to be new and more salutary paths of life. Hadot writes, "The Stoics, for instance, declared explicitly that philosophy, for them, was an exercise. In their view, philosophy did not consist in teaching an abstract theory—much less in the exegesis of texts—but rather in the art of living .... The philosophical act is not situated merely on the cognitive level, but on that of the self and of being. It is a progress which causes us to *be* more fully, and makes us better. It is a conversion which turns our entire life upside down, changing the life of the person who goes through it." Hadot, *Philosophy as a Way of Life*, 82–3. Hadot believed that twentieth-century philosophers like Ludwig Wittgenstein and Michel Foucault also conceived and practiced philosophy in this way.
54 Wiktionary contributors, "psychosis," *Wiktionary, The Free Dictionary*, https://en.wiktionary.org/w/index.php?title=psychosis&oldid=59403337

(accessed November 6, 2020); Wiktionary contributors, "-osis," *Wiktionary, The Free Dictionary,* https://en.wiktionary.org/w/index.php?title=-osis&oldid=59718351 (accessed November 6, 2020).

55 The poem with these words, "Patmos," has become famous through Heidegger's admiration of it and has been translated into English by many translators in many ways.

Chapter 3

1 Virginia Woolf, *The Essays of Virginia Woolf: 1919-1924,* ed. Andrew McNeillie (New York: Harcourt Brace Jovanovich, 1988), 195-8. Virginia Woolf's nonfiction explored in this chapter is found in the third and fourth volumes of her criticism: Virginia Woolf, *The Essays of Virginia Woolf: 1919-1924,* and Virginia Woolf, *The Essays of Virginia Woolf: 1925-1928,* ed. Andrew McNeillie (London: Hogarth Press, 1984). I will give references parenthetically in the text with volume and page numbers.
2 See Phillips, *Becoming Freud,* 18.
3 It can remain useful to make a phenomenological distinction between the world of the text and the world outside it, even if these worlds influence each other and even permeate each other.
4 While the scope of Woolf's claim that Mrs. Brown is indeed human nature may sound strange to contemporary ears (many of us would be more sensitive to the diversity of "meanings" of life, in the plural), she does seem to mean that fiction can investigate and try to represent something essential to the meaning of human life at a universal level.
5 In this chapter I discuss Woolf's understanding of the fiction of her contemporaries; I bracket the question of whether her understanding was fair.
6 See Wikipedia Contributors, "Fictional Character," *Wikipedia, The Free Encyclopedia,* https://simple.wikipedia.org/w/index.php?title=Fictional_character&oldid=7404750 (accessed March 16, 2021).
7 This form of philosophical fiction is not the only form, as we will see.
8 Erich Auerbach, *Mimesis: The Representation of Reality in Western Literature,* trans. Willard R. Trask (Princeton, NJ: Princeton University Press, 1953), 552.
9 Pericles Lewis, *The Cambridge Introduction to Modernism* (New York: Cambridge University Press, 2007), 7.
10 Interiority is a vexed category of human existence, and Woolf is only one player in a twentieth-century movement to exteriorize interiority. The most famous explicit critic of self-contained interiority probably remains Ludwig Wittgenstein. See, for example, Ludwig Wittgenstein, *Philosophical Investigations,* 3rd ed., trans. G. E. M. Anscombe (Oxford: Blackwell, 1958), part 2, 178, and Ludwig Wittgenstein, *Last Writings on*

the *Philosophy of Psychology: The Inner and the Outer*, vol. 2, trans. C. G. Luckhardt and Maximilian A. E. Aue (Oxford: Blackwell, 1982).
11 Sue Roe, "The Impact of Post-Impressionism," in Susan Sellers and Sue Roe, eds., *Cambridge Companion to Virginia Woolf*, 1st ed. (Cambridge: Cambridge University Press, 2000), 165–6.
12 Here I am obviously echoing the ideas in existential phenomenology of the "worlded" and "being-in-the world." For examples, see Martin Heidegger, *Being and Time*, trans. John Macquarrie and Edward Robinson (Oxford: Blackwell, 1962), 12; Jean-Paul Sartre, *Being and Nothingness: A Phenomenological Essay on Ontology*, trans. Hazel E. Barnes (New York: Washington Square Press, 1956); Maurice Merleau-Ponty, *Phenomenology of Perception*, trans. Colin Smith (New York: Routledge and Kegan Paul, 1962), part 3.
13 Auerbach, *Mimesis*, 529.
14 Lewis, *The Cambridge Introduction to Modernism*, xviii, 5.
15 Michael Whitworth, "Virginia Woolf and Modernism," in Sellers and Roe, eds., *Cambridge Companion to Virginia Woolf*, 1st ed., 151.
16 Auerbach, *Mimesis*, 534.
17 The notion and language of "affordances" are found in the work of J. J. Gibson, *The Ecological Approach to Visual Perception* (Boulder, Colorado: Taylor and Francis, 1979).
18 The notion of the underdetermined nature of evidence came to prominence in the work of Quine. See W. V. O. Quine, "Posits and Reality," in *The Ways of Paradox and Other Essays*, 2nd ed. (Cambridge, MA: Harvard University Press, 1955), 246–54.
19 For a sophisticated discussion of the phenomenology of fantasy and imagination, see Edmund Husserl, *Phantasy, Image Consciousness, and Memory (1895–1925)*, trans. John Brough (Dordrecht: Springer, 2005).
20 Roe, "The Impact of Post-Impressionism," 177.
21 There is a vivid parallel, however unwitting on Woolf's part, between her idea of Mrs. Brown's subjectivity and Husserl's idea of subjectivity in his transcendental phenomenology. See, for example, Edmund Husserl, *Cartesian Meditations: An Introduction to Phenomenology*, trans. Dorion Cairns (The Hague: Martinus Nijhoff, 1973).
22 Virginia Woolf, *To the Lighthouse* (New York: Oxford University Press, 1992), 220. Further citations will be given parenthetically in the text.
23 Incidentally, it bears saying that Woolf seems to show Mr. Ramsay doing to his daughter exactly what, mutatis mutandis, the Edwardian authors did to their literary subjects—another example of how the logics of literature and life reflect one another.
24 Even though for Freud immediate psychological experience occurred mainly "in the head," it would have implications for life in the world. A hysteric, once healed, would like Elisabeth von R. enjoy an opportunity

to participate in public life in the world again, an opportunity they lacked when they were caught in the grip of neurosis.
25 Michael Lackey, "Modernist Anti-philosophicalism and Virginia Woolf's Critique of Philosophy," *Journal of Modern Literature* 29, no. 4 (Summer 2006): 87. Lackey's discussion about the broader implications of Woolf's novel, viz. "the philosopher's inability to respect the inner life of another" is on the same page.
26 Rosenthal, *Virginia Woolf*, 103.
27 Michael Whitworth, "Virginia Woolf, Modernism, and Modernity," in Susan Sellers, ed., *Cambridge Companion to Virginia Woolf*, 2nd ed. (Cambridge: Cambridge University Press, 2010), 108.
28 Phillips, *Becoming Freud*, 31, 15, 40.
29 Lackey, "Modernist Anti-philosophicalism and Virginia Woolf's Critique of Philosophy," 94.
30 If attempts at renewal and reformation are thwarted, of course, then revolution may be the next step.

Chapter 4

1 Maurice Merleau-Ponty, "Phenomenology and Psychoanalysis: Preface to Hesnard's *L'Oeuvre de Freud*," in Alden L. Fisher, ed., *The Essential Writings of Merleau-Ponty* (New York: Harcourt, Brace, and World, 1969), 86. I will give further citations parenthetically in the text.
2 Recently, significant work has been done in the relational school of psychoanalysis with Merleau-Ponty. See, e.g., Norman Gabriel, "Beyond 'developmentalism': A relational and embodied approach to young children's development," *Children and Society* 35, no. 1 (January 2021).
3 Citations of Merleau-Ponty's works will be in the text. I draw on two translations of *Phenomenology of Perception*: Maurice Merleau-Ponty, *Phenomenology of Perception*, trans. Colin Smith (New York: Routledge, 2002), cited as "*PhP-CS*," and Maurice Merleau-Ponty, *Phenomenology of Perception*, trans. Donald A. Landes (New York: Routledge, 2012), cited as "*PhP-DL*." Although the focus of my discussion is the famous "Preface" to *Phenomenology of Perception*, I will also draw on the main body of the book. Maurice Merleau-Ponty, "The Primacy of Perception and Its Philosophical Consequences," trans. James M. Edie, in his *The Primacy of Perception: And Other Essays on Phenomenological Psychology, the Philosophy of Art, History and Politics*, trans. James E. Edie et al. (Evanston, IL: Northwestern University Press, 1964) will be cited as "PrP." Maurice Merleau-Ponty, "Cezanne's Doubt," in his *Sense and Non-sense*, trans. Hubert L. Dreyfus and Patricia Allen Dreyfus (Evanston, IL: Northwestern University Press, 1964), will be cited as "CD." Merleau-Ponty's *The World*

of Perception, trans. Oliver Davis (New York: Routledge E-Book, 2004), will be cited as "*WP*."

4 Merleau-Ponty uses the language of "immediacy" in multiple senses, but in this chapter, I focus on what may be the most important sense.

5 See Thomas Nagel, "What Is It Like to Be a Bat?" in his *Mortal Questions* (Cambridge: Cambridge University Press, 1979), 165–80.

6 I am leaving "man" in the quotation because it is the term he used; were he writing today, he would probably use the nongendered word "person" or "human being" instead of "man."

7 In this passage, Merleau-Ponty was focused on the way reflective analysis "works back *toward the subject* as if toward a condition of possibility distinct from our experience." He was concerned particularly with the metaphysics or psychology of the subject of knowledge, but his point applies to any kind of "working back" as explanation.

8 Merleau-Ponty's discussion of empiricism and idealism in *Phenomenology of Perception* is complicated and extensive, and I am only drawing out one dimension of it.

9 In one sense, we have done phenomenology implicitly in the first three chapters of this book. With Merleau-Ponty, we turn to phenomenology performed in an explicit way.

10 My discussion will not engage every dimension of Merleau-Ponty's discussion of the nature of the body-subject. Other aspects—such as his notion of the embodied subject as an "I can" in the world—are fascinating but cannot be dealt with adequately in this project.

11 I saw columbines when I was a child and spent time camping in the Colorado forest, but I pieced together this description from various descriptions of them I found online.

12 Robert Sokolowski's discussions of presence and absence in perception and phenomenology are very helpful in formulating these issues. See, for example, Robert Sokolowski, *Introduction to Phenomenology* (New York: Cambridge University Press, 1999).

13 Donald Landes, *The Merleau-Ponty Dictionary* (New York: Continuum, 2013), 145. I acknowledge my debt to Landes's work as I have sought to understand Merleau-Ponty.

14 Here I am echoing but altering Wilfrid Sellars's famous definition of philosophy's project: "The aim of philosophy, abstractly formulated, is to understand how things in the broadest possible sense of the term hang together in the broadest possible sense of the term." See Wilfrid Sellars, *Science, Perception and Reality* (New York: Humanities Press, 1963), 1.

15 Quoted in Donn Welton, *The Other Husserl: The Horizons of Transcendental Phenomenology* (Bloomington, IN: Indiana University Press, 2001), 343. Welton notes the way that Husserl did not see being as a predicate: "Being itself 'is not a real predicate,' is never itself one of the determinations and is certainly not one of the objects perceived.

But though never apprehended, it is ever delivered in all determinate experience" (88, contents in single quotes are from Husserl). Merleau-Ponty's work shows one way this theme might take shape.

16 Romand Coles, *Self/Power/Other: Political Theory and Dialogical Ethics* (Ithaca, NY: Cornell University Press, 1992), passim. I am deeply indebted to Coles's interpretation of ontology in Merleau-Ponty.

17 Emmanuel Alloa, *Resistance of the Sensible World: An Introduction to Merleau-Ponty*, trans. Jane Marie Todd (New York: Fordham University Press, 2017), 86, also passim.

18 Cf. Hartmut Rosa, *The Uncontrollability of the World*, trans. James C. Wagner (Cambridge: Polity, 2020).

19 Wonder may even be a kind of affective posture. In an unpublished manuscript, Anna Bortolan explores how emotions, including wonder, can play a crucial role in the activities of knowing. I am grateful to Dr. Bortolan for sharing her research with me. Considered in such a framework, Merleau-Ponty may have been in his own way as much concerned with affect as Freud even when he is engaging in ontological reflection. This issue merits further reflection.

20 Virginia Woolf, *To the Lighthouse* (New York: Houghton Mifflin Harcourt, 1989), 202.

21 Iain McGilchrist has shown how the written program for a concert or a written description of a work of art does not replace the music or art but rather supplements and enriches the first-order experience of the music or the painting. See Iain McGilchrist, *The Master and His Emissary: The Divided Brain and the Making of the Western World* (New Haven, CT: Yale University Press, 2009).

22 George Marshall, *A Guide to Merleau-Ponty's Phenomenology of Perception* (Milwaukee, WI: Marquette University Press, 2008), 73.

23 For reflections on the dynamic of wonder in philosophy, and on how it can be foreclosed or opened, see Mary-Jane Rubenstein's *Strange Wonder: The Closure of Metaphysics and the Opening of Awe* (New York: Columbia, 2010).

24 David Michael Kleinberg-Levin, *Reason and Evidence in Husserl's Phenomenology* (Evanston, IL: Northwestern University Press, 2018), xviii.

25 Welton, *The Other Husserl*, 58.

26 See Gary Brent Madison, *Understanding: A Phenomenological-Pragmatic Analysis* (Westport, CT: Greenwood Press, 1982).

27 Coles, *Self/Power/Other*, 108.

28 Alloa, *Resistance of the Sensible World*, 98, 86, 85.

29 Jessica Wiskus, *The Rhythm of Thought: Art, Literature, and Music after Merleau-Ponty* (Chicago, IL: University of Chicago Press, 2013), 123, 1.

30 Marshall, *A Guide to Merleau-Ponty's* Phenomenology of Perception, 75.

31 Here we can recall what Husserl refers to as passive synthesis. The world as I find it before reflection or cognitive activity; the given before all

thinking that is the soil of thought. For Husserl the realm of passive synthesis has to do with association—the way consciousness links up its various moments into coherent wholes, for example, through inner-time-consciousness—and cultural and historical influence—the way that things in the world are given to experience in inherited ways, for example, the given meanings of friendship in the culture into which we are born. See Edmund Husserl, *Analyses Concerning Passive and Active Synthesis: Lectures on Transcendental Logic*, vol. 9 (Husserliana: Edmund Husserl—Collected Works), ed. Anthony J. Steinbock (Dordrecht: Kluwer, 2001).

32 These formulations are obviously Heideggerean, but I hope they are not unfaithful to Merleau-Ponty's way of thinking about being. See, e.g., Hubert Dreyfus, *Being in the World: A Commentary on Heidegger's Being and Time, Division I* (Cambridge: MIT Press, 1991).

33 Lawrence Hass, *Merleau-Ponty's Philosophy* (Bloomington, IN: Indiana University Press, 2008), 8. Original italics.

34 Here we can listen to Husserl in a late remark: "Perhaps it will even become manifest that the total phenomenological attitude and the epoché belonging to it are destined in essence to effect, at first, a complete personal transformation, comparable in the beginning to a religious conversion, which, then, however, over and above this, bears within itself the significance of the greatest existential transformation which is assigned as a task to mankind as such." See Edmund Husserl, *The Crisis of European Sciences and Transcendental Phenomenology*, trans. David Carr (Evanston, IL: Northwestern University Press), 137. I thank Alessio Rotundo for bringing this passage to my attention.

35 Katherine Morris has investigated the nature of "Sartrean therapy" for "intellectual prejudices." See Katherine Morris, *Sartre* (Malden, MA: Blackwell, 2008). I thank Tom Sparrow for bringing Morris's work to my attention.

36 The inspiration for my consideration of Merleau-Ponty's phenomenology as a form of philosophical therapy is, of course, Pierre Hadot, who himself recognized that Merleau-Ponty has practiced philosophy as a way of life. See Hadot, *Philosophy as a Way of Life*.

37 Spiritual exercise does not have to connote anything necessarily religious. Again, see Hadot's *Philosophy as a Way of Life*.

Conclusion

1 I certainly do not claim that Freud, Woolf, or Merleau-Ponty was the only or the first figure to explore the topic of experiential immediacy. The issue, in some fashion, goes back to Plato and Aristotle, and in more recent times, Hegel and William James have given serious attention to immediate experience in human life. In the twentieth century, a discussion of the

irrationalism and celebration of instinct of someone like Herbert Marcuse would need to be studied. What Freud, Woolf, and Merleau-Ponty did was to put immediate experience at the center of human nature and at the center of psychological, social, and philosophical existence. They sought to explore the risks and possibilities of putting immediate experience at the center of our humanity.

2. Two prominent examples of studies on revolutions in human identity and of ideals of flourishing are Alasdair MacIntyre, *After Virtue* (Notre Dame, IN: University of Notre Dame Press, 1981), and Taylor, *Sources of the Self*.

3. Frederik Westerlund also briefly explores the connection between phenomenological philosophy and therapeutic self-transformation in his *Heidegger and the Problem of Phenomena* (New York: Bloomsbury, 2020), 226–7.

4. The phrase "truth of the world" is found in Hans Urs von Balthasar's *Theo-Logic, vol. 1: Truth of the World* (San Francisco: Ignatius, 2000).

5. For reflections on the "blessings of more life," see Eric Santner, *On the Psychotheology of Everyday Life: Reflections on Freud and Rosenzweig* (Chicago, IL: University of Chicago Press, 2001), 26. Santner takes the phrase from Harold Bloom.

6. W. H. Auden, "In Memory of Sigmund Freud," in Edward Mendelson, ed., *W. H. Auden, Collected Poems*, (New York: Vintage International, 1991), 275.

7. Focusing on the ways in which Freud, Woolf, and Merleau-Ponty engaged immediate experience has meant there are many important dimensions of their thought that are not covered in this book.

8. See, for example, Jacques Derrida, *Of Grammatology*, trans. Gayatri Chakravorty Spivak (Baltimore, MD: Johns Hopkins University Press, 1976).

9. See, for example, Jacques Derrida, *"Speech and Phenomena" and Other Essays on Husserl's Theory of Signs*, trans. David B. Allison (Evanston, IL: Northwestern University Press, 1973).

10. Merleau-Ponty, *The Primacy of Perception*, 30. The specific text "Primacy of Perception" is translated by Edie.

11. And we know from the work of Roland Barthes that even photographs are not simply mirrors of what they represent. See Roland Barthes, *Camera Lucida: Reflections on Photography*, trans. Richard Howard (New York: Farrar, Straus, and Giroux, 1981).

12. Merleau-Ponty, *The World of Perception*, 83.

13. Here I echo Jonathan Lear's remark about his interpretation of Freud: "As a philosophical introduction, our aim is to work out the possibilities of human mentality, the possibilities of interpretation." Lear, *Freud*, 33–4.

INDEX

abreaction 38–47, 51–2, 57–8, 61–3, 105
acute hysteria 50
aggression 47–9, 59, 61, 63, 67, 96, 105, 194 n.22
Alloa, E. 163
anomalous experience 16–19
arising 16, 25, 37, 48
Aristotle 124, 204 n.1
Auden, W. H. 180
Auerbach, E. 81, 86
autobiography 53, 195 n.32

Barthes, R. 205 n.11
biography 53, 195 n.32
Black, M. 31
Breuer, J. 15, 25
Brown, N. 58

Coles, R. 149, 163
commonplace 17–18
conscious emotional experience 34, 41
conscious life 23–4, 31–2, 35, 41, 43–4, 52, 63, 67–8, 70, 81
conscious psychological phenomenon 26, 29, 32, 40, 43, 49, 51, 60, 64, 69–70
cultural artifact 4, 139
cultural sources 4–5

Dalí, S. 182
Derrida, J. 181–2, 189 n.4
desire 47–61, 63, 93–7, 100, 105, 108, 117, 196 n.37
differently conscious 33, 53, 57, 196 n.37
Dreyfus, H. 4

emotion 16–18, 25–6, 29–47, 55–6, 58–64, 67–8, 81, 93, 95, 169
ethics
  in Europe 185–6
  of experience 11, 58, 69
  and history 173–4
  of immediacy 65–9, 104–11, 114–15, 166, 171, 173–80, 184–6
  and morality 105–8, 188 n.6
existential revolution 1–5, 7, 9, 12, 102, 104, 113–14, 166, 175–6, 180–1, 184

fantasy 28–30, 40, 45, 47, 51, 64, 69, 89, 104, 113
feeling 16, 19–21, 26–30, 33, 36–7, 40–2, 44–5, 51, 53–6, 59–64, 66–9, 93, 95–100, 169
Ferenczi, S. 65
Fräulein Elisabeth von R (case study) 25, 47–67, 193 n.20, 193–4 n.21, 196 nn.37–8, 197 n.43, 200 n.24
Freudian age 5–10, 12, 104, 114, 118, 166, 173, 176, 178, 180–1, 184–6
Freudian Fiction 73–4
Freud, S. 5–12, 20–1, 25–70, 73–4, 191 n.4, 193 n.15, 193 n.21, 194 n.22, 195–6 n.35, 195 n.27, 196 n.38, 197 nn.46–7, 198 nn.51–2, 200 n.24
  and consciousness 23–4, 44
  immediate experience 15–18, 180–6
  immorality 28, 54
  incoherence 51–7, 60–1, 63, 68, 70
  literature 104
  psychoanalysis 118, 180

Hadot, P. 66, 188 n.7, 198 n.53, 204 n.36
Harjo, J. 131
hermeneutics 181–3, 197 n.47
Hesnard, A. 117
Hölderlin, F. 70, 115
Homer 3–5
human life 110–11
  in Europe 9
  fantasies 89
  quandaries 19–21
human subjectivity 1, 16, 20, 64, 81, 86, 92–3, 141, 154, 190 n.3

Husserl, E. 121–2, 127–8, 134, 139, 143, 156, 158, 181, 187 n.3, 189 n.3, 200 n.21, 202 n.15, 203–4 n.31, 204 n.34
hysteria 25–30, 33–4, 38, 47, 50
hysterical 17–18, 30, 33–7, 39, 41, 43, 45–7, 50–1, 53–4, 57, 59, 61–3
neurosis 24–5, 47, 54, 62
psychosis 50

idealism 90
immediacy 190 n.3
conscious 24
creative 87–91
ethics of 65–9, 104–11, 114–15, 166, 171, 173–80, 184–6
experiential 18, 83–4, 102, 204 n.1
intersubjective 92–4
perceptual 11, 119, 124, 130, 132–5, 140–4, 146–8, 150, 152–3, 158–61, 165–7, 170
promise of 178–80
psychological 11, 34, 40, 66, 178
and relocation 98–9
therapeutic 108–12
immediate experience 5–12, 15, 21, 23–4, 27, 29, 38, 52, 57, 63, 67, 69–70, 81–93, 174–5, 178, 187 n.3, 189 n.4, 191 n.4, 204 n.1
dangerous experience 18–19
defamiliarizing and dangerous 174–5
interruption and anomaly 15–18
stymied position 19–21
immorality 28, 54
inauthenticity 17, 36–7, 165, 167
incoherence 51–7, 60–1, 63, 68, 70
insensibility 36
intellectual revolution 180–1
interiority 85–7, 93, 99–100, 109, 120, 137, 192 n.9, 199 n.10
interminable 43
intersubjective experience 11, 93–115, 150, 166, 173, 175

joy 24, 62–4, 69, 106, 112, 179
Joyce, J. 82–3

Kant, I. 176, 192 n.10
Keats, J. 131

Kleinberg-Levin, D. M. 156
Kohut, H. 190 n.3
körper 33
Kristeva, J. 191 n.3

Lacan, J. 191 n.3, 196 n.37
Laplanche, J. 23, 190 n.2, 195 n.35
Lear, J. 20, 23, 63, 190 n.8, 193 n.16, 193 n.18, 196 n.35, 197 n.43, 205 n.13
Leib 33
Leibniz, G. 125–6, 144
Lewis, P. 81–2, 86
Locke, J. 125–6

Marshall, G. 164–5
McGilchrist, I. 203 n.21
McWilliams, N. 58
Merleau-Ponty, M. 7–9, 11, 117–18, 166–71, 174–84, 188 n.5, 202 n.4, 202 nn.7–8, 203 n.19, 204 n.36
Cézanne's Doubt 130, 139, 169–70, 182
explication and explanation 119–20
givenness 122–3, 136–7, 143, 145, 147–9
human life 183
interrogation 124
logic of being 144–9
menace and danger 149–53
miracle and mystery 149
nascency 121
ontology and reason 163–5, 168
pastness 122
perception, immediacy, and predication 119–24
perceptual immediacy 119, 124, 130, 132–5, 140–4, 146–8, 150, 152–3, 158–61, 165–70
phenomenological ontology 140–4
phenomenological philosophy 125, 127, 149, 157, 162, 182
phenomenological thinking 159, 162
phenomenology and reduction 127–32
phenomenology as a way of life 166–7, 169
phenomenology as reflection 132–5

Phenomenology of Perception 118–20,
    127, 136, 141, 152, 161–2, 164–5,
    167, 170, 187 n.3, 202 n.8
phenomenology of phenomenology
    153–5
pre-reflective perception 126–7, 132,
    136, 148, 152
presence and absence 135–40
psychoanalysis 117–18
psychological depression 129
responsibility 165–71
scientific philosophy 125–7
Spinoza 141
temporality 156–7
therapeutic action 130, 161, 168, 171
thetic intentionality 123
thinking and time 156–62
miraculum 154
Mitchell, S. 31
Monet, C. 131–2, 182
Mooney, J. 197 n.42
morality 28–9, 35, 45–6, 61, 105–8
Morris, K. 204 n.35

neurosis 37–9, 45–7, 56, 58–9, 69, 105,
    190 n.8, 196 n.37
neurotics 24, 49–50, 55–6, 194 n.22,
    196 n.37
    insanity 49, 56, 69, 178
    life 27–8, 35–8
    psychosis 56
Nietzsche 3, 11
nomos 19–20

pain/painful 2–3, 16–17, 19–21, 24, 26,
    32–9, 41, 43–5, 58–64, 69, 101,
    112, 175
pensée du survol 162
perceptual experience 11, 121–2, 124,
    127–37, 139–40, 142–50, 152–3,
    155–6, 164–6, 169, 171, 175, 182
Phillips, A. 18, 53–6, 74, 104, 195 n.30
philosophical existence 7, 11, 134, 175,
    178, 185
Plato 3–5, 124, 144, 176, 204 n.1
positive psychology 64
Preliminary Communication (Freud)
    15–16, 25, 41, 47
producing 17

psúkhōsis 69
psychological experience 10–11, 24–6,
    28–31, 33–52, 54, 56–70, 85, 93,
    104, 166, 173, 190 n.8
psychological immediacy 11, 34, 40, 66,
    178
psychological life 24, 28–9, 34–7, 40–6,
    49, 51–6, 58, 60–1, 63–5, 67–70,
    93, 118, 166, 175–6, 180–1, 189
    n.7
psychosis 56, 191 n.3, 196 n.37
psychosomatic pain 59
psychosomatic symptom 36, 38, 50–1
psychotic insanity 49, 194 n.23
psychotic psychosis 56

repression 30–4, 36, 39, 45, 47, 51, 57, 60,
    105, 196 n.37
Rosenthal, M. 102

sanity 50–1, 68, 70
Sartre, J.-P. 156
Schmitz, H. 187 n.3
self-enclosed phenomenon 35, 85, 120
Sellars, W. 202 n.14
sex/sexuality 47–9, 56, 58–61, 63, 67, 96,
    104–5, 117–18
social existence 11, 92–6, 98, 102–4,
    108–15
social identity 94–5, 97–103, 106–15,
    179
Socrates 5
Sokolowski, R. 202 n.12
spontaneity 192 n.10, 196 n.35
Stern, D. 20, 189 n.7
Strauss, R. 131
suppressed/suppression 16–17, 20–1,
    25–6, 33
symptom relief 44, 51, 53

Taylor, C. 4
Thrasymachus 5
trauma 26–33, 39–40, 42–3, 47–9, 53, 58,
    62, 65, 67, 104, 192 n.6

unconscious 23, 32–3, 41–2, 46–7, 51–3,
    57, 118, 190 n.2, 191 n.4, 193
    n.18, 196 n.37
unsettling experience 21, 53, 68, 152, 184

vicious immediate psychological experiences 46
virtuous experience 35

Whitworth, M. 86, 103
Williams, B. 188 n.6
Wissenschaft 133
Wittgenstein, L. 192 n.9
Woolf, V. 7–8, 11, 73–4, 112–15, 166, 199 n.1, 199 n.4, 199 n.10
  body feeling 95–6
  creativity 107–8, 112, 115
  Edwardian fiction 78–80, 85, 91–2
  experience and social revolutions 99–102
  experience and world 84–7
  fictional character 74–6
  goodness and thriving 105–8
  human nature 74–6, 101
  identity and conflict 94–7
  immediacy 87–91, 98–9
  immediate experience 82–7
  immediate intersubjective experience 11, 93–115, 166, 173, 175
  improbable 82–4, 89–90, 110, 113
  To the Lighthouse 92, 94, 102, 113, 154, 187 n.1
  literature of death 76–80, 112
  literature of life 79–82, 102–4, 112–13
  radical reversal 104–5
  realism 86
  recalcitrance 94–7, 100–2, 105–11, 113, 115
  relocation 99
  representation and sociality 102–4
  social existence 92–4
  therapeutic immediacy 108–12

www.ingramcontent.com/pod-product-compliance
Lightning Source LLC
Chambersburg PA
CBHW052041300426
44117CB00012B/1919